Knapton

Twentieth-Century Village Voices

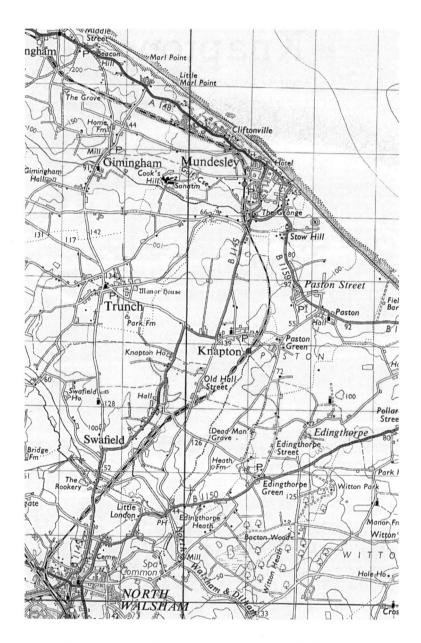

Knapton on the Ordnance Survey map published in 1954.

Knapton

Twentieth-Century Village Voices

edited by
Gillian Shephard

with a foreword by
Peter Hennessy

Biteback Publishing

First published in Great Britain in 2011 by
Biteback Publishing Ltd
Westminster Tower
3 Albert Embankment
London SE1 7SP

ISBN 978-1-84954-103-9

10 9 8 7 6 5 4 3 2 1

A CIP catalogue record for this book is available from the British Library.

Set in Caslon and Archer

Printed and bound in Great Britain by
TJ International, Padstow, Cornwall

CONTENTS

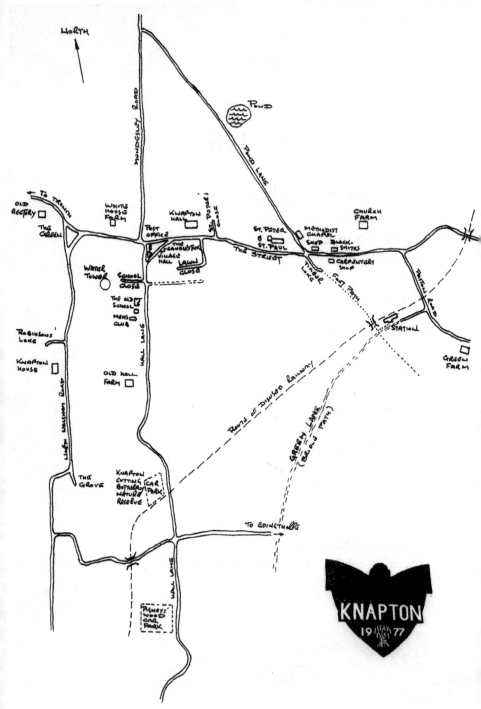

'Sketch of Knapton showing key locations', drawn by
David Glaze to mark the Silver Jubilee, 1977.

FOREWORD

History, when it works, is all about recapture. This book works. Reading it, one sees, breathes, feels and smells a rural England that is no more – a world of wild flowers; of steam trains on branch lines; of quiet but palpable religious faith; of working lives in the fields and in the pantries of great houses; of communal vitality and social peace, albeit within a very pronounced hierarchy.

It is, in a way, the stuff of which novels are made. Yet there is nothing fictional about the world recreated in these pages. It was real and it spanned a considerable swathe of time. Queen Victoria and Edward VII would have recognised much of it, as would the RAF National Servicemen and American airmen who flooded into East Anglia in the early 1940s and stayed ready to fight the Cold War in the 1950s and 1960s, placing the serenity of North Norfolk in the front line of the world's great struggles.

A multitude of English villages could tell their equivalents of the Knapton story if they possessed, say, a former Cabinet Minister to help organise them – one who had always remained rooted with her own people as Gillian Shephard has. But such combinations come scarce.

This is a book to be savoured like the seasons and the rural rhythms it describes. For a professor who spends far too much of his time reading old Whitehall minutes and grand political diaries, absorbing the Knapton story has been a pure delight, as it will be for every reader fortunate enough to pick it up.

I'm not at all clear what is meant today by 'The Big Society', but I am sure that the relationships caught in these pages is what it was.

Lord Hennessy of Nympsfield FBA
Attlee Professor of Contemporary British History,
Queen Mary, University of London

ACKNOWLEDGEMENTS

More than 100 people have contributed their memories and experiences to make this book, some by writing accounts of their memories, some by providing photographs and other memorabilia, some by organising meetings and discussions. Thanks are due to everyone who has helped, in whatever way.

June and Richard Wild have worked tirelessly, not only to provide their own memories, and memories from members of their families, but also by helping to keep the wider group in touch with what was going on at each stage. In addition, Richard has provided a number of excellent photographs. Janet Munro has contributed very interesting material from her own research on Valentine's Day observances in Norfolk, and with June Wild and Clifford Self formed a committee to oversee the project's finances. Pearl Eves, Linda Risebrow and Renie Turner have provided much appreciated arrangements for our meetings, at the chapel and in the Village Hall in Knapton

I am indebted to David Yaxley, Marion Daniels (née Wright), William Stubley and William Schamp for allowing the wonderful accounts from their parents to be included. Malcolm Wild discovered the splendid account of the Knapton Home Guard and Home Front, written by his father Willie Wild. Peter Amis generously gave his permission for me to use an unlimited number of quotations from his father Arthur Amis's book *From Dawn to Dusk*, and a photograph. Stella Dixon, grand-daughter of Sir George Edwards, kindly provided the photograph of him in the chapter on politics.

Thanks are also due to Susan Yaxley, whose Larks Press published our group's last book *Knapton Remembered*, for her encouragement with this one, and to Thomas Yaxley for some of the early typing work.

Some of our writers are members of the Knapton History Group, which has supported and helped them with their research, with the encouragement of the chairman, Alison Glaze. Her husband David Glaze provided the beautiful map of Knapton to be found on page vi.

Not all our writers are from Knapton, notably John Capes (from Paston), his cousin Mary Helyar (born in Norwich), Philip Almey (born and brought up in Paston), and Elizabeth Purdy (whose family farmed Green Farm in Paston, which she still owns). All have strong links with Knapton. Philip Almey allowed extracts from his mother's diaries to be used in the chapter on agriculture; his mother Adeline was the niece of Walter Watts of Knapton.

Margaret West has provided valuable proofreading assistance, and Anna Williams some very useful research for the chapter on politics. Professor Peter Hennessy and Keith Simpson MP have been towers of strength and encouragement throughout the writing of the book, as has our editor with Biteback Publishing, Sean Magee.

My husband Tom Shephard has throughout provided invaluable support and technological guidance.

I am grateful to Paul Damien for allowing the photographs of The Street and the blacksmith's shop to be used in this book.

Thanks are also due to the House of Lords Library and the Norfolk Records Office.

Gillian Shephard
June 2011

LINKS AND CONNECTIONS

This list does not seek to give a comprehensive history of everyone involved in the production of this book. The writers in any case speak for themselves in what they have written. Since, however, there are family, marriage and friendship connections between some of the writers and others mentioned in the book, I thought it might be helpful to give a brief explanation of some of the links.

ALMEY Philip (1935–2011) Son of Adeline and Laurie Almey. Grandson of Philip and Augusta Gaze. Husband of Marion (née Scott). Born in Paston; farmed in Paston and Antingham, near North Walsham. Attended Knapton School for a time.

AMIS Arthur (1905–2000) Born and lived in Trunch. Methodist preacher, union activist, Labour Party agent and local politician. Attended Knapton School and worked for a period in Knapton, where his sister Ellen lived with her husband James Steward and their four children: Janet (Munro), Ruth (Matthew), Eric and Mary (Lewis).

BANE Josiah (1882–1972) Known as Joe. Married to Elizabeth. Father of five daughters, including Queenie (Wild) and Marjorie (Schamp).

BANE Marjorie (1924–97) Daughter of Joe and Elizabeth Bane. Sister of Queenie. Married to Bill Schamp. Mother of William and Steven.

BANE Queenie (b. 1917) Daughter of Joe and Elizabeth Bane. Married to Sidney Wild, brother of Willie Wild. Mother of Brian, Jennifer (Lambert) and Richard, married to June (née Wild).

BURLINGHAM Ivy (b. 1931) Married name Austin. Daughter of Burt and Lily Burlingham. Sister of Grace (Ellis).

CAPES John (b. 1930) Born and brought up in Paston. His grandparents Herbert (Captain) and Elizabeth (Libby) Wright lived in The Street, Knapton, where John spent a lot of time as a boy. Cousin of Mary Helyar (née Wright).

CLAYDON Arthur (b. 1925) Farmed at Parrs Farm. At the time of writing, his son Andrew is farm manager for the Clan Trust and at Knapton Old Hall Farm.

CLOVER Bertha (1911–2006) Daughter of Bill and Millie Clover, wholesale greengrocers in Sheffield. Married to Jack Watts. Mother of Jill Watts (Shephard).

COE Leslie (b. 1922) Son of Elijah Coe, station master at Paston and Knapton station until around 1950.

DIXON Barbara (b. 1938) Married name Jarvis. Adopted sister of Pamela Dixon. Evacuee who arrived in Norfolk in 1944 and was adopted by the Dixon family in 1946.

DIXON George (1898–1972) Uncle of Roger Dixon. Served in First World War. Lived with his brother Hubert and sisters Ruth and Lucy Dixon at Parrs Farm, where he farmed for a time.

DIXON Pamela (b. 1935) Married name Garnham. Daughter of Albert Dixon, poultry farmer and keeper of Knapton shop. Niece of Margaret Townshend. Adopted sister of Barbara Dixon. Founded the Busy Bees in the 1960s with Margaret Hicks, a group for girls and women in Knapton.

DIXON Rev. Roger (b. 1933) Son of Bertie and Eva Dixon. Nephew of George Dixon. Husband of Stella (née Edwards), granddaughter of Sir George Edwards.

FAWKES Linda (b. 1950) Married name Risebrow. Daughter of Ronald and Barbara (née Wilkins). Sister of Rene (Turner). Helped run the Knapton Friendship Club from 1970 until 1976. Mother of Christopher (b. 1972) and Sadie (b. 1974).

FAWKES Rene (b. 1952) Married name Turner. Daughter of Ronald and Barbara (née Wilkins). Sister of Linda (Risebrow). Also helped run the Knapton Friendship Club as above. Mother of Paul (b. 1970).

FAWKES Ronald (b. 1926) Son of Herbert and Ethel Fawkes. Married to Barbara (née Wilkins). Father of Linda and Rene. Brother of Mervyn, Ursula, Sylvia, Megan and Roy.

FAWKES Roy (b. 1932) Son of Herbert and Ethel Fawkes. Brother of Mervyn, Ursula, Ronald, Sylvia and Megan. Served motor mechanic apprenticeship in North Walsham with Hannants. National Service in RAF.

FAWKES Ursula (1918–77) Daughter of Herbert and Ethel Fawkes. Sister of Mervyn, Sylvia, Megan, Ronald and Roy. Strong supporter of the Methodist Chapel and for many years organiser of the Christian Endeavour Group for young people in Knapton.

GAZE Adeline (1900–1973) Married name Almey. Daughter of Phillip and Augusta. Married to Laurie. Niece of Walter Watts of Knapton. Mother of Philip Almey.

HARRISON Gordon (b. 1942) With his sister Patricia and brother John, lived at Paston and Knapton station from around 1950, when his father William became station master after the death of Elijah Coe.

HICKS Pearl (b. 1951) Married name Eves. Daughter of Harold Hicks, Sunday School superintendent, trust treasurer and historian of Knapton Methodist Chapel, and of Margaret (née Turner). Sister of David and Christopher. Chapel steward at Knapton Methodist Chapel.

HOOKER Desmond (b. 1941) Lived with his family for the first ten years of his life at The Grove in Knapton. His mother, Barbara (née Farrow), was the best friend of Olive Wild (Webster).

JOHNSON Kathleen (b. 1936) Married name Suckling. Daughter of Kathleen (Kitty) Johnson, headmistress of Knapton School from 1934 to 1961, and of Arthur Johnson, clerk to the Knapton and Paston Parish Council, who served in the Knapton Home Guard during the Second World War.

HAMMOND Betty (b. 1920) Step-daughter of Norman May of Church Farm, Knapton. Married to Phil. Her younger son Stephen now farms Church Farm.

KIRK Llewellyn (b. 1930) Lived in The Street with his parents, until they moved back to his mother's native Wales after the war. Gives first-hand account of the Knapton 'bomb' incident in the Second World War.

LANGHAM Josephine (b. 1936) Married name Hourahane. Came with her brother Edward as an evacuee to Knapton School House in 1944.

LEE Anne (b. 1936) Married name Isitt. Lived as a child with her widowed mother and brothers and sisters at Knapton Green. Attended church Sunday School and sang in church choir.

MARKHAM Anne (1907–90) Married name Stubley. Mother of William.

MILLER Renie (b. 1921) Married name Morris. Daughter of George Miller, who worked for Walter Watts from time to time. Sister of Molly, Nancy, Derek and Michael.

MILLER Michael (b. 1938) Son of George Miller as above. Brother of Renie, Molly, Nancy and Derek.

MILLER Nancy (b. 1932) Married name Lynch. Daughter of George Miller as above. Sister of Renie, Molly, Derek and Michael.

PUNCHER Mary (b. 1948) Wife of Eric Steward. Daughter of Victor and Hilda Puncher. Lived in Hall Lane with her parents and seven brothers and sisters. Cousin of Willie Puncher.

PUNCHER Willie (b. 1937) Son of Willie and Ethel Puncher. Brought up with his brother John at Parrs Farm, Knapton, where he still lives and farms. Cousin of Mary Puncher, married to Eric Steward.

PURDY Elizabeth (b. 1941) Daughter of Tom and Helen Purdy of Green Farm, Paston. Granddaughter of Tom Purdy senior. Lived as a child with her two sisters, first in Footpath House, Paston, and from 1960 at Green Farm. She now lives at River Mount, where she has done important conservation work.

ROBINSON Miss Constance, (1879–1968) Daughter of Henry Robinson. Devoted to the village of Knapton and supporter of the church (where she played the organ), the Women's Institute, the Men's Club and many other causes. Her companion was Miss Leather, Sunday School teacher.

SELF Clifford (b. 1942) Cousin of Janet, Ruth, Eric and Mary Steward, with whom he lived in Knapton as a child during his mother's illness. Nephew of Arthur Amis. An ordained lay reader in the Church of England.

STEWARD Eric (b. 1944) Brother of Janet, Ruth and Mary. Married Mary Puncher, cousin of Willie Puncher. Nephew of Arthur Amis. Cousin of Clifford Self. Chapel treasurer and property steward of his local Methodist Chapel in Norwich.

STEWARD Janet (b. 1940) Married name Munro. Sister of Eric, Ruth and Mary. Niece of Arthur Amis. Member of the Methodist Chapel. Cousin of Clifford Self.

STEWARD Ruth (b. 1943) Married name Matthew. Sister of Janet, Eric and Mary. Niece of Arthur Amis. Has played organ at her local Methodist Chapel in Suffolk for many years. Cousin of Clifford Self.

WATTS Jill (Gillian) (b. 1940) Married name Shephard. Daughter of Jack and Bertha Watts. Granddaughter of Walter Watts. Great niece of Adeline Watts. Third cousin of Philip Almey. Great niece of Virtue Small, wife of Mick Small, carpenter.

WILD Brian (b. 1941) Son of Sidney and Queenie Wild. Brother of Jennifer (Lambert) and Richard.

WILD Henry (1911–2005) Married to Vera (née Rouse). Father of June. A Knapton Parish councillor until the age of ninety-four.

WILD Jennifer (b. 1944) Married name Lambert. Daughter of Sidney and Queenie Wild. Sister of Brian and Richard.

WILD June (b. 1951) Daughter of Henry and Vera Wild. Married to Richard Wild.

WILD Olive (b. 1919) Married name Webster. Daughter of John Wild, gardener at Knapton House for Miss Robinson. Sister of Henry Wild and aunt to June Wild. Best friend of Barbara Farrow, mother of Desmond Hooker.

WILD Richard (b. 1946) Son of Sidney and Queenie Wild. Married to June. Brother of Brian and Jennifer (Lambert).

WILD Willie (1913–83) Husband of Marjorie. Father of John, Margaret, Malcolm, Keith and Gerald. Brother of Sidney. Uncle of Brian and Richard Wild and Jennifer Lambert, among others.

WILKINS Barbara (1930–2009) Married to Ronald Fawkes. Mother of Linda (Risebrow) and Rene (Turner).

WILKINS Brenda (b. 1941) Sister of Barbara. Aunt to Linda Risebrow and Rene Turner.

WRIGHT Archie (1904–95) Father of Marion (Daniels). Born at Post Office Cottages, Knapton Cross Roads.

WRIGHT Mary (b. 1940) Married name Helyar. Born in Norwich. Granddaughter of Herbert (Captain) and Elizabeth (Libby Wright); spent much of her childhood with her grandparents in Knapton.

WRIGHT Shirley (b. 1938) Married name Conquest. Lived with her parents, brothers and sister at Knapton Green. Keen attender at church and chapel organisations, and supporter of village activities.

YAXLEY Alfred (1900–74) Started life as a farm worker. Became gardener at Footpath House in Paston. Father of David, writer and historian, who is married to Susan of Larks Press – publisher, among many other successful books, of *Knapton Remembered* and the reprint of *From Crow Scaring to Westminster* by Sir George Edwards.

INTRODUCTION

Nearly one hundred people have been involved in producing this book. Some have written accounts of their memories of Knapton or helped others to do so, or discovered and provided the written memories, diaries, photographs and letters of relatives now dead. Others have helped organise our meetings, and kept people in touch with the project. Many of that hundred were also involved in writing *Knapton Remembered*, which we published in 2007 and which gave an account of Knapton School between 1934 and 1961, the time in office of its inspirational head teacher Kathleen Johnson.

In *Knapton Remembered*, I wrote: 'Much more could be written. Many of us feel that we have only scraped the surface of our memories, and what they tell us about our own lives and the history through which we have lived. But we have made a start.' It was only a matter of time before we realised that we wanted to take a wider view of our village and its place in the shifting social history of Norfolk. This book is the result. Its title describes the process we have employed: the accounts are the authentic voices of those who have lived through two world wars, revolutions in agriculture and educational opportunity, sweeping economic, social and political change and all that that has meant for our small community, and for other communities like it.

Knapton has had a remarkably stable population of around 300 throughout the period covered by this book. Before we started writing, I believed I knew a great deal about the village and the people in it. But I have learned a great deal more – not least about the sheer rapidity of the decline in agriculture which transformed this part of Norfolk in the space of thirty years between 1940 and 1970. I might have imagined that the influence of church and chapel were roughly equal, but the memories recorded in this book demonstrate that the Methodist Chapel in Knapton, which continues to provide a strong social and educational network, was the greater force, notwith-standing the experience of individuals. The influence of the school and its teachers, graphically recorded in *Knapton Remembered*, was heart-warmingly recognised even by those who might have felt their schooldays were not the most successful period of their lives.

I have often described the community of north-east Norfolk in which I grew up as close-knit, but the family and friendship links revealed in this book are even more interlocked than I had thought. This, far from being a limiting factor in our lives, has given all of us a closer experience of the full social spectrum than if we had been born in a middle-class suburb, for example, or even in a large city. We have certainly had an intimate knowledge of how things are run, since we and our parents and grandparents have been closely involved in running them. Most would agree that doing things for and in the local community, and the voluntary principle, are among the best characteristics of British life. Much lip service is paid to that principle these days by politicians and others. But the village voices recorded in this book tell us, for example, that the upkeep of the church, chapel and Village Hall, the organisation of activities for local young people or the provision of a Men's Club were regarded as a matter of course, as the responsibility of all. The book abounds in examples of literally decades of devotion to local causes, often on the part of people whose working lives were physically punishing and far from affluent.

The number of people involved in producing this book has meant that it has been as much an exercise in organisation, involve-ment and communication as in writing. The process itself has been a pleasure and a revelation − of what people found they could do and of what they could discover about their origins. Our circum-stances are now widely divergent. But the voices in this book reveal what we share, and the value we put on our sense of place, on our roots in that place, our families, the land and the seasons. Above all, we share the view that community is precious, as is the privilege of knowing where we have come from, a privilege shared by people in communities like ours, everywhere.

ONE

VILLAGE AND VILLAGERS

K napton is in north-east Norfolk, a mile and a half inland from the North Sea at Mundesley and about four and a half miles from its nearest market town, North Walsham. Its population has hovered around 300 for at least the past 150 years. It is not a beautiful village, composed as it is of small scattered settlements and with no discernible centre, apart perhaps from The Street, where the church, chapel and Village Hall are to be found. Its church is remarkable, described by Arthur Mee as 'a landmark and a magnet, drawing us to one of the finest treasures of its kind in the land', a reference to its extraordinary double hammer-beam roof, dating from 1503. Unlike its neighbouring villages, Trunch and Paston, Knapton had a school from 1837 until the early 1980s, when it was closed. And unlike Trunch, Knapton never had a pub. Trunch had two, but it also had a brewery.

The map of the village (see page vi) shows its scattered nature. The church and chapel stand on and just north of The Street, while the station, which was provided to serve Paston and Knapton, is reached by a 'loke' – lane – off The Street for Knapton people, and by a series of small lanes for people from Paston and Edingthorpe. Some of the main settlements are along The Street. Church Farm is there, below the shop and blacksmith's shop; Knapton Hall is next to the church. At the top of The Street are to be found 'The Candlestick', described below by Richard Wild, and the Parish Room, now the Village Hall. Hall Lane runs in a southerly direction past the school, the Men's Club and Knapton Old Hall. The main road towards North Walsham travels west to Knapton Green and then veers south past Knapton House and The Grove.

Richard Wild describes The Candlestick as the roads that surround the Village Hall and its neighbouring cottages. He suggests that the Village Hall belonged to Miss Selina Shirley, who is commemorated by a plaque in the church and who owned Knapton Hall. The Village Hall started life as a thatched barn, and Miss Shirley supported the setting up of a school there, described in *Kelly's Directory* of 1892 as 'erected in 1837 for sixty children, average attendance sixty'. Jack Watts, who was born in 1903, always referred to the Village Hall as the old school. He himself attended the new school that was built further along Hall Lane in 1897. A couple of large, thatched cottages on The Candlestick, where Alfred Yaxley was born in 1900, were pulled down in the early 1900s. Photo 1 (in the plate section of this book) clearly shows these cottages and what is now the Village Hall, with its thatched roof. The cottage known as Crossways, where Mrs Sexton, postmistress, and later her son Harry lived, stands on the corner of The Street and Hall Lane. It was built in 1806. The two neighbouring cottages were owned by the Robinson family, and when Miss Robinson put them up for sale in 1957, the shared open garden at the back had to be divided and fenced off.

It may seem strange that so small a village should have different communities and be described as scattered. However, in the days before almost universal car ownership, the settlements were somewhat separate, especially seen through the eyes of a child. Desmond Hooker (b. 1941) writes: *'I was born and lived for the first ten years of my life at The Grove, Knapton, this being a small hamlet on the outskirts of the village. It was quite an isolated childhood in many ways, as the only other child living there was my young soulmate, Paddy Fisher, but we had so much freedom and space to play it was quite idyllic too.'*

Desmond's account also vividly illustrates the close-knit nature of Knapton up to and including the 1940s and 1950s: *'I lived in the last house down the lane with my parents, Albert and Barbara Hooker, my grandparents, Jack and Myrtle Farrow, and my mother's sister, Grace. Three other houses there were occupied by my relations. These were Fred and Edie Hedge (great uncle and aunt), George and Hilda Turner (cousins), and Billy and Barbara Lancaster (great uncle and aunt). Myrtle Farrow, Fred Hedge, George Turner and Barbara Lancaster were all from the Hedge family.*

'*As we lived out on a limb we had many tradesmen call. The coalman was my great uncle Boardman Hedge. Mr Alden of North Walsham brought clothes and drapery. Groceries were delivered by Mr Miller of Skeyton and Mr Dixon of Knapton. Mr Bridges of Mundesley supplied batteries and accumulators for the wireless. Edwards and Fayers bakeries also delivered. My favourite was Mr Ward of Trimingham who brought his fish and chip van every week. Four shillings and sixpence was enough to feed five people in the late forties.*

'*On Saturdays my grandmother would bake bread, large loaves and small ones, which we ate with cheese. There was always enough for the relations. It was my job to deliver these and in return I would receive many sweets.*

'*When I was a young lad, I spent many hours with my great uncle Fred Hedge, nicknamed Puffer. He worked as team-man at Church Farm, Knapton. I loved helping and being around horses and they became my passion. Knapton had a great influence on my life.*

'*Just down the road from The Grove towards Swafield is Straithern Farm, where Mr Basey-Fisher lived with his wife and daughters, Brenda and Stella. They ran a small farm with a dairy herd. On Saturday mornings I would go on the milk round, mostly driven by Brenda. She used an Austin 7 with all the seats removed to make room for the milk crates, on which I sat. No problems then with Health and Safety. The round took in Swafield council houses, Swafield Street, over the bridge and into Little London, left at Royston House to the Wherry, left again at River Mount to Stone Cottages, and then home via Steadman's Hill, delivering to most properties en route. I was paid sixpence for my help, plus some sweets. I recall Brenda visiting me once when I was unwell and bringing a present of a bar of soap in the shape of PC 49, which I kept for years.* [PC, or Police Constable, 49 was a popular character in a radio series at the time.]

'*At the age of ten I moved to Trunch and to Mundesley School from Knapton. This was not my choice and Knapton School will always stay in my memory as the very best.*'

Knapton's situation is exposed to the cruel north and east winds and sea frets common in this part of Norfolk. Some of its buildings are distinguished: the church is fine, by any standards. The sea can be seen from various parts of the village – from the churchyard, for example – and the air has the biting freshness and clarity that sharpens and illuminates even the most commonplace of views. The curve of The Street, dropping down past Church Farm on its way to Paston, shaded by the farm wall, has a gentle prettiness. But the combination of nostalgia, the sense of a world lost to us now and our shared memories of a gloriously free childhood in the wonderful north Norfolk setting of Knapton, give our village a beauty remembered and loved in the six accounts that follow.

Roger Dixon (b. 1933) writes: *'The title of Thomas Hardy's novel* The Return of the Native *is just right for what I want to share. One of the nicest things about coming back to Knapton when I first retired was being able to retrace familiar fields and paths, places which I knew well as a boy and enjoyed seeing again. Some things had changed. The greatest loss, to my mind, is Allison's Loke* [a lane linking Hall Lane and the Swafield Road near Straithern's Farm]. *It was a lovely place and was used a great deal by my family. Primroses grew there in profusion and there were violets and other flowers. I searched very carefully for the wild anemones that used to grow where the Loke came out into what were then by-roads leading to The Grove and Swafield Hall. I found just one, and wondered if it was the last of the species at that site. My aunt Ruth used to gather pussy willows there too, for Palm Sunday, and when she became too lame to do so, one of us in the family would get them for her. I suppose it was necessary to clear and plough it up when every inch of soil needed to be cultivated, but I can't help wondering about it. After all, it survived the war.'* (Allison's Loke was ploughed up by a local farmer, and brought into cultivation in the 1970s, destroying a priceless example of age-old hedgerow lining an ancient footpath.)

Roger continues: *'Great sweeps of marsh marigold – king cups – grew on the meadow in front of Beeches Farm. The house was in Swafield, but the meadow was in Knapton. It is better drained now and the king cups have gone. There used to be orchids in an old sand-pit bordered by the same loke and the railway, but they have gone too and the pit is over-grown with blackthorn. Moving from flora to fauna, sand-martins used to nest in the sides of the big sand-pit that faced Straithern Farm and Swafield Hall. Now, there are animals about which were not there in my childhood, like Muntjac deer.'*

King cups were, for us, mythical flowers, not least because we sang in the infant class, 'King cups, king cups, let us take you home/ Put you in a green glass and call our very own.' We were obviously not aware at that stage that the *Observer's Book of British Wild Flowers,* our bible as we went on to become wild flower collectors, states unequivocally: 'The plant is poisonous.' With no apparent irony, it continues: 'The unopened flower-buds are sometimes pickled and used as a substitute for capers.' I still look for king cups wherever I find marshy ground.

Roger describes *'another loke, Wallage's Loke. This was entirely different. It had banks all the way down, rather than hedges, and a very windswept feel to it. I liked the pit at the very end. Unlike most other pits and ponds, this one was entirely clear and usually dry. I was often there because at one time my mother "helped" Mrs Wallage and I was frequently around, sometimes helping in the garden.*

'This is describing a Knapton fifty or sixty years ago, when the land counted for so much in people's lives. Many of the men knew every corner of the fields they worked on in an intimate way, unlike the view from a big machine. This detailed knowledge was passed on to us children. We were free to roam where we wished and our mothers did not suffer the anxieties of today as to who would be around and what moral dangers we might fall into. They weren't that bothered about the physical dangers either. Llewellyn Kirk and I climbed a difficult tree in Green Lane. I took some owl pellets to Mrs Johnson (head teacher of Knapton School) and we teased out mouse bones, beetle shells and whatever else the bird had eaten.

'Another favourite place of mine was called the Rough Piece, down the North Walsham road. Mr Claydon grazed cattle there in the area nearer the road. The far end, down to Water Lane, was covered in gorse and bracken, tall enough for me to be hidden as a child. There were some strange, deep hollows running across the field. I never knew what they were, and wondered if they dated back to the Middle Ages and an older

system of agriculture. They have been ploughed out now, and in spite of trying many times to trace them, I never could do so.

'I know these are very personal memories, made warmer perhaps, or kinder, than the events were at the time. But they are part of my story of Knapton and they are very dear.'

Richard Wild (b. 1946) continues the idyllic theme of wild flowers and animals, observed during his family's Sunday walks round Knapton: *'Some of my favourite walks were across footpaths because of all the wild flowers and animals and birds we would see. In spring there were primroses and violets on the banks and bluebells in the woods. In those days we were allowed to pick them and we would take a bunch or two home to have indoors. We would see rabbits playing in the meadows, and the occasional hare, weasel or stoat would run across the road in front of us. On the freshly drilled fields there were partridges, pheasants, pigeon, crows and rooks looking for grubs.*

'Summer walks were more limited because my father worked as a labourer for Mr May of Trunch and he had to work in the harvest field, as the crops had to be cut when it was fine and dry. We sometimes took dad's tea and our own and sat on a bank or shoaves [sic] of corn. We took sticks with us to chase the rabbits that ran out as the binder went round. I remember being in one field, and when they had finished cutting, the bottom of the binder was covered with rabbits and hares, so we had plenty of meat for a week or two.

'Autumn time was nice for a walk. There would be all the berries in the hedgerows and chestnuts, horse chestnuts, beechnuts and acorns on the trees as well as on the ground. The acorns we would take home for our popguns, which were made from elder trees. The pith in the centre was burnt out by a red hot poker; the ramrod was made of ash. The sweet chestnuts we roasted on the fire; conkers were threaded with a leather shoe lace to play to see whose conker lasted the longest. Then of course there were the blackberries, one of my favourite fruits, with which mum made jam or apple and blackberry pudding with custard. Some people would pick them and take them to chapel to decorate up at harvest festival with hips and haws ...

'*Looking back I think how lucky we were to have good parents who made time for us and to teach us about the countryside.*'

Leslie Coe (b. 1922), whose father, Elijah Coe, was station master, also has happy memories of autumn bounty and of his Knapton childhood: '*One thing I remember quite clearly is that Mr Purdy from Paston Green used to send his shire horses to graze on a meadow by the station. We were pleased as we were able to pick lovely mushrooms, which my mum would often cook for breakfast. I used to pick blackberries, crab apples and sloes from the hedgerows, which we used in the house, and of course chestnuts from Witton Woods …*

'*I still keep thinking of my life in Knapton and I guess I will until the final curtain.*'

John Capes (b. 1930) and Mary Wright (Helyar) (b. 1940) are cousins. Their grandparents, Herbert (Captain) and Elizabeth (Libby) Wright, lived in Knapton Street. Their memories are of family visits to Knapton and a closely observed way of life that has gone for ever.

John Capes writes: '*My maternal grandparents were Herbert and Elizabeth Wright, who lived in a wooden bungalow called "The Shrubs" opposite the church in Knapton, which grandad had built himself during 1930. At that time, my parents were living in Edingthorpe, but I was born at my grandparents' bungalow in December 1930. We moved to Paston when I was ten months old, and there I stayed until getting married in 1963. All through the 1930s and 1940s we almost always went as a family to my grandparents' on a Sunday afternoon, and some-times my mother would take me and my brother there during the week in the school holidays. After I was about eight or nine I would often go there on a Saturday morning by myself. Thus I saw quite a lot of my grandparents, and knew some of the village people.*'

Mary Wright writes: '*I was never a resident of Knapton but used to visit my grandparents in the holidays and alternate weekends. My grandfather, a carpenter by trade, built the bungalow with the help of his son-in-law and before that they had lived, I think, in Pond Lane, Knapton.*

'The bungalow consisted of four rooms, two bedrooms, a lounge and a kitchen. There was a verandah along the back, off which there was a scullery and a washing room. As a young child, I was frightened to walk along the verandah in case I fell through the boards, as you could see through them. The front bedroom was where I slept, in a large double bed with a feather mattress and a brass head board with knobs at the end. These, after years of use, had worked loose and rattled when you turned over in bed. The back bedroom belonged to my grandparents.

'In the centre of the lounge was a large, round, wooden pedestal table. To one side of this was the sofa, made of horsehair so I was told. It was so prickly and uncomfortable that people very rarely sat on it. My grandfather had a wooden-armed chair in front of the fireplace, and my grandmother had a smaller chair on the other side. I sat on a small stool or the floor in front of the coal fire. Against another wall was a sideboard, which housed the best china.

'The kitchen did not contain things associated with today's kitchens. There was a wooden table on which my grandmother would make pies, shortcakes and pastry. I can still taste her raspberry tart with runny custard. A couple of chairs in case anyone called in, and the fireplace and oven in the wall. There was a built-in cupboard in an alcove where stood a radio to which my grandmother loved listening.

'The kitchen was also the place where you had a bath, in front of the fire, after it had heated the water. As a child, I got in the tin bath first and then I think more water was added for the adults after I had gone to bed. Of course there was no running water. This had to be fetched from the two water butts outside the back door. Drinking water had to be drawn from the well at the bottom of the garden, which was shared between the neighbours on either side.

'You went out of the back door and down two steps into the scullery. Again there was a wooden table or bench, on which there was a bowl for hand and face washing and also washing up crockery and cutlery. On another shelf there was an oil cooker, which I think was mainly used in summer when the fire in the kitchen was not lit.

'Through this small room was the wash room, where there was a boiler for the clothes, sheets and towels. There was a wooden mangle, *through which the clothes were put to squeeze out the water before they were taken down the garden to hang on the washing line. This always seemed a rather cold damp room and was not my favourite place.*

'The last little room was the toilet, which of course was right at the end of the building and could only be reached by going outside. It was a wooden bench with the hole in the middle and a nail on the wall with newspaper hanging there. Of course it had to be emptied regularly but I didn't ask too much about that!

'Although electricity came to the village in 1948, it was not installed in the bungalow until after my grandfather's death in 1953. Until then oil lamps were used and were not really very bright to read by. I was always given a candle in a metal holder to see me to bed.

'As an evening occupation, I would help my grandmother to make rag rugs. These were made from any old clothes or fabric that were cut into strips and woven through a hessian base and looped to secure them in place. When finished, they were put beside the bed or fireplace.

'There was quite a lot of land behind the bungalow, so my grandfather grew all his own vegetables and fruit. I remember there were gooseberries, raspberries, currants, broad beans, peas, lettuces and tomatoes. I was allowed to pick the very tiny ones, which my grandfather called "dibs", from the tomato plants in the greenhouse. Sometimes, when there was a bumper crop of lettuces all developing at the same time, he would put them in a box and place them outside the gate for passers-by at a cost of 3d each. Occasionally we would sit on the bank and wait for custom or just a chat with anyone passing.

'Granny and I would go on the train to North Walsham to do a bit of shopping and then visit her two sisters for a cup of tea before catching the train home. She always put on her best clothes, which were usually a long navy coat, hat and court shoes. Grandad never came with us and did not seem to leave the village. He was content working in the garden or doing a bit of carpentry in the shed. Sometimes he would take me down the road to see the blacksmith shoeing the horses or to visit someone, but it was never far.

'My grandfather died in 1953 followed by my grandmother in 1956. The bungalow was sold and so my contact with Knapton ended.

'I have brought my children on a couple of occasions to see the home of their great grandparents. I was also fortunate to have one last look before it was pulled down to be redeveloped, which I believe was some time in the 1990s. The wooden outside toilet was still there, the water butts and still no taps. I also plucked up courage to walk on the verandah and nearly did fall through as the wood was completely rotten! I will always remember Knapton as it played a very special part in my childhood.'

Mary is remembering her grandparents' home and life as they were in the 1940s and 1950s. Others give descriptions of how life was lived in a later chapter, but Mary's account is so evocative of Knapton in that period that it is included here.

Clifford Self (b. 1942) remembers Knapton for different reasons. His experiences there, as a boy and as a young man, eventually changed his whole life.

For part of his childhood he lived in Knapton with the Steward family, his cousins, as his mother was terminally ill with cancer. While he was there, he got involved in the Methodist Church, *'travelling on the back of uncle Arthur's tandem to different chapels where he would take the service, being a Methodist lay preacher'*. (Arthur Amis's career in politics and the Methodist Church are described later in this book.) After Clifford left school in 1957 he worked as a farming apprentice in Trunch for a time. He writes: *'During this time, I would bike to Knapton to attend the Methodist Chapel, and afterwards with several youngsters we would meet at Herbert and Margaret Hicks's house for fellowship. We had great times eating Margaret out of house and home and causing mayhem. I have good memories and thank them for what they did for me. Herbert was a Methodist lay preacher, and on some occasions when he had an evening service he would ask if any of us would like to join him and read a lesson. Several of us did, and travelled with him in his Vanguard car.'*

After a professional career that eventually led him to a position as a manager with British Telecom, Clifford writes, *'I felt something missing from my life, but was not sure what. I started going to church in our village, Hainford, and found that I was being called to get involved in the church. I spent three years studying and at the end received a licence as a lay reader in the Church of England.*

'In 2008 I got a phone call from Pearl Hicks to see if I would take Sunday service at Knapton chapel. I accepted, and very nervously took my first Methodist service. I have been asked back again, so it must have been all right! John Hicks of Trunch chapel has also asked me to take a service there. It is a great privilege to be able to preach at places where as a boy I used to attend and listen to others.

'Knapton and Trunch are very dear to me; the people from both villages are to me what village life is all about, the Christian values of looking after and caring for one another. As you can see from these few words, Knapton has influenced and played a large part in who I am today.'

This strong affection for the village itself and its surrounding fields, woods, lokes, pits and lanes comes through in all the accounts of the contributors to this book. For us, when we were children, Knapton was our world. For many of us, the values and experience it gave us have sustained us throughout our lives.

The pictorial map of Knapton by David Glaze on page vi shows the layout of the various settlements that made up the village and the position of the most important buildings. These were the church, the chapel, Knapton House, the Old Hall, the Hall, the Parish Room (later the Village Hall), the school, the Men's Club, Church Farm, White House Farm, the shop, the blacksmith's shop and the station.

There is an old rectory at Knapton Green but during the whole time that Knapton and Paston shared a rector, he lived at the Rectory in Paston. The sharing arrangement ended in the 1970s, when both villages were absorbed into the Trunch Group of parishes and a team ministry was set up. With the exception of the blacksmith's shop, which was burnt down in 1958, and the shop, school and station, which have become dwellings, the appearance of these buildings, and indeed of the whole village, remains today very much as it was at the start of the period covered by this book around 1880. Many of the cottages from that date are also still in place, built in their distinctive mix of brick and flint, some extended and modernised but easily recognisable. Knapton has not had the overwhelming additions of new housing estates found in many Norfolk villages, nor has it been swamped by second-homers. Willie Puncher (b. 1937) writes: '*Since 1945, eighty-one new houses have been built in Knapton, and nine old barns and out-buildings have been converted to dwellings. Miss Robinson's old home, Knapton House, has been converted into flats.*'

Among the additions have been significant numbers of council houses. Richard Wild writes: '*The first twelve council houses were built about 1927 at Knapton Green. The next council houses were built in 1950–51. Four were built in School Close and in 1956 four more. These were three-bedroomed houses with kitchen, pantry, sitting room, downstairs toilet, and toilet and bathroom upstairs. There were back boilers to heat the water and radiators to heat the rooms. Eight more houses were built in 1956 and four bungalows. The bungalows had two bedrooms, kitchen, sitting room and bathroom. Later, six more bungalows were added in School Close.*'

The biggest private residential development in Knapton has been Lawn Close in The Street, when twenty-three bungalows and chalets were built in 1964–5 opposite the Hall.

Roger Dixon, writing in the Knapton newsletter of summer 2002, explains the name of Lawn Close: '*In the days of horse-drawn carriages and pony traps most substantial farmhouses and all the local halls had a "lawn", usually on the opposite side of the road to the house. There the horses and ponies grazed. There was one opposite White House Farm, where the celebrations for the Coronation were held in 1953. The one opposite the Old Hall is now covered with trees. The rather grand piece of rising ground opposite Knapton House is now cultivated as a field.*

'*The lawn that gave its name to Lawn Close played quite a significant part in village life. Celebrations for national events such as coronations and royal jubilees were held there, and school sports too. Some will remember the event held on Coronation Day in 1937, when among other events there was a Ladies' Tug of War. Quite apart from all this, the Lawn was an attractive piece of land. Two large sycamore trees stood halfway across it, exactly in line with the Hall drive, and a dip in the land gave the impression of a continuation of the drive. There was a large spread of wild violets, some of them white, under the hedge, and the "country house" iron railings, railings like those restored opposite the Old Hall.*

'In the corner near what is now Autumn Cottage where I lived as a boy with, next door, first the Gedges and then the Thomsons, was a copse of oaks and sweet chestnuts with wild anemones growing beneath them. Along the west side of the meadow was a line of trees sheltering the gardens there, and on the eastern boundary was a deep and wide hollow where I remember playing with Llewellyn Kirk. My great uncle Dan Dixon pastured his horses and cows on the Lawn during and after the war.'

TWO

PLACES OF INFLUENCE

The section that follows describes some of the most important buildings in Knapton, through the eyes and memories of the people who used them. It also recalls some of the people associated with the buildings. The church and chapel were perhaps the most significant buildings in the village, although as becomes clear from other chapters, the shop, the blacksmith's shop and the station played an important economic role in Knapton life.

We start with the church and the chapel.

The church of St Peter and St Paul is largely fourteenth-century, and according to Pevsner its roof is one of the finest in Norfolk. He describes the font and font cover as 'almost as striking'. The roof is remarkable because it is double hammer-beam, and adorned with a total of 138 wooden angels. It stands high in the village and, like so many churches in north-east Norfolk, its tower can be seen for miles around. The weather vane, in the shape of an elegant cockerel, is said to have been designed by John Sell Cotman, during the course of a drawing lesson he was giving at Knapton House. Inside, the feeling is one of space and light from the great Norfolk skies outside. Outside, the church towers above the village street, its flint walls and tower and plastered chancel glittering in the cold, clear Norfolk air. It is surrounded by a substantial graveyard, enclosed by a flint wall. The church is approached from the street by steps and a graceful lych gate arch. Until recent years there was a carnser on the church side of the street. The word carnser is explained by Roger Dixon in the Knapton Newsletter of autumn 2002 as 'an old Saxon word for high path'. He writes: *'The carnser on the north side of The Street is now grassed over but it used to be maintained as a gravel path, the grass verge clipped and the edge to The Street carefully kept sharp rather than sloping. My earliest recollection of it is of Mr Rouse, Henry*

Wild's father-in-law (and June Wild's grandfather), looking after it, to be followed after the war by Tom Coe (son of Elijah Coe, station master, and brother of Leslie Coe). It dates of course from the times before roads were properly surfaced. The carnser provides a dry, well-kept path to church, Knapton Hall, and shop.'

I too can remember the carnser, but more than the path, I remember the bank above it being first gold with celandines, then buttercups, and then white with dog daisies, or marguerites as we called them.

For the first nine years of my life I lived with my parents opposite the church, in a bungalow called East Side, built by Mr Sayer of North Walsham in the late 1930s. It cost £400, and my mother's mother lent my parents the money. They had been married in Knapton church in February 1932, and had had their first home in two rooms in the house of my great-aunt Adeline Watts, about a hundred yards further up The Street

My mother had been brought up a Methodist in her home city of Sheffield. She used to tell me of the hearty, hymn-thumping services she attended in chapel, and most particularly of the Whit Sunday parades through the city streets, with everyone dressed in their Whit Sunday new clothes. She would occasionally attend services in Knapton chapel, especially at Harvest Festival, but I was christened in Knapton church by the Reverend Prichard and as a matter of course went on to attend church Sunday School, at first in church with Miss Leather, and then in the Parish Room with Mrs Dixon (mother of Pamela and Barbara) and Miss Townshend (their aunt). I also attended church fairly regularly and was roped in to help decorate the church at Harvest, Easter and Christmas. In about 1954, a group of us attended pre-Confirmation instruction from Mr Thur, Mr Prichard's successor, and went on to be confirmed in North Walsham church. At the same time, Ursula Fawkes, sister of Roy, Ronnie and Melvyn, ran Christian Endeavour meetings in the chapel for the young people of the village, and together with many others I attended these.

For me, the church calendar was completely intertwined with

the passing of the seasons, and with so many of the village events which marked our childhood lives in Knapton.

On Mothering Sunday, at Sunday School, the gentle Miss Leather, companion to Miss Robinson, would give us bunches of sweet-smelling violets that she had picked in the grounds of Knapton House to take home to our mothers. We gathered armfuls of pussy willow to bring to church for Palm Sunday. At Easter we would pick baskets of primroses from the railway bank and gather thick damp moss, which we laid on the steps of the font to keep the small flowers fresh for the week. The moss, starred thickly with violets, polyanthus, and tiny daffodils, reminded me of early Renaissance primavera paintings. But Harvest Festival was the high point of the year, when church, village life and farming all came together in heart-felt celebration. The church was filled with late summer flowers and foliage, all beautifully arranged, and tomatoes, scrubbed potatoes, onions, carrots, beetroot and eggs adorned the edges of the aisle and the windows, like Greek friezes. Sheaves of wheat, barley and oats stood against the pew ends, and a huge loaf baked in the shape of a sheaf of wheat was laid in the chancel. At school we were asked to bring harvest produce to put in the church, and we would walk down The Street carrying our plums, apples, vegetables and flowers, to arrange in the doorway (never opened) on the north side of the church. The whole building smelled of the bountiful fruits of the earth, and the service, with the special harvest hymns, heartily sung, seemed always to me entirely at one with that moment in the life of our village. 'All is safely gathered in' had a profound meaning for all of us.

The church at Christmas too was moving and exciting, the old, familiar carols ringing out in a church decorated with great swathes of holly and ivy, Chinese lanterns, white chrysanthemums. I so loved the church at Christmas, with all its associations of warmth, friendship, peace and joy, that I chose to get married, in 1975, on 27 December, when the Christmas decorations were still in place.

In other ways, too, the life of the church was indissolubly linked with the rhythm of our village year. Although ours was not a church school, the vicar was a school manager and visited on occasion, and we were involved in raising money for church funds, like others in the village. Our parents would attend church sales of work in the Parish Room, whist and beetle drives to raise money for church funds, and there was of course, every year, the summer fete in the garden of Miss Robinson's house. I eagerly looked forward to this (and to its chapel counterpart, held at Church Farm). For one thing, there was often an interesting guest invited to declare the fete open; for another, we children usually had to do country dancing, with Mrs Johnson's wind-up gramophone scratching out the familiar tunes. There was 'bowling for the pig' to watch, and darts – a serious business – and games to try, like bean bags, the bran tub and treasure hunts. The bric-a-brac stall would sometimes yield a treasure for a few pence, like a tiny piece of china or an old scarf. There were refreshments – mounds of sandwiches, scones and slices of Victoria sponge, tea and orange squash for us. I can still smell the particular combination of steam, tea leaves and clean tea cloths which pervaded the kitchen, presided over by very busy women who could not be disturbed, at the risk of a stern rebuke. Above all, there was the perfection of the beautifully kept gardens, with the newly mown lawns and banks of sweet peas scenting the whole afternoon. Even when we had a wet day for the fête the impromptu arrangements were exciting, the games being housed in Miss Robinson's old coach houses and outhouses, with their scent of mouldy hay and hard, old, earth floors.

So for me the church was an integral, tightly linked part of our village year and village life, underscoring the passage of the seasons in the countryside. Although I enjoyed Christian Endeavour meetings, which were organised and held in the chapel, I regarded myself as an Anglican. Others, however, attended both church and chapel, as Alfred Yaxley (1900–1974) recalls: *'Sunday School caused me a great deal of worry as I got older. The trouble started when I was old enough to be in the class taken by the rector himself. (The rector in 1908 was the Reverend Leonard Chesters, rector since 1895.) At first we had to learn the collect of the day and recite it on Sunday mornings, then as we got older it was the Collect and the Gospel, or at least part of it, if the Gospel was a long one. If I had had the sense to start learning these on a Monday, it wouldn't have been so bad, but usually on Saturday evenings mother would suddenly say, "Have you learned your Sunday School lessons?" There would then follow a frantic hour or so with the Prayer Book in my hand. It was not easy with three younger children being prepared for bed and the hubbub that goes with this ritual. When they were taken upstairs it was easier, but more often than not I would be standing outside the Church Rooms on Sunday morning completing the job. I can truthfully say that I never once missed fulfilling my task. Whether all this did me any good spiritually, I don't know. What I do know is that for years after I left school I would dream that I was on my way to Sunday School and then suddenly realise that I hadn't learned a word of the Collect and the Gospel. These dreams were like little night-mares. I even had one of these when I was in the Army.*

'After Sunday School we would go off two by two to the 11 a.m. service at the church. Very few children dropped out, although I must say that church services were an ordeal for youngsters in those days; they were so long, or seemed to be especially when we had the Litany. Sermons always seemed to be longer than they are nowadays and children natu-rally got fidgety. I shall always remember the rector suddenly stopped in the middle of his sermon and said sternly, "Bessie Wright, will you stop talking?" – the only time I remember a rebuke from the pulpit.

'I recall one occasion when the rector brought politics into his sermon – he was a Tory – and two or three women Liberals got up and walked out. That sort of thing needed a good deal of courage to do in those days.

'Our Primitive Methodist chapel had no Sunday School in those days, but my grandmother was a Primitive Methodist so I often used to go with her to chapel on Sunday afternoons, perhaps go and have tea with her and then to chapel again in the evening. The preachers then were mainly working men and would come from miles around, on foot or bicycle and sometimes in pony carts. Between services they would be invited to have tea with a member or members of the congregation. If it fell to my grandmother's lot to do the inviting, she often asked me to tea too, and those occasions were milestones in my life. The preachers

would often come in pairs and it was a great joy to me to have tea in the company of Messrs Raspberry and Bacon. One was a fat, jolly man with mutton-chop whiskers, and one was tall and thin and rather more solemn, but both I thought were sincere Christians, indeed with one possible exception they all seemed to me to be very genuine in their belief.

'The exception was a tall, thin, youngish man with a little, fair moustache. He had the gift of the gab and I adored him. My enthusiasm was modified when I heard my grandmother talking to another woman about it. "Did you know," she said, "that he thack [beat] his wife?" My adoration went in a flash.

'The pulpit in our chapel had an oil lamp at each end, raised on a standard and each with a chimney and outer globe. One Sunday afternoon the preacher, an elderly man with a long beard, started to pray. Closing his eyes, he worked himself into such an ecstasy that he flung both arms out sideways and scored a perfect knockout on both lamps. The crash was a bit startling. He opened his eyes for a couple of seconds and then went on praying as if nothing had happened. It was after the service that I felt sorry for him, when I saw him taking money from his pocket to pay for the damage.

'Other preachers who came in pairs were the brothers Robert and Henry West, fishermen from a coastal village a few miles away. If I knew they were coming I would never miss chapel on that Sunday if I could help it. In their fishermen's garb they were a complete contrast to the usual run of preachers and in addition they were very fine singers, and they certainly could preach. I well recall the Saturday afternoon when the news came through to the village that the brothers West had been drowned when their boat overturned in a sudden squall at sea. This news proved to be wrong in one respect: only Robert had been drowned, along with his mate. The brothers had not been together that afternoon. The news was bad enough as it was and I think everyone felt sad and shocked. I know I did.

'In the later days of my chapel-going the music was provided by an American organ, but when I first attended the music for hymns was played by two little old gentlemen. Each had a violin, and they always did a vast amount of tuning up. As everyone sang very heartily it

didn't matter if they made mistakes. Perhaps they didn't make any – I don't know. I did my share in singing those wonderful old hymns in the Primitive Methodist hymn book, and enjoyed doing it until I heard someone after the service say to my grandmother, "Hasn't he got a nice voice?" "Yes," replied my grandmother, "he sings like a girl." That remark offended me and my singing in chapel almost ended.

A few more words about church and chapel. I like church services and certain of the rituals – the beautiful words of the Prayer Book are a joy – but for sheer religious fervour the chapel services were hard to beat. Members of the congregation were often asked by the preacher to offer a prayer, and pray they did. Grandmother didn't much care for praying in public, but she didn't shirk it. When she prayed, I prayed too, but it was a silent prayer that she wouldn't make any mistakes and let the side down, so to speak. It is not to my credit that I would bet with my other self that when a certain man was called on to pray he would begin by saying, "O Lord, thou hast said that when two or three are gathered together in thy name", etc. This chap never failed me. I always won my bet.

'I very seldom attended chapel when my schooldays had ended, mainly because I lived away from home, but as long as I keep my senses, I will remember it and its services, and I will always connect it with my dear old grandmother, a simple, good-living country woman if ever there was one.'

Olive Wild (Webster) (b. 1919) remembers Miss Robinson (of Knapton House) playing the church organ on Sundays: *'It was at the time when somebody would have to sit behind it and pump a lever by hand. My brother Henry did this, and would pull faces which could only be seen by the congregation!*

'We had Sunday School outings to Mundesley beach and were taken by horse and wagon from Wallage's Farm (now White House Farm). Barbara Farrow and I were confirmed at North Walsham church, where we had to wear veils which were given to us.

'I would take the Sunday papers – I think they came from North Walsham and were left at ours – to the Brocklehursts's back door at the Hall (in The Street). When Mr Brocklehurst was taken ill they only lived there in the summer, then spent the winter down south. My sister Lily worked for one season in service at the Hall.

'Also I would take the Sunday paper down to the Dixon family in Hall Lane. They were very good to me; for doing this, they bought me a present. It was an umbrella.

'My mother would not allow me to go to chapel, only church, though we had chapel preachers in the family, but because the Robinson family owned our cottage, and my father worked for them as a groom and gardener, and as they were church-going people, my mother told me, "That is where your bread is buttered." That was how it was then.'

Leslie Coe (b. 1922) writes: *'During my schooldays I also attended Sunday School in the Parish Room, where we were taught by Miss Montford, and I think Nina Swan. Every Sunday we were given a small card with words on it which we had to learn for the following Sunday. After Sunday School I usually went to the morning service in the church, conducted by the Rev. Prichard, and the organ was played by Miss Robinson. Going back to the Sunday School, I shall never forget the lovely Christmas parties, beautiful Christmas tree, and every one of us had a present given to us by Father Christmas.'*

In the Parish magazine for North Walsham and District in March 1932, the rector, Mr Prichard, writes in the 'Paston with Knapton' entry: *'To our great regret, no record was made last month of the most successful Christmas Party for the children of our Sunday Schools, which was held on January 8th. Needless to say that the children appeared to enjoy themselves, as did the teachers; these gatherings do help us to feel that we are part of one big family. This year, it was marked by the number of people who sent donations, cakes etc., which not only helped the teachers to see that their work is valued, but helped us to make real the fact that the church's children are the care of the church's grown-ups, and that they see the necessity of providing amusement as well as teaching. It was a most happy evening and we thank all who helped to make it so.'*

Llewellyn Kirk (b. 1930) remembers a summer Sunday School party held *'in Miss Montford's garden. The sandwiches were chocolate spread and nasturtium leaves. We could not eat them so we ended up with apples from the tree above.'* There is more about Miss Montford in the chapter 'Transport'. The occasion described by Llewellyn here was obviously a non-meeting of minds.

The parties – and the Sunday School treat, their summer counterpart – continued up to and beyond my time as a Sunday School pupil. The parties were held, in the 1940s and 1950s, alternately in Knapton and Paston Parish Room. Games such as Pass the Parcel, Musical Chairs, The Farmer's in his Den and Musical Statues gradually became more uproarious until the relative peace of tea, when sandwiches, jellies, cakes, biscuits and squash would be served. For us, the novelty of being with Paston children, who mostly did not attend our school but went instead to Edingthorpe or Mundesley, made the occasion noteworthy.

Pearl Hicks (Eves) (b. 1951) retains affectionate memories of the Methodist chapel Christmas parties in the 1950s, and writes: *'One particular game stands out in my memory. Three or four people lay on the floor with a blanket covering their legs. The children were called one by one from another room. We had first to shake each person's hand, then their leg, when to our horror one of them had got a false leg and it would come off in our hand. Lots of other games were played. The schoolroom's lino-tiled floor would become very hot and wet. This caused us to slide around a lot, which of course all added to the fun.'*

Church and chapel summer treats took the form of a visit to Great Yarmouth, with a very long walk along the promenade to the Pleasure Beach, and fish and chips for lunch. I can remember feeling that our school trips to Blakeney Point or to London were very much more interesting, because they had been carefully prepared, and we had to write about them afterwards. Even so, the journey by train to Yarmouth was a novelty.

The chapel children travelled by Starling's coach, and Pearl writes: *'We were very excited and got more so as the journey went on. The morning was usually spent on the fun fair. For many years, everyone met in a restaurant for a fish and chip lunch at the cost of one shilling and sixpence. This was paid for from Sunday School funds. In the afternoon most people visited the circus. This event was certainly the highlight of the year.'*

Anne Lee (Isitt) (b. 1936) remembers weekly choir practice being taken in the church by Miss Robinson, and also that Miss

Robinson *'started a club for us in the Parish Room where we had beetle drives and played board games'.*

Shirley Wright (Conquest) (b. 1938) writes of church and chapel. She recalls singing in the church choir and attending Sunday School. She adds: *'A few of us when we reached the age of around fifteen would also go to the Methodist chapel for a Sunday service, alternating with the church service. Mr and Mrs Herbert Hicks, who were Methodists, would hold a Youth Group at their house once a week, and also an invitation back to their house on a Sunday evening. We were all made so welcome and they really enjoyed having us, as we were a good crowd and got on so well together; we would often have evenings out, such as visiting their farm for supper, a walk along the beach from Bacton to Mundesley in the summer evenings, or activities with other Methodist groups. We always spent part of the evening discussing religion. It was lovely to participate with other people of the same age, and gave us something to do in such a quiet village.'*

Roger Dixon (b. 1933), who after a teaching career was ordained, writes of Knapton church: *'I absolutely loved church as a boy. It was like being at a beautiful play, performed every week, mostly the same, but with fascinating changes as the seasons came round. Mr Prichard, the rector at the time, was a wonderful visitor to my father, who had quite serious heart trouble. He called one day, chuckling to himself. He had visited Mr Wallage at White House Farm, and had asked whether he thought we should pray for rain. He got the answer, "What's the good of that with the wind where it is?" I think Mr Wallage may have been having him on, but he was greatly amused. One thing I remember about Christmas time is that Mr Prichard would not allow carols to be sung until Christmas actually came, unlike today, when we sing them all through December.*

'Sunday School was run by Miss Montford, who had a great enthusiasm for the Melanesian Mission to the South Sea Islands. A whist table was always arranged like a little altar with a cross and flowers. The child whose birthday fell that week took home the flowers. I, or perhaps my mother, lost out because my birthday is in late December.'

In contrast to others, Roger adds: *'As a teenager, I started*

going to the Christian Endeavour at the chapel, but my mother and
father, strongly Anglican, did not really approve. Happily, those days
have gone, and in my later life I have had wonderfully happy times
with the Salvation Army, the Methodist and Baptist churches, and
even the Brethren, although they did not invite me any more after
I was ordained.'

The Rev. Chesters, the Rev. Prichard and the Rev. Thur were rectors of the churches in Knapton and Paston during the period covered by this book. In the 1970s, both villages became part of the Trunch Group of parishes, which continues to this day. The influence of the church on the lives of many of us was considerable, since our contributors include an ordained priest of the Church of England and a licensed lay reader in the Church of England.

The chapel stands close to the church, near the junction of Pond Road and The Street. The *Historical Atlas of Norfolk*, edited by Ashwin and Davison (2005), devotes an entry to 'Protestant Noncomformity in Norfolk'. It states (p. 144): 'Dissent was a significant feature throughout eastern England from the seventeenth century. Baptist and Congregational membership was strong in Norfolk ... But by 1851 Methodism was the dramatic force in the county, with Primitive Methodism attracting exceptional support.'

The establishment and development of Knapton's Methodist chapel was part of this movement, as is illustrated in a short history of it written by Herbert Hicks to mark its centenary in 1990. Mr Hicks was Trust Treasurer of the chapel and for many years the Sunday School superintendent. He and his wife Margaret ran the extremely successful and influential youth fellowship mentioned in many accounts in this book.

Mr Hicks relates that the chapel began its life as a barn. In 1880, a retired minister, Rev. E. S. Shields, bought the building with its adjoining cottage and turned the barn into a chapel, registering it for worship. In 1890, the North Walsham Primitive Methodist Circuit hired the building and began organising services. For some reason services were discontinued in 1902, although the rent continued to be paid by someone unknown. The chapel reopened in 1916. A new

head teacher at the school, Miss Carpenter, had come to Knapton
with her mother. Photo 4 shows Mrs Carpenter at Knapton School
House, together with Granny Bowman and others, sewing items to
raise funds for the chapel. They were keen to have services restarted
and improvements began to be made to the building, including a
wooden floor and a tortoise stove. Knapton School was a county
school, but the rector at any one time was a member of the school
managers, later governors, and it is interesting to note that Miss
Carpenter, a highly respected and successful head teacher of the
school, was such a strong Methodist activist. For a time there was
also a Methodist infant teacher, Miss Cox.

Other improvements followed over the years, including, in 1944,
seats from the chapel at Trimingham, which had closed, and later
an extension of a schoolroom, kitchen and toilets.

Mr Hicks writes that in about 1946 special evening services
were organised by the Young Laymen's League: *'One of the results
was that a newly-wed young man became a member. For many years,
he and his wife, Mr and Mrs James Steward, were a great blessing.
They brought all their family through the chapel, and many of them still
serve in other churches.'* Contributors to this book and to *Knapton
Remembered* include Janet, Ruth, Mary and Eric, the children of
James and Ellen Steward, and Clifford Self, a cousin. Arthur Amis,
well known lay preacher, political activist and councillor, was a
brother of Ellen Steward. More about his career and of the work
of Labour/union/Methodist activists like him is included in the
chapter on politics.

Mr Hicks, writing in 1990, concludes his history of the chapel
with these words: *'We have a very happy, loving fellowship in our
society today. There are twenty-four members, six under twenty years
old. There are fifteen children, Women's Own has twenty-five members,
and Men's Fellowship fifteen members. We have a monthly prayer circle,
and regular united worship and other shared activities with our friends
in the Parish Church. We praise God for all that is past and trust that the
future may be fruitful and bring glory to His Name.'*

An interesting account of the early days of Knapton chapel

was provided by Ursula Fawkes, who died in 1977 at the age of fifty-nine. She was a strong supporter of the chapel, and ran the Christian Endeavour group for young people described by many contributors to this book. A photograph of a meeting of Christian Endeavour in the early 1950s is shown as Photo 6. It was taken in the chapel, and Ursula can be seen on the right, at the back. Ursula describes the chapel in her parents' time, and continues with some memories of her own:

'When my parents, Herbert and Ethel Fawkes, first joined the Methodist Church at Knapton, it was vastly different from what it is now. [Mr Fawkes was born in 1895, so this description dates from the 1920s.] This is what it looked like. There were railings right round the cottage [next door] and the chapel you entered by a small door between the large windows. On opening the porch door you faced wooden bench seats, different in lengths and heights ... Having taken your seat facing what is now the altar rail, you would see a double cupboard where books were kept on the top shelves, and coal underneath. Next to this was a black-top stove, then the pulpit, under which stood a small organ. At the other side of the pulpit a door led into the cottage, so that the tenant could walk through the chapel to the door at the back, which led into three small rooms. In one was the copper and oven.

'The walls of the chapel were blue distemper and the floor red flag brick, with pieces of natural colour coconut matting across the front. Two ladies who occupied the front seat had their own cushions, one green mixture and one red. Granny Bean and Granny Bowman had these seats. On the left hand side of the stove there was a seat sideways where the caretaker, Mr Hewitt, sat. On the rails, which go across the chapel now, there were two hanging oil lamps on each side which pulled up and down on chains. There was also one fixed to each side of the pulpit. These had to be cleaned with Brasso and filled each week with paraffin, sometimes twice when there were week-night meetings.

'We had a Christian Endeavour: anybody could come, and two teachers from the day school provided the music. Miss Mary Carpenter, who was the head teacher, played the organ, and Miss Cox, the junior teacher who lodged with Granny Bowman, played the violin.

'The building was closed for some time, and Grandfather Hedge said that if a Sunday School were started again, there would be a sovereign (a gold coin with the worth of a pound) to start the funds off. This is still in the Sunday School funds. Although there have been many hard times, someone has always come along to help and see that this is not changed.

'The first children to come to Sunday School were Walter Abbs, Walter Pardon, Bill, Blanche, Sidney and Victor Wild, Ursula and Sylvia Fawkes, Fred, Vic and Stanley Watts, Herbert and Edith Grey and Owen Blake. The family of Wilds had to walk from Stone Cottages (at least a mile and a half beyond the Old Hall) twice on a Sunday, Sunday School at 10 a.m. and 2 p.m., afternoon service at 2.30.

'There were four on the staff: Miss Mary Carpenter, Mr Scott, Mr Blake and Mr Appleton, and then Mr Watts when a few more children came along. Mr Scott rode a three-wheel bike and went round selling books. He was taken ill on the train from Knapton to North Walsham one Saturday morning and died before the train reached North Walsham.'

Pearl Hicks writes that her mother Margaret (née Turner) collected and sold jumble all the year round to raise money for chapel funds. The money she raised went into the funds for the fête, which was held annually at Church Farm. Before her marriage to Herbert Hicks, she visited every house in Knapton once a year with a missionary box collecting money for overseas missions on behalf of the chapel.

Janet Steward (Munro) (b. 1940) writes vividly in *Knapton Remembered* about her Methodist upbringing, and her account echoes Alfred Yaxley's description of his grandmother's household, sixty years earlier. Janet writes: *'My mother came from a chapel family so it was obvious that I and any siblings I might have would be brought up to attend the Methodist Church. This we did – three times on a Sunday. Sunday School in the morning and chapel services in the afternoon at 2.30 p.m. and 6.30 p.m. Often the local preacher would stay to tea, having been "planned" to attend and preach at both services.*

'The most favourite of all the local preachers was Arthur Amis from Trunch, my mother's brother and our uncle. He was an excellent story teller. He was, in addition to his many years as a Methodist

local preacher, at various times a parish, district and county councillor. He started his working life as a cowman at Hill Farm in Mundesley, immediately joining the National Union of Agricultural Workers. He was very active in the union and helped to marshal their forces in the 1926 General Strike. In 1958 he became the first secretary-agent for the North Norfolk Labour Party, firstly serving Edwin Gooch MP and then Bert Hazell MP.'

Janet's sister Ruth Steward (Matthew) (b. 1943) continues the story of this Methodist household: *'In May we held our Sunday School anniversary. For weeks we learned new hymns, choruses and recitations. On the special Sunday we sat at the front of the chapel in our finery. Most present had new clothes to wear. The chapel was overflowing with parents and relations. Recitations were said, solos or group songs were sung, action choruses enjoyed, as were the hymns, sung with gusto. The collection on this day went to Sunday School funds, these being used for our outing to Yarmouth in the summer, the Christmas party and medals with additional metal bars, added each year, for full attendance. At one time we had stamp books for attendance and pictures with texts were attached for each Sunday the student was present. I can remember going for five years with no Sundays absent.*

'We had a houseful of relations and friends for tea because there was an afternoon and an evening service. We had salad, bread and butter, jelly, cakes, quite a party. We were not encouraged to play in the garden in case we got our clothes dirty.

'When my sister Mary was born I spent four weeks staying with others, one week was with Mrs Johnson at the School House. On this Sunday I went to the church Sunday School. I was just six and made to feel so welcome. I could answer the questions Miss Townshend asked and of course I wanted to be allowed to join this Sunday School. Mum had other ideas, however, and I was soon back at the chapel! I must say I have the chapel Sunday School to thank for my biblical knowledge and my love of hymns, which enabled me to be organist for a short time before I left Knapton in 1959 to work as a nursery nurse.

'Harvest Festival at the chapel produced a lot of groceries and produce. We spent much of the Saturday before helping decorate the

chapel which always looked and smelled terrific. During the week there was a service and a sale of produce. All monies raised went to the chapel funds.

'The chapel was always decorated for Easter Sunday; the window sills were covered in primroses and moss (there were many places to find primroses then). I can also remember having a service of songs, telling a special story with songs in between readings, these were very popular at one time. Sometimes we had lantern slide evenings.

'Holy Communion was held every few Sundays, when the minister came: small squares of bread and non-alcoholic wine, probably blackcurrant juice. Children left after the closing hymn, then Communion was held. Now it is taken during the service.

'A special service was held at North Walsham Methodist Chapel, for some of the teenagers from Knapton and other chapels to be welcomed into membership of the Methodist Church on St George's Day 1959. My brother Eric and I were included. The Women's Own met fortnightly on a Tuesday and still meet today. Members of this group would meet once a year to spring clean the chapel.

'What is now called the church council would meet once or twice a year to discuss the affairs of the chapel and make plans for repairs, etc. Hence the chapel now has a purpose-built school/general purposes room, and a kitchen and toilet.

'At one time, there was a stable to house the preacher's horse and a washroom for the person living in Chapel House [the adjoining cottage], *for their wash-day. A copper was in one corner, and washing was hung up in the chapel to dry. There was a door from the chapel into Chapel House at the time.'*

Both church and chapel continue to exert a lively influence on what goes on in Knapton, and their cooperation in joint ventures is now regarded as a matter of course. In 2009, for example, there was a flower festival with a wedding theme, involving both church and chapel and other village organisations.

Knapton also has some Catholic families. The Kiernans, who lived at Knapton Old Hall in a period which spanned the Second World War, were Catholic, as were the children of Tom

Purdy junior, of whom Elizabeth Purdy (b. 1941) was the eldest. My father's brother Leslie married an Irish Catholic girl during the war, and their three children, my cousins Brian, Josephine and Patrick, were brought up as Catholics. The nearest church was at North Walsham, and a bus went round the villages on Sundays to collect the congregation and take them to church. Two evacuees, Edward and Josephine Langham, who stayed with Mrs Johnson, the headmistress of Knapton School, and her family towards the end of the war, were also Catholics, and Josephine Langham, now Hourahane, writes: '*North Walsham's Catholic church was too far for us to attend so Miss Mary Kiernan of Knapton Old Hall took us to Mundesley where Mass was said for the servicemen in the Grand Hotel.*'

Some of the large houses and other buildings in Knapton, and the people who lived and worked in them, are recalled below.

Knapton House was the home of the Robinson family, who appear in all the *Kelly's Directories* quoted in this book. The first member of the family commemorated by a plaque in Knapton church is George Robinson, born in 1761. His son, Henry Robinson, was born in 1804 and died in 1879. He was knighted and had been a Gentleman at Arms. He was also a Deputy Lieutenant and a JP. His son, Henry Matthew Cooper Robinson, mentioned in Olive Wild's account below, was born in 1851 and died in 1922. His daughter, Constance Ellen (1879–1968), is the Miss Robinson so lovingly remembered by many contributors to this book. The commemorative plaque dedicated to her in the church describes her as 'Most gracious benefactress of this church'.

Olive Wild (Webster) describes Knapton House as she remembers it during the 1920s and early 1930s: '*When going through the front door, the dining room and the stairs were on the right. On the left was the drawing room. Going down the hall, the study was on the right-hand side, with the breakfast room, where the family lived, on the left. It had doors leading out on to the lawn. It was also known as the library. Going back into the hall, at the back door a passage was to the pump house where the water would be pumped into the house. Then came the kitchen with a cooking range and big shiny saucepan lids hanging on the wall. Agnes Gee and another person from North Walsham worked there. Then came the scullery. Upstairs there were several bedrooms, bathrooms and the maids' quarters.*

'I can remember peaches hanging in the greenhouse beside the house, also the vegetable garden. Lawns on three sides of the house, which were cut with a pony pulling a mower. The pony had sacks tied around its feet to stop it sinking into the grass. Flowerbeds were cut into the lawn, and there was a maze. Going down the drive from the Knapton Green end you would pass the coach house and the wooden billiard room [the predecessor of the Men's Club]. *The drive swept round in front of the house, and out on to the road near the Driftway cottages.*

'There was a gardener's shed where I would find my father [John Wild] *and the head gardener, Mr Appleton, dozing on the benches! My father was coachman, but when Sir Henry died he became gardener. After my father died George Turner was the gardener.'*

The last member of the family to live in the House was Miss Constance Robinson, who died in 1968 at the age of eighty-nine. It was said that she never spent a night away from the village. Indeed, throughout the whole of her long life Miss Robinson was devoted to Knapton and the people in it. It would be impossible to exaggerate that devotion, and possibly difficult for today's reader to understand it. It is also the case that because of Miss Robinson's devotion to the Knapton community, the majority of people in the village were extremely familiar with her house and garden, as they were opened to us so frequently.

I have very clear memories of Miss Robinson in the 1940s and 1950s, dressed like an Edwardian lady in coat and long skirt, and always a large hat, accompanied by her companion Miss Leather, driving a huge Lanchester car at a snail's pace round the village, making calls, visiting the sick, and delivering gifts. When I was six I had a bad ear infection, which without antibiotics was a serious condition, necessitating three weeks in bed. Miss Robinson came to visit several times, bringing very old children's books, no doubt her own, which I devoured voraciously, even if I found *Straw Peter* rather bizarre.

She was devoted to the church, where she ran the choir, played the organ and helped decorate for all festivals. All church fêtes were held in the garden of Knapton House. She was for many years the President of the Women's Institute and was instrumental in setting up the Men's Club and the provision of the playing field. She was a magistrate and served on the North Walsham bench. She, together with Mrs Johnson, the headmistress of the school, was a great enthusiast for National Savings, taking part in the many campaigns during and after the war. She was a school manager and frequent visitor to Knapton School.

Olive Wild remembers Miss Robinson's father: *'I was very ill when I was four years old with pneumonia; prayers were said for me in church. I had a bed under the window in the front room, and my father told me that when he drove past in the pony and trap with Sir Henry Robinson, he would have to stop so Sir Henry could get down and look at me through the window.'*

Leslie Coe remembers *'Miss Robinson, who at Christmas used to give tins of tea to people in the village, aided of course by Miss Leather.'*

Kathleen Johnson (b. 1936) writes of Miss Robinson thus: *'In Knapton, Miss Robinson was very much the Lady of the Big House. In the days before the NHS and social security, it was said that most of the villagers wore false teeth and spectacles paid for by Miss Robinson. Every house was given a sack of coal at Christmas and all "church" girls were given a very nice present when they got married.'*

Ann Lee writes: *'Miss Robinson and Miss Leather lived at Knapton House and were key figures in village life. They were the "gentry". Miss Robinson played the church organ and held choir practices, and ran a club for us in the Parish Room. Miss Leather took Sunday School and I remember each year on Mothering Sunday she gave each child a posy of beautifully tied violets for their mothers. We were rather in awe of these ladies but they were very kind, and when I was ill with whooping cough and pneumonia Miss Robinson called at our house with good things to help me get better. Calves' foot jelly was something I remember well, and have never tasted since all those years ago.'*

Knapton Old Hall is remembered by Alfred Yaxley as his first place of work for the farmer and auctioneer Herbert Barcham, and his vivid description of the farm buildings is given in the chapter on agriculture. Roger Dixon, writing in *Knapton Remembered*, recalls that his mother *'used to go one afternoon a week to Knapton Old Hall to do the washing in their laundry. I always joined her after school. One day I was singing as I played in the garden and Mrs Kiernan, who I think had been an opera singer, heard me and called down from her window, "Who's that singing?" I hid in the shrubbery but it transpired that she wasn't cross but simply interested. She offered to give me singing lessons and train my voice, but soon after that she became more frail and nothing came of it. I often wonder what might have been.'*

The performance of *A Midsummer Night's Dream* which the Kiernan family produced in their garden at the Old Hall is remembered by Roger Dixon, who writes: *'The production was in the open air, under an enormous beech tree. A girl called Dorothy Green and I were in it, as bumblebees! Mr Twigg from the dairy at Mundesley was one of the players. He had a quick draw on his pipe in the bushes backstage, but was called for the next scene and stuffed the pipe into his pocket. Part way through the scene his jacket began to smoulder and a thin spiral of smoke began to rise. The other actors were all local people. Mr Claydon senior was one, and my uncles George and Hubert. They were Bottom the weaver and the other "mechanicals".'*

Knapton Hall is mentioned by some contributors to this book, not least the fact that in the late 1950s it became a hotel run by the Spankie family, and later by Derek and Madeleine Heath. Photo 8 shows a tennis party during the 1920s at the Hall when the Brocklehurst family lived there. The Village Hall, which began life as a thatched barn, was opened as a school for sixty pupils in 1837 – by Selina Shirley (1787–1870), who lived at Knapton Hall. The school was replaced by a purpose-built school in 1897, and after that became known as the Parish Room.

The Parish Room is so frequently mentioned in this book that the importance of its role to the village is obvious. It was the place where Sunday School for the older children was held each week; the parish council met there; the Women's Institute held its monthly

meetings there; and a host of social events took place there. During
my childhood in Knapton I can recall concerts, film shows, dancing lessons, socials for church and chapel funds, Sunday School
parties, and whist and beetle drives. There were official events too:
we had to go there to be issued with ration books. It is impossible
to imagine life in the village without the Village Hall, despite its
imperfections. These are numerous: it is not large; it is difficult to
heat; the kitchen is dark and steamy; and the lavatories (a relatively
recent addition) likewise. Nevertheless, it is a much-loved public
space and holds happy memories for everyone.

Olive Wild writes: *'My mother was caretaker of the Parish Room
and we held a key which would hang on a hook just inside the door.
When people wanted the key they would just open the door and take it,
not always knocking first. So my mother had a curtain hang beside the
door and behind it we could sit and have our meals in privacy.*

*'My memories of the Parish Room in the 1920s and early 1930s are
as follows. The main entrance was from the Hall Lane side. The present
main entrance from the Little Road was almost never used at that time.
The Hall Lane door brought you into the room where the stage is now,
into what we called the little room. This had a brick floor. There were two
rooms upstairs which were not in use, only for storage, including trunks
full of clothes for when plays were performed. When it was wet and we
children could not play outside we would take the key, go into the Room
and dress up in the clothes out of the trunks.*

*'There was a fireplace in the little room and in the big room and both
were lit when there were functions. A wicker wheelchair was kept in the
Parish Room for use by people in the village when needed.*

*'On Saturday mornings, after I had cleaned the spoons and forks
indoors for my mother, I had to go into the Parish Room and lay the fires
and put out the chairs ready for Sunday School the next day at 10 a.m.
My Sunday School teachers were the two Miss Pains, Miss Robinson and
Miss Leather. It was followed by going to the church service at 11 a.m.*

*'When my mother helped at functions I would go in with her. I will
never forget, as a child, the best wedding I saw in Knapton. It was Rose
Wright's (sister of Archie Wright), who married Jack Davies, a Cromer*

*Lifeboat man and fisherman. The men were wearing their uniforms and
danced a clog dance.'*

The school was built in 1897. The importance of its role and its
influence on the lives of its pupils have been described in detail in
Knapton Remembered, which focused on the time as headmistress
of Mrs Kathleen Johnson between 1934 and 1961, when sadly and
prematurely she died. In the introduction to *Knapton Remembered*
I wrote: 'The importance of the school, and of its inspiring head
teacher, Mrs Johnson, illuminates every page of this book. The
school was small, not more than between thirty and forty pupils
except when evacuees swelled its numbers during the Second
World War. Yet pupils were given as broad an education as was
possible, given the obvious constraints, in a way which would not
shame the most modern of today's schools.'

Our education and our memories of it inspired that book and
led to the writing of this one.

Knapton Men's Club, next to the school house on Hall Lane,
has a fascinating history that illustrates the tradition of self help
frequently found in small, isolated communities like Knapton.

In 1938 a General Meeting was held in the Parish Room to form
a Men's Night Club (sic) in the village. It was decided that the Parish
Room should open on Mondays, Wednesdays and Fridays from 6.30
p.m. to 10 p.m., so that men and boys could meet to play darts, cards,
table tennis and bagatelle. Meanwhile, money would be raised for
a 'rebuilding fund'. The progress of the project, including plans for
money raising, are meticulously recorded in the minutes of General
Meetings and committee meetings, which continue throughout the
war. After the war the club activities transferred to Miss Robinson's
billiard room in the grounds of Knapton House. For a short time
during 1947 and 1948 there were club activities in the Parish Room
on three nights a week, and in Miss Robinson's billiard room on two
nights a week during the season. Eventually in 1949 a piece of land
belonging to Mr Cargill and next to the school house in Hall Lane
was acquired on a 99-year lease for the new building. Work began on
the building in 1949 and the new room was completed in 1950. The

whole project was achieved by people giving their time on a voluntary basis, and the official opening took place on 3 October 1950. At the General Meeting on 25 September, just before the official opening, Miss Robinson had been elected Life President, as it was her initiative and support that had made the whole project possible.

The above account, based on research by June Wild, gives only the bare bones of a sustained effort by a whole community to provide a simple facility for the common good. Money raising, which mostly took the form of whist drives, fêtes and members' subscriptions, was pitifully slow. The minutes record some of the proceeds of, for example, a barn dance and whist drive at Church Farm: £15 6s. The Men's Club share of the proceeds of a fête held jointly with the Women's Institute in 1951 was £23 16s 7d. But Knapton got there in the end.

One building that played a key role in the economic life of Knapton was destroyed by a disastrous fire in 1958. This was the blacksmith's shop, shown in the plate section as Photo 9. Mr Bussey, the blacksmith during my childhood, was very well known to my parents, who were friends with Jack Bussey, Mr Bussey's son. Jack was in the Merchant Navy.

Pam Dixon (Garnham) (b. 1935) writes: *'As a child, I spent hours at Mr Bussey's blacksmith's shop, watching him shoe the horses from the farms in the area. He also made parts for the horse-drawn ploughs used locally and harrows, which consisted of a square metal framework with several curved and shaped metal pieces attached, used to smooth the ground after it had been ploughed. The fire was kept going by pumping bellows. Mr Bussey would use tongs to put the metal in until it was red hot, and then hammer it into shape on the anvil.'*

All of us would hang about The Street, near the shop, watching the comings and goings of the horses and savouring the extraordinary smells of burning and noises of hissing steam and hammering as Mr Bussey did his dramatic work.

But no one could have foreseen the drama that befell Mr Bussey and his shop in 1958, and which is recounted here by Babs Dixon (Jarvis) (b. 1938) and Linda Fawkes (Risebrow) (b. 1950).

Babs writes: *'A spark flew from the blacksmith's shop to the thatched roof of Mr Bussey's house, as he lived next door to his shop. It went up in one big blaze, very frightening to watch. I had never seen a fire engine in action till then, but the sirens made me feel quite ill as it brought back memories of my childhood living in London. (I was evacuated to Norfolk at the age of six.)'*

Linda writes: *'I was about eight years old when mum sent me to Mrs Coe's with a note. When I went down the path I got to the gate where two firemen were rolling a hose down the street. I ran back to tell mum. We walked back outside the door and could see the thatch round the chimney well alight at the blacksmith's shop. As the fire took hold, it moved along the roof of Mr and Mrs Lubbock's house. They brought all their furniture into our house, then as the fire crept along to Mr and Mrs George Wild's house they put all their furniture on our lawn. Mr Bussey would not come out of the house. People were trying to talk to him as the fire took hold. In the end they had to send for his son to come and coax him out. Auntie Ursula came to take me and my sister, Rene, to Christian Endeavour, so by the time we got back the fire was out. We went indoors, and mum told us to go into the kitchen as all Mr and Mrs Lubbock's furniture had been put into our front room. There was just enough room to walk through when we went upstairs to bed. Next day we went to school, and by the time we got home all the furniture had gone as Mr May had given the Lubbock family a temporary home in Pond Road, next to the Stewards, until their property had been repaired.'*

Knapton had a shop for almost the whole of the period covered by this book. *Kelly's Directory* of 1892 records a Miss Rebecca Grimes, grocer; a George Rolfe, grocer and draper; a post office for the issue of stamps only; and a Joseph Sexton, receiver. In 1922 the shopkeeper is named as Miss Ada Watts. Mrs Sarah Sexton is described as the sub-postmistress. In 1932 Mrs E. Webster is described as tobacconist and keeper of the post office. The business then passed to Mrs Smith, who ran it at her house at the bottom of The Street, opposite the house where the Miller family lived.

Pam Dixon takes up the story: *'When we first moved to the Shop House in Knapton Mrs Smith had the shop and Post Office in her front sitting room at the bottom of The Street. In 1948 or 1949 she sold the business because of ill health. My father bought it.*

'*Everything was still on ration books and in short supply. Someone came from Norwich Head Post Office for several days to teach us to do the accounts etc. Ration book customers had to register with a shop. It was very difficult when we were allocated a few tins of fruit or salmon. We tried to be fair to our registered customers. Biscuits came in big, square tins. We could also get tins of broken ones which were much cheaper.*

'*When clothes came off coupons I can remember large boxes of wellie boots, caps, braces, men's trousers, socks, ladies' underwear, nighties, aprons, jumpers, and lisle stockings and nylons (if we could get them). Everything sold very quickly as clothing was scarce after the war.*

'*When sweets came off ration they were still very short and we could never seem to get enough to meet demand.*

'*We used to go to Fayers' bakehouse in North Walsham every Friday and bring back trays of cakes to sell. Later we had a weekly delivery of Melton Mowbray pies, which were very popular – mince, steak and kidney and chicken, as well as pork.*

'*The post office accounts had to be added up and tally every week, and pension dockets etc. sent to Norwich. That had to be done every night. Pay wasn't very good. When I finished in 1981 the wage was just over £30 per week.*

'*Later we did the newspaper round. My sister Barbara and I used to cycle before work. On a Saturday we would load up the van with orders to deliver also a selection of groceries and a lot of Corona, very popular at that time. Dad and I used to go round the village collecting newspaper money and delivering groceries and selling from the van.*

'*In later years, as supermarkets started to open and more people got cars, the trade slowly dropped, until at the end, my cousin Violet Thompson and I just kept it going until we could sell up after my mother died.*'

Mrs Dixon lived in the house which adjoined the shop.

Knapton station and its role in the life of the village is mentioned throughout this book. Detailed accounts of the station appear in the chapter on transport, but it is worth noting here that the railway line that ran through Knapton and Paston from North Walsham to Cromer was built in 1898 and closed in 1964. During its life it was a vital link not only for passengers, but also for freight and especially for agricultural produce, fertiliser, feed and livestock.

Knapton itself has no particularly unique features. Rather, its life and its decline as a self-sufficient community are a microcosm of the change that swept through rural England from the end of the nineteenth century to the end of the twentieth, told here by the authentic voices of those who have lived that change.

THREE

THE LAND

Knapton is described in the 1892 *Kelly's Directory* as a parish of 1,442 acres with mixed soil, whose chief crops are wheat, oats and barley. The Lords of the Manor are given as the Master and Fellows of St Peter's College in Cambridge (Peterhouse), and Lord Suffield of Gunton Hall. The principal landowners are given as Henry Matthew Robinson; the trustees of the late Henry Atkinson, Maris Collings and John Coleman; and the Master and Fellows of St Peter's College, Cambridge. The farmers are listed as Herbert Barcham of Knapton Old Hall, Timothy Blanchflower, Samuel Brady, Robert Hewitt, John Pain, and William Tice. George Watts is listed as a cattle dealer. The other occupations include a blacksmith, carpenter and bricklayer, as well as shopkeepers and a shoemaker. While *Kelly's* by no means provides a comprehensive list of jobs and occupations, it is clear that the principal economic activity was farming, with associated trades to support it.

The hundred years from 1880 to 1980, roughly the period covered by this book, have been marked by dramatic ups and downs in the national fortunes of the farming industry. These ups and downs cannot disguise the overall direction of travel of the industry, which has been a steady decline in terms of its percentage of the national economy, as an employer and, above all, in influence. Obviously, its fortunes are closely linked with the import or otherwise of cheap food. Just before the First World War, for example, Britain was importing 5 million tons of wheat, three times its domestic production. Arable acreage was therefore reduced, but because cheap grain meant cheap cattle feed, beef, sheep and dairy production increased.

Concern about the fortunes of farming and the setting up of farm workers' unions led to the creation of the National Farmers' Union in 1909. The Norfolk Agricultural Station was set up in 1908.

At the outbreak of the First World War half of Britain's food was imported. Predictably, it took the restrictions imposed by the war to make the domestic food supply an issue of concern and in 1917 the Corn Production Act was passed, guaranteeing the price of wheat and oats.

Equally predictably, some would say, once the war was over the corn subsidies were scrapped again in 1921, a measure described as 'the Great Betrayal'. An indirect consequence of the decline in farm incomes was the Norfolk farm workers' strike in 1923, although there were many other legitimate grievances.

Agriculture went back into decline during the late 1920s and 1930s, the consequences of which are vividly described by Henry Williamson in *The Story of a Norfolk Farm*. It became clear that by the time of the Second World War some lessons had been absorbed from the First. Agriculture was made a reserved occupation and food production became a priority of the war effort. Lease-lend brought new machinery from the USA and farming prospered. EU grants and subsidies during the 1970s and 1980s made fortunes for many farmers, their production helped by advances in science and technology, drainage, plant breeding, agronomy and marketing.

During the 1930s, 1940s and 1950s Norfolk's regional newspaper the *Eastern Daily Press*, could not have been mistaken for anything other than a paper that covered a powerful farming area. Even on 3 September 1939, the day war broke out, the line on the front page above the title announcing 'First Day of War' is dwarfed into total insignificance, appearing above a solid page of agricultural advertisements and announcements of farm sales. The news coverage of the outbreak of war with Nazi Germany was carried on page 5.

For at least those three decades the *Eastern Daily Press* was dominated by agricultural news and opinion. It carried regular features written by the National Farmers' Union Secretary of the day, articles about farming for the general reader by such journalistic stars as Adrian Bell, and features on crop yields and machinery innovations. There were regularly whole supplements devoted to the Royal Norfolk Show, the sugar beet harvest and prominent members of Norfolk's farming community. Norwich had a Corn Exchange and a Corn Hall, the market town of Swaffham has the figure of Ceres surmounting the Butter Cross in the Market Place, and King's Lynn's Corn Exchange, crowned by its own Ceres, is described by Pevsner as 'jolly and vulgar'. The National Farmers' Union was extremely influential and on the whole respected, and the farming community played an important part in civic and community life. The Royal Norfolk Agricultural Association, which runs the Royal Norfolk Show, was founded in 1847. It is an example of the many associations and clubs founded in rural areas throughout Britain from the eighteenth century onwards with the aim of improving farming and animal husbandry. The RNAA is still a powerful voice in Norfolk. The Stalham Farmers' Club (Stalham is about 8 miles from Knapton) was founded in 1841 with the same objective of farm improvement. It too is still going strong, with a regular series of winter and summer meetings, lectures and visits. Its members exerted their considerable influence on the decision to build the sugar beet factory at Cantley, near Great Yarmouth, in 1912. The father of Elizabeth Purdy, who provides an account of farming later in this chapter, was at one time the President of the Stalham Club. Young Farmers' Clubs were numerous and important organisations for young people, combining as they did socialising with agricultural education. Farmers were to be found on the Bench, as school managers and governors, serving in voluntary organisations and in local government. In 1977 twenty-two of the eighty-three members of the Norfolk County Council were farmers. The county was peppered with farm machinery outlets and manufacturers, mills, manufacturers of animal feed, food processing factories for canning and later for freezing produce, flour and mustard milling, and breweries. Until the end of the 1950s at least the county lived and breathed farming. When I got to Oxford in 1958 some wit asked if I had travelled there by seed drill.

Knapton Remembered covers the period between 1934 and 1961. The employment analysis of that period, detailed in Appendix 1, makes it clear that agriculture, for the parents of children at Knapton School during those years, remained the principal economic activity. Of the thirty-five fathers of the forty-five schoolchildren who contributed to *Knapton Remembered* twenty were either farmers or farm workers, variously described as team-men, foremen, pigmen, stockmen, cowmen or farm managers. Four of the fathers were gardeners and, interestingly, three of the mothers also did farm work. Small wonder that all of us had an intimate knowledge of the fields that surrounded Knapton, what was grown in them and what machinery was used to get the crops in.

We were acutely conscious of the weather and the wind direction and their effect on the crops and those working outside. The land was and still is in our souls, and yet of those forty-five children in the earlier book only three became farmers, all three sons of farmers who took on the family farm. Only two became farm workers.

Willie Puncher was one of those farmer's sons who has continued to farm. He has been at Parrs Farm in Hall Lane, Knapton, all his life, his father before him. He writes: *'In the 1940s and 1950s there were eight farms in Knapton, ranging from 5 to 300 acres. There were also two farms in the village that were owned by farmers in the neighbouring villages. Of these farms five had a diary herd and sold the milk to the Milk Marketing Board, which collected it daily. The Milk Marketing Board was established in Norfolk in 1933. Female calves were mostly kept for replacing the dairy herd. Some were kept along with the male calves to fatten up for beef and were sold at about eighteen months to two years old. The farms that did not keep cows bought in young calves from the other side of the county and fattened them for beef. There were also four egg-producers in the village. Many kept pigs. Two people had an acre or so and grew vegetables, which were sold at North Walsham market. Now these have been built on. I can remember that the first combined harvester that I saw working was at Norman May's Church Farm in Knapton, around 1948–50. This combine was a Marshall, pulled by a tractor – and very different from the monsters of today.*

'In 2010 there are only three farms in the village. Farms have been amalgamated and put out to contract farming. There is not one farm

animal in the village, just one or two people with a horse or pony. The four egg-producers have all ceased production.

'A lot of the old farm buildings and barns that were in everyday use in the 1940s and 1950s are no longer suitable for modern farming and have been converted into homes.'

Willie adds: *'That's how farms have changed in the last sixty years. I wonder how they will change in the next sixty.'*

Willie Puncher is describing agricultural change as he has experienced it at first hand over the past seventy years. A clear account of the background to this change in Norfolk agriculture is given in *An Historical Atlas of Norfolk*, which states: 'In 1914 the pattern of Norfolk farming had hardly changed in four generations. By 1972, the eve of entry to the European Economic Community, it had been revolutionised.' That book divides Norfolk into broadly east and west, and states that before 1914, while across the county farming was based on the traditional Norfolk four-course rotation of crops, in the east, on the stronger land, wheat and fodder roots predominated, the latter used to winter-fatten store cattle. After the First World War foreign competition caused prices for cereals and livestock to fall drastically. The four-course rotation was no longer economic, not least because the fodder roots, mangolds, swedes and turnips brought in no cash until the livestock that had been fattened on them were sold.

It was the introduction of sugar beet by the Dutch and the establishment of the first factory at Cantley on the marshes west of Great Yarmouth in 1912 that helped provide an answer. Sugar beet was (and is) grown under contract to the factories. It is therefore a cash crop, and can almost without exception be harvested no matter what the weather conditions. The Norfolk Agricultural Station demonstrated that the pulp and tops could also be used for feeding livestock. And therefore, from the mid 1920s onwards, sugar beet became *the* break crop for farmers.

Alfred Yaxley, who was born in 1900, was working on Mr Barcham's farm at Knapton Old Hall from 1914. He does not mention sugar beet at all in his account, but it looms very large indeed in all the accounts that follow, starting with that of Arthur Claydon, born in 1925, and ending with the account from Philip Almey, born in 1935, whose three sons and a grandson still farm today, and from Elizabeth Purdy.

It would be difficult to overstate the importance of sugar beet to the Norfolk economy, right up to the present day. Not only does the crop have the advantages for the producer described above, its transport and processing provide jobs throughout the 'campaign', as the harvesting period is called, between September and February. The sugar beet factory at Wissington, near Downham Market, was built in 1922 and, in addition to processing beet, also manufactures bio-fuel and provides the heat for a 27-acre glass house, about to increase its capacity by a third, which produces tomatoes for the commercial market during ten months of the year. The cultivation, harvesting and transporting of beet have been transformed by mechanisation over the decades, but the descriptions – in particular the one by Arthur Claydon – of the hoeing, lifting, carting and transporting involved before machines could help bring tears to the eye. The famous Boy John letters written by Sidney Grapes to the *Eastern Daily Press* between 1946 and 1958 are punctuated by references to the hoeing and lifting of sugar beet. On 22 February 1951 his letter begins with the words, 'Well, tha's orl over, sugar beeten I mean, the last load went away a Tharsday. Bor, we never worked in so much mud an sluss in orl our lives.'

On 6 September 1952 he writes to say the harvest is in, but 'now them oul sugar beet lay ahid on us'. On 23 November 1953 he writes: *'We're a gitten them oul sugar beet orf the land farster than wot the factory can teark 'em in. Thas acos we're hed a nice lot o' open weather, thas why when you Norridge people, when you go about (if you go about), see grate oul lumps o' beet a layen alongside o' tha rud.'* It is worth remembering that the beet had to be hoed and lifted by hand, the former in the biting easterly spring winds, the latter in the dark and often wet days of autumn and winter, and this before the days of proper work clothing. No wonder sugar beet dominated life and conversation in those parts of Norfolk where it was a staple and vital crop.

And no wonder, either, that as the agricultural depression continued into the 1930s farmers continued to diversify, some into soft fruit, pulses, bulbs and flowers, and even into taking in paying guests, all described later in this chapter. Another cash crop, the production of peas for freezing, was a very positive development for farmers in this part of Norfolk, from the early 1960s until very recently. Freezer plants were established at Yarmouth and Lowestoft, King's Lynn and – crucially for Knapton – at Westwick, near North Walsham. There was also a canning factory in North Walsham itself. These plants were a useful source of employment, especially in the summer when huge numbers of students were brought in to help process the crop. The production of peas and beans was also a useful cash alternative for local farmers.

The harvesting or vining of the peas was extremely dramatic to watch, accomplished by enormous pea viners that went through the fields in what seemed no time at all in order to get the crop to the plant and frozen in the hour and a half from field to pack so vaunted in the Bird's Eye advertisement. Changes in public taste have caused many of these plants to close, and I suppose we have to await the discovery that peas are a miracle food to cure all ills before they re-open.

There were two important changes in livestock production in the inter-war period. The first came about because many farmers from dairying areas elsewhere in Britain came to Norfolk, where land was cheap and plentiful. Many of those arriving in Norfolk were from Scotland. The Cargills, mentioned in Elizabeth Purdy's account later in this chapter, were one such family, while among the others were the Patersons, Alstons, Moores, Ritchies and Scotts. These 'Scotchmen', as they were called locally, quickly established a reputation for being skilled and canny farmers. They were certainly a progressive influence on farming in Norfolk, an influence which continues to this day. They introduced winter milk production on the arable farm, and by 1939 Norfolk had become a major milk producing area. The second change was the decline in the number of sheep, as British producers found it increasingly difficult to compete with the flood of imported lamb.

'Dig for Victory', the campaign to increase and improve food production during the Second World War, meant that agriculture was controlled and grants were provided for farm improvements. Poor land was reclaimed and some permanent pasture was ploughed up. Farm Advisory Services were improved. The War Agricultural Committee, or War Ag as it was known, was a powerful and influential force. By 1954, when national controls were finally removed, the industry had become much more prosperous, and improved machinery, crop varieties, fungicides, insecticides and artificial fertilisers raised yields to hitherto undreamt-of levels.

As mechanisation advanced there were fewer farms, requiring fewer farm workers. At the end of the 1950s the number of farms in Norfolk under 100 acres and the number of workers on them had hardly changed since the beginning of the century. In the next ten years the numbers of both were almost halved. These facts alone provide both explanation and background to the view expressed and reiterated by the writers of this book that time seemed to linger up until the 1960s; since then there has been an escalating avalanche of change in every aspect of their lives. Land ownership, too, was restructured. In 1914 fewer than one farmer in six owned the land he farmed. By the early 1970s two out of three farms were owner-occupied.

That is the background to the vivid accounts of farming that follow.

An early account of farm work is provided by Alfred Yaxley (1900–74). He spent the first part of his working life doing farm work, although he went on to be a gardener. He describes some encounters with farm machinery: *'The hay kicker was a horse-drawn machine that had sets of long tines or prongs geared to move to and fro. These tines were spaced so that each set took a swathe of cut hay and by its movement kicked and tousled up the grass so that wind and sun could ripen the hay ... I finished the field where I was working and as I went back along the deeply rutted cart track I could see the steward waving* his arms at me. I stopped, he rushed to the rear of the machine and pulled or pushed a lever which stopped the kickers working, shouting, "Don't never do that again, you might have broke them there kickers right off!" I humbly apologised. I was not and never have been mechanically minded and it never occurred to me that the kickers could be stopped from working. I never made the same mistake again, as I never did the job of hay kicking again.

'Another implement was the "toppler", a thing like a huge double-toothed comb, which was used at haysel time to gather up the hay and topple it into ridges across the field, making it easier for cocking. The toppler was worked by a man, who of course couldn't drive the horse at the same time, so somebody had to ride the horse. I enjoyed riding the horse at toppling, especially when the horse happened to be one of my favourites, a gentle mare named Peggy.

'One of the most unpleasant and dirty jobs I had to do was to deal with the "colder", the barley beards and rubbish that comes out of the threshing drum. I don't think it has any food value, unlike wheat chaff and oat "flights", and was usually burnt, although I have a faint memory of my great uncle feeding it to his poor unfortunate donkey. It was most unpleasant stuff to deal with and, as far as I remember, the method of working was to hang big sacks at the openings of the drum and when they were full to drag the sacks a short distance away from the stack and empty them into a heap. Between the unhanging of the sacks and fixing replacements the colder poured out and had to be forked away as it accumulated. I had never done this work before, and if I had I might have made easier work of it. It was a hot, windy day and as time went on I got very tired My eyes and ears were full of dust and muck, my head ached, my throat got sore and I felt like nothing on earth. It was a long day's threshing, and as it was past my normal leaving-off time my father came to see where I had got to. He must have found his son a pitiful little object – indeed, I could see in his eyes a look of distress – but the job was nearly finished and I was soon on my way home to have a good wash and a good meal and soon recovered from a nasty day's work …

'The farmyard was in a loose sort of way separated from the area that contained the barn, cart sheds and stables, which housed the farm horses. *It was a big, open space bordered by the house at one end and at the other end a range of buildings that consisted of stables, a cow stall, cart sheds and a harness room. I had been familiar with this part of the farmyard all my school life, so that before I even worked there I knew the place. My father had worked there as a gardener and yard-man until I was ten or eleven years old and I would take his breakfast most mornings. I well remember falling down one morning spilling all his tea, which was in an enamel container with a sort of cup-shaped lid more in the shape of a vacuum flask. Back home I trotted to get a refill. On the return journey I fell down again at exactly the same spot. Fortunately, the bag fell upright and I was able to grab it before it fell over.*

'The place where father had his breakfast was the harness room. It was long and narrow and I loved it; it was so warm and snug in there, especially in the winter time when there was a fire in the little Tortoise stove. There was a bench near the stove covered with a horse rug for the men to sit and have their meals. At the other end were corn and meal bins. The walls were hung with saddles and harness, which gave out a lovely smell of horse and polish, and best of all, a collection of whips of various sizes, which I often examined and sighed with envy as I did so. My own whips were only bits of cord tied to a brotch or stick, not be compared to the beautiful plaited leather of a real whip.

'Many a winter's day have I sat in the harness room plucking pheasants that were so ripe that big lumps of skin came off with the feathers. The old man [Alfred's employer] *certainly liked his game well hung. My work in the yard was varied and on the whole pleasant. I had certain set jobs to do, and between times I was given other work to do, but I was never rushed, and nobody bothered me much. One of my regular jobs was to feed fifty young pigs twice a day, which wasn't so bad when they were small but they would insist on growing rapidly and became a bit of a problem later in the summer. They were all kept in one open yard and fifty hungry growing pigs hadn't much difficulty in knocking over a skinny boy of fourteen at feeding times. However, it didn't take me long to find out that a good, thick cudgel in the hand of the feeder is a disincentive to rowdiness on the pigs' part. Mucking out*

stables and cow stalls, working in the garden and sometimes in the house all occupied my time.

'In those days farm workers "took" harvest, which really means that they undertook to get the harvest in for a certain sum – in that year I think it was £7 or £7. 10s. This arrangement suited farmers as well, and the men worked long hours and worked very hard to finish harvest in the shortest possible time. The extra money earned was often the only means of getting the extra clothes, boots etc. for men and their families, and the harvest sales in the shops of the nearest town were always well patronised by farm workers after harvest. The regular wage at the time was 13s a week, so you can see how much it meant to men if they could take home £7 or over for two or three weeks' work.

'Of course the length of the harvest largely depended on the weather. I know one farm that finished harvest in a fortnight, but I have known harvest to last a month or even more if wet days came along. In the event of long, wet times, farmers would usually give their men "day work" so the men didn't lose too much money on the deal. Terms for harvest were usually agreed some time before harvest started. That was why early one morning the old man, still in his dressing gown, said to me, "How much d'ye want for your harvest, boy?" "Thirty bob," I said. "Shan't give it to you." "All right, I shan't work for you," I said. The old man had a lot more to say about boys in general and then finished off by saying, "I was going to give you some old clothes, now I shan't." I said, "I don't want your old clothes, I want thirty bob," and stalked off. Later in the morning, he came to me and said he would like to make a bargain with me: he would give me 9s a week as long as harvest lasted. I accepted and inwardly hoped for a long, wet harvest. As it happened, it lasted exactly three weeks, and I got 27s. I have often wondered why the old man made all that fuss over what turned out to be a mere 3s. When I went home and told mother what I had said to the boss she was half frightened at first, but soon all was well.

'The old man had friends at North Creake who wanted a house boy and he asked me if I would go. I said I would ask my parents. I didn't think much of the idea myself. I had never heard of North Creake, but of course if my parents wished me to go I should have gone. However, *they didn't and I stayed on. The thought did cross my mind that if the old man had offered me a job elsewhere he didn't value my services as much as I thought they should be valued, but I didn't brood over that for long.'*

Arthur Claydon (b. 1925), father of Andrew Claydon, gives a detailed description of his life in Knapton's farming community: *'I was born at Sunnyside in Hall Lane, at the south end of the village, where my father, Thomas, and my mother, Edith, rented land off the Norfolk County Council. It was a mixed farm of arable, cows, bullocks, pigs, chickens, goats and a pony. It was mainly arable, growing wheat, barley, oats, root crops of sugar beet, mangolds, and potatoes, and sometimes broad beans.*

'The most labour-intensive crop was sugar beet. The soil had to be worked to a fine tilth before sowing the seed. There were no precision drills in those days, so when the seed came up it had to be thinned out by men using a hoe, or as we called it, chopping out. This was back-breaking work. The beet would be left about nine inches apart, and between the rows had to be done by pulling a set of hoes, either by horse or tractor. This had to be done several times to keep the weeds down.

'When the crop was ready to harvest it was dug up with a two-pronged fork and topped with a beet hook, before squeezers and harvesters came in. They would be put in small heaps ready to be forked onto carts, and taken to the edge of the field and put into one heap. They would then be taken to the railway station and loaded on to trucks that held between ten and eighteen tons. The ten-tonners had lower sides so it was not so high to throw them. The trucks were allocated by the station master, Elijah Coe, by putting tickets on the trucks with the producer's name on it. There would be other farmers from around the area also loading up.

'When all the trucks were full the train came with empty trucks to replace them, taking the full ones off to the sugar beet factory at either Cantley or in Yorkshire [there was a sugar beet factory in York] *where it would be processed into sugar. The pulp came back for animal feed. I was once asked by David Cargill Senior (Mr Cargill's son Alan now farms Old Hall Farm in Knapton) to take two loads of beet to Cantley by tractor and trailer as the chap who usually did it was laid up. I was*

not too happy about it as there was no cab on the tractor. I had an old Army coat, a cap and gloves, and old sacks over my legs, but I was frozen stiff by the time I got there; it was a round trip of about fifty miles.

'I remember once at Knapton station the goods train was shunting trucks in to a siding when one hit the buffers so hard it jumped up on top of the buffers. They had to bring a crane to lift it back on to the track.

'I would take sacks of potatoes to the station to be loaded into covered trucks, two ton at a time. I would see Jack Larke and Mr Hedge sacking up coal in hundred-weight bags and loaded on to a lorry or horse and cart ready to deliver round the villages. Also Mr Trivet from Little London came round with coal.

'The wheat, barley and oats we grew were harvested by binder. The sheaves of corn were then stood up in eights or tens in rows to dry out, before being picked up onto a wagon and taken to the corner of the field and made into stacks that looked like houses with loose straw on top to keep the corn dry.

'Then Mr B. J. Aldridge would come with his thrashing [sic] *tackle, which was a drum, elevator and buncher, and of course the steam traction engine. He would charge £9 15s; the corn would be sacked up, also the chaff, and put in the barn. The straw was made into a stack and used for bedding for the animals. I would take some of the corn to the millers, either Mr Gaze of Gimingham or Mr Larter of the Dell at Mundesley. They were both watermills. It was ground up for animal feed.*

'I kept six cows, and milk would be put in churns and taken by lorry to the Milk Marketing Board. The bullocks we reared were sold at H. Plumbley's cattle market in Yarmouth Road, North Walsham, and sold for about £66, a cow for £35, a calf £3 6s. The pigs also were sent to market or to the slaughterhouse; a store pig would fetch £5.

'I bought twenty pullets in 1948 for £14 19s. The eggs were sold to the North Walsham egg packing station. I also did ploughing, hay cutting, combining and sugar beeting for other farmers and allotment holders. There were allotments up the Mundesley Road and also in Hall Lane opposite the school. I also let out a meadow to a man from Great Yarmouth who had Shetland ponies [possibly for rides on the beach in the summer season]. *They would be there over the winter. I bought*

a pony and named him Copper. He would help on the farm, but I also bought a trap so I could go out for a drive, weather permitting. I was asked if I could do weddings too. So I took Richard and June Wild from the church after their wedding to the Crossroads, where they had a car waiting to take them to Skeyton for their wedding reception.

> *'Here are some prices from 1948:*
> *5 coombs or 20 bushels of seed wheat £16 7s 6d*
> *5 coombs or 20 bushels of seed barley £18 0 10d*
> *2 tons fertiliser £36 15s*
> *12 tons of lime £8 13s 6d*
> *1 ton of salt £7 15s*
> *1 milking pail and 1 bushel £1 16s*
> *A digger plough £3*
> *Motor car in 1955 £207*
> *Pair of glasses £7 15s 4d*
> *Wages per month £24*
> *In 1959:*
> *A television £88 2s 6d*
> *In 1965:*
> *For combining 25 acres £106 5s*
> *For combining 4 acres barley £17*
> *For ploughing 6 acres £25 8s*
> *For cutting hay 4 acres £12 10s*
> *For harvesting sugar beet 1 acre £8 10s*

Michael Miller (b. 1938), brother of Renie Morris and Nancy Lynch, writes: *'I lived all my life at the bottom of The Street, Knapton, with my father, mother and one sister. My two older sisters, who were sixteen and seventeen years older than me, had left home. I was at Knapton School until I was fourteen, then had a year at North Walsham Secondary Modern and finally left at fifteen. I then went to work at White House Farm.*

'My father bought one and a half acres of land. Every three years we grew sugar beet, which was hoed by hand by my father, brother and me. We dug up the beet and topped them by hand. We then carted them

to Knapton station by tractor and trailer, which were borrowed from White House Farm. They were then loaded into a truck, as were other farmers' beet, and sent to Cantley sugar beet factory to be processed into sugar. Some local farmers would have pulp sent back to them to feed their cattle. Others would have seed potatoes and artificial [fertiliser] sent by the then steam trucks. There was also a coal yard at Knapton station, which was then distributed by Mr Larke to the local villages. Another year we would grow wheat and then the next, barley. This would have been cut by a tractor and binder and stacked in the field. A threshing machine would come and thresh it in the field, and it would then be bagged up and stored in one of our sheds. Some would be sold and some kept for grinding up to feed pigs, chickens and guinea fowl. My father made a two-wheeled barrow to pull with his bike. We took the corn to Mundesley Water Mill to be ground up. He would then go with his bike to pick it up. I cycled beside him with a rope attached to the barrow to help pull it along. We grew all our own fruit and vegetables. We sold the eggs that we did not need.

'We had two ferrets and two dogs to use when we wanted to catch rabbits, with permission from the local landowners. The ferrets were sent down the holes. We used nets to put over the holes as we were not allowed to carry guns to shoot them. We caught anything between ten and twenty rabbits per weekend. We ate two ourselves and sold the rest for half a crown each.'

Ruth Steward (Matthew) (b.1943) remembers her early life as the daughter of Jimmy Steward, horseman for Mr Norman May at Church Farm. There were four children in the family: Janet, Ruth herself, Eric and Mary. *'We lived in a tied cottage belonging to Church Farm. Our father, Jimmy Steward, was horseman and also looked after bullocks and pigs, as well as being a farm labourer. Later he became foreman.*

'We used to help dad when he was chopping out sugar beet and lifting beet by hand. We also enjoyed searching for eggs after harvest, as our chickens went out onto the fields to feed on any corn left after the binder had cut the corn and the shocks had been carted and stacked. Next the combine arrived and corn was carted by the sackful and taken

to the thatched barn at Church Farm, the Ferguson and trailer being used for this. Here the corn was dressed and re-sacked. Dad worked on this machine. Of course, it meant that we no longer saw the threshing machine, which we called Queenie, in the stack yard each autumn.

'We saw several farm labourers and their families come and go in the cottage adjoining ours. We just got used to one set of neighbours when they suddenly moved on.'

Today Church Farm is farmed by Stephen Hammond, step-grandson of Norman May. Stephen's mother, Betty Hammond (b.1920), talked to June Wild. She told June: *'Norman May's parents were farmers and lived at Little Farm at Trunch Tee. Later they moved to Ivy House Farm in Trunch, where Norman was brought up with his brother Arthur and their thee sisters. In the early 1900s Norman went to work in Chamberlin's Multi Store in Norwich, and then went to Rhodesia where he had a general store, which did very well. However, he contracted malaria and had to come back to England.*

'There was a farm for sale in Knapton called The Aspens, owned by the Pain family. Norman bought it and changed its name to Church Farm, which he thought was more businesslike.

'The house still has the old brewhouse, with the old chimney still in place, where beer was made, and many outhouses and other buildings around a courtyard. A number of tied cottages went with the farm. These included the cottage further down the street, where Mrs Smith kept the post office at one time. [Her daughter, Hazel Gooch, still lives there.] *There were two cottages in Church Close, Pond Road, in one of which the Steward family lived. There were four more on each side of the road in Pond Road, next to the pond. When the detached gardens were no longer needed they were used to grow peonies.*

'Some of the farm workers over the years included Herbert Gee, who was foreman until his retirement, Jimmy Steward, Ronnie Harris and Maurice Cutting.

'When farming was hit by the recession in the 1920s Norman decided to diversify by taking in paying guests in the summer. My mother knew Norman's sister, Kathleen, when they shared a house while teaching in Leeds, and through their friendship we came as a family for our six

weeks' summer holiday. It was a big change for my brother Kim and me, coming from Bolton in Lancashire, where my mother taught to support my brother and me after my father died. Later, my mother married Norman and Church Farm became our home.

'Eva Wright was housekeeper at Church Farm and when the house was full of guests her sister Alice would help by doing the cooking. Guests could not be taken in during the war.

'It was after my mother married Norman that the Whit Monday fêtes for the chapel were held in the garden, and village fêtes are still held here today but on the first Sunday of September.'

Adeline Almey (Gaze) (1900–1973), mother of Philip, was born at Poplar Farm in Paston. Her mother Augusta, sister to Walter Watts, married Phillip Gaze; Adeline was their only child. Phillip Gaze had been the miller at Paston windmill before taking over Poplar Farm. A picture of Phillip Gaze harvesting mangolds is shown as Photo 10. His cousin Walter was the miller at Gimingham water mill. Adeline married Laurence Almey in 1928. They had one son, Philip, who until his death early in 2011 continued to farm the land at Poplar Farm as well as at Tavistock Farm, Antingham, near North Walsham, which he took over in 1963.

Adeline was a most unusual woman for her time. She was extremely knowledgeable about farming, a keen horsewoman and a canny business woman. Photo 11 shows her outside Poplar Farmhouse, dressed for the weather and preparing to set off on her milk round with her horse and cart. She had a postcard prepared from this photograph and wrote on the back, 'This is Adeline with her can, / Delivering milk just like a man.'

She kept a diary for many years of her life. The entries are terse, to say the least, partly because the diaries themselves were very small indeed, and she often wrote in pencil, red crayon or whatever came to hand in her extremely busy life. She moves between brief comments about the family's health, visits to doctor and dentist, shopping in North Walsham and Norwich, and seeing friends for tea, with notes about the farm livestock, the harvest yields and the weather. Entries for the week beginning 12 January 1947 are fairly typical:

Sunday 12 January

Had W. Gaze to tea and went to look at mare.

Monday 13 January

Philip started school. Nellie came.

Thursday 16 January

Went NW [North Walsham]. *Got shoes and pillow cases.*

Saturday 18 January

Went Norwich. 10 bullocks, then football match, Stalham.

Sunday 19 January

Nice day. Walk on Cromer cliffs, then tea at Roughton [where Laurie's brothers farmed].

Monday 20 January

Washed, nice day.

Tuesday 21 January

Not much. Went to look at mare at Ingham, too much money.

Thursday 23 January

Snow and very cold. Got sausages. W. Gaze

Friday 24 January

Mack's Sale [at Paston Hall Farm] *Got house and stack knife.*

Sunday 26 January

Very, very cold and a lot of wind

Monday 27 January

Snow. In for a bad time with weather.

This was indeed the start of the Great Snow of 1947, which was catalogued by Adeline throughout. She continued to record the snowfalls and her precautions. On 3 February she went to North Walsham to the ironmongers and agricultural suppliers Randalls to buy a kettle and stove. On Sunday 9 February she wrote: 'Bad day very cold and bad. Brrh. Yaxley to tea.' On 10 February it was 'still cold, a lot of snow fell at night, and there were electricity cuts everywhere'. Bread had to be fetched (because there could be no deliveries) from Mundesley across the fields on 11 and 13 February, but on 15 February 'the baker got through'. For the next week she described the weather as very cold with frost, but on 9 March 'went

Gimingham for tea, (thawed)'. Alas, this was a temporary respite, and she continued to record heavy snowfalls, frosts and very cold temperatures until on 21 March when 'it rained all day' – the start, at last, of the thaw.

In April that year electricity arrived in Paston, and Adeline wrote on 16 April, 'Had lights and pump done,' followed the next day by an entry, 'Had cooker put in. Ordered barley.' She and Philip went to the Royal Norfolk Show on 25 June, and the following week she ordered a plough at Randalls and 'went North Walsham. Put Philip's pig money in bank'.

Her 1953 diary recorded the terrible East Coast floods, which killed 100 people in Norfolk alone. On 31 January she wrote, 'Did not go out all day. Very cold, bad day, worst gale I can remember, floods of sea everywhere, and lots of lives lost.' The 2 February edition of the *Eastern Daily Press* of that year reports the scale of the disaster and describes the scene at Walcot, no more than two or three miles from Paston and Knapton: 'At Walcot, debris littered the cliff edge. A newly painted cream and red bungalow hung a quarter over the cliff, its neighbour stood half-suspended ... Some distance on was a house whose bay windows appeared from the air to be overhanging the cliff edge.'

Other, happier times see Adeline recording her school managers' meetings at Mundesley School; her visits to see her mother, recovering from an operation in hospital in Norwich; bullocks and pigs being sent to North Walsham market on a Thursday and the prices they fetched; on Whit Monday 25 May, 'washed, went ride'; and on 27 May, 'went ride, Philip hoed beet all day'. Not much time seems to have been devoted to leisure, but that year on July 1 'went Show, had nice day'. At Christmas: 'Nice day. Mother for dinner.' The year ends on 31 December, with 'Philip ploughs in big field'.

Philip Almey (1935–2011) remembered that his mother much preferred outside work to housework and washing. She was not very enthusiastic about cooking, and on wet washdays was not in a good humour. Nor was anyone else when wet washing was draped all around the kitchen to dry. She was extremely knowledgeable about everything that went on at the farm, as is obvious from her diaries, but she found time to be a school manager (governor) at Mundesley School. Philip remembered a land girl working on the farm during the war and recalled Mundesley Holiday Camp being used to house soldiers.

Like Willie Puncher, he lived the farming revolution in his lifetime. In 1957 he married Marion Scott, daughter of a Scottish farmer, Alec Scott, who with his wife had moved down to Norfolk from Scotland in 1928 to farm at Alby. For a time, Mr and Mrs Scott lodged with David Cargill (father of Alan, now at Knapton Hall Farm), until David himself married.

Philip and Marion Almey took over Tavistock Farm, Antingham, in 1963, while continuing to farm Poplar Farm in Paston. With his three sons Philip built a farming business, which now includes a haulage operation with four lorries, livestock (finishing bullocks for sale now directly to a supermarket), and arable farming concentrating on cereals and sugar beet. While one grandson is now part of the farming business, two are agricultural engineers and the fourth is also in farming, but working for another local farmer.

Green Farm at Paston Green is owned by the Purdy family. Olive Wild writes of her early experience in domestic service at Green Farm in 1935 in the jobs chapter of this book. The Mr Purdy senior of whom she writes was also known to my family. He would telephone my father, Jack Watts, when he needed cattle or pigs. I would frequently answer the phone, and he would say, 'Purdy Paston here.' When aged about five I was convinced for some time that Purdy Paston was his name. He used to come regularly to our house in Knapton on Christmas Eve to have a Christmas drink in the early evening, when he and my father would talk over all the local news, and I would occasionally be given a half crown Christmas present on these occasions. My father genuinely liked and respected Mr Purdy, but also knew that he was an invaluable business contact, so a fair amount of attention was paid to whether he was sitting comfortably and that his drink was to his liking.

Mr Purdy's granddaughter Elizabeth (b. 1941) is now in charge of Green Farm. She writes: *'My grandfather, George Thomas Purdy, always known as Tom, was born in 1877 and died in 1960. He was married to Helen Constance née Candler, who died in 1965. He inherited the farm from his uncle, also Thomas, who had come from Salthouse. My grandfather sold the Salthouse farm to buy Rivermount and Austen Bridge Farm in the early 1900s. My grandfather kept a lot of bullocks. He had three children: Mary born 1910, died 2002, and Thea, born 1911, died 1989, both unmarried; and my father, Tom, born 1914, died 1990.*

'The children were looked after by nanny, Florence Gee, sister to Agnes who worked for Miss Robinson, and Walter. I also remember Mabel who worked in the house. George Pye was my grandmother's gardener. She loved her rose garden. When I was a child Charlie Burgess was foreman and George Fincham was head horseman. He was succeeded by Fred Thirtle as foreman. I remember Mrs Roberts who lived at the bottom of Knapton Street in a house called Little Duddo. She was the widow of Joe Roberts, gamekeeper. She came from County Durham and Joe met her when he went to work in the mines for a spell in the 1930s.

'My grandfather never learned to drive a car. Fred would drive. My grandfather would clear his side of the windscreen and tell Fred it was all right to go. He used to go to North Walsham once a week for a shave. He attended the cattle market in Norwich most weeks, as well as the markets in Stalham and North Walsham. I can just remember the horses. One of them used to go round and round to drive the elevator for the stack-making, and Mr Gooch would come to do the threshing. When I was a child the men wore old Army clothing for farmwork. Most always wore a hat or cap.

'We stopped keeping bullocks in the 1950s. My father was a great innovator and was keen to modernise the farm. He had many arguments with his father about this, to the extent that he once wrote "T. PURDY" in fertiliser in a field of wheat, which came up much greener than the rest, just to show his father the benefit.

'We kept horses into the 1950s, when mechanisation and tractors took over. My grandfather was reluctant to replace the binders with a combine harvester, but was persuaded when someone sent a photograph

of "Paston old and new" to the Eastern Daily Press, *comparing Paston Hall Farm, with its modern combine, and our farm, still stacking the sheaves and cutting with a binder.*

'My father was married during the war to Helen, née Lavery, who died in 1984. She was from Ireland; hence my two sisters and I were brought up as Catholics. They lived at first at Bacton, and after the war he worked as a fieldsman for the British Sugar Corporation, as well as helping with the running of the farm. In the early 1950s we moved to Footpath House in Vicarage Road, Paston. When my grandfather died in 1960 we swapped houses and our family moved to Green Farm, and my grandmother and aunts went to Footpath House.

'Many people in Paston and Knapton will remember my aunts, Mary and Thea. Mary, in particular, had a lot to do with Paston Church and taught the children in Sunday School for many years. She was renowned for the hats she wore to church! Thea was also very well known in the village. She was quite an expert on goats, which she kept on the tennis court at the farm during the war.

'After my grandfather died my father ran the farm full time. By then we only grew arable crops – wheat, barley, sugar beet – and then in the 1960s peas for freezing became the thing. My father was one of the founder members of the Aylsham Farmers' Pea Group. We also started growing fruit – strawberries and blackcurrants – at that time. Jimmy Myhill was in charge of the pickers and was very strict with anyone putting mushy fruit or too many leaves in the bottom of the pail. Pay was 2s 6d a pailful.

'My father was a great sportsman. I think he was a good shot. When we were children, we were never allowed in the woods for fear of disturbing the pheasants and he grew stands of kale as cover for the birds. He had a legendary dog called Curly who was rather a character and did not always do as he was told, but my father said, "Never call a dog unless it is coming towards you!" Brian Myhill was foreman. Joker (Robert) Myhill, his brother Cuppa Myhill and his father Jimmy Myhill also worked for us. Jack Self replaced George Pye in the garden, and Audrey Pye helped my mother in the house. Gordon Brett at first helped Jack Self in the garden and helped with the pheasant-rearing

and became my father's right-hand man. He now looks after me! Audrey looked after my father and cooked all his meals until he died in 1990.

'I lived and worked in London for a time and then in Essex. Towards the end of his life my father was struggling with ill health and with running the farm. I therefore decided to move back to Norfolk. I attended Writtle Agricultural College for a year and then we moved to Rivermount. The house had always been rented out and was in a very sorry state, so we renovated it and I start working with my father on the farm with our farm manager, Brian Myhill, to help me after my father died in 1990.

'By the mid-1990s farming was becoming more and more technical and required enormous investment in machinery and marketing, so we went into a farm agreement with the Cargills [Alan, based at Knapton Old Hall], *who are still doing a great job for us.'*

During her time in sole charge of the farm Elizabeth introduced a number of wildlife and conservation schemes, of which she wrote movingly in *Paston 2000,* a book produced in Paston to mark the Millennium. Here is an example: 'Since we have fenced the marsh (near Rivermount) we have low-level grazing by horses and sheep, which keep the reeds at bay and allow the grass to flourish and keep it short, which also allows wild flowers such as ragged robin, vetches, fleabane, meadowsweet and valerian to grow ... In the unfenced area the reeds and scrub will prosper and are home to many marshland birds, such as snipe and reed warblers, the favourite host to cuckoos who lay their egg in their nests.'

In the 1950s I cycled every day past these marshes on my way to school in North Walsham. What Elizabeth restored fifty years later is the landscape I knew and loved then.

And so the wheel of agriculture turns on. The voices in this chapter tell of hard, back-breaking work, grinding poverty and insecurity, busy prosperous markets and traders, the inexorable rhythm of the farming year, all now changed for ever yet still just discernible to the loving eye. The agriculture industry has undergone nothing less than a complete revolution in the last century. Even so, and despite what sometimes seems like wanton neglect from government, Britain still produces food, and British farmers are now more conscious of their consumers, and of the needs of the environment which provides their living, than ever before in their history. And for those of us with the land and its rhythms in our blood, the rural life is still the only one which counts.

FOUR

GETTING ABOUT

In many ways, the social history of the late nineteenth and twentieth centuries is encapsulated in the story of transport in this part of Norfolk during the period. We see the building and the closure of the railway line that linked Knapton to the rest of the world. We see the ending of the horse era, and with it the final closure of the blacksmith's shop and the loss, except in the memory, of a whole world of skills, language, vocabulary, culture and legend. We see the arrival of the bicycle, and therefore the delivery man. We see the arrival of motorised transport, the bus and the car, for a few at first – the rector, the lady of the village, the doctor, the cattle dealer – and then gradually for almost everyone, and the resulting transformation in trade, business, shopping, opportunities and, ultimately, horizons.

We will start with the railway. Norfolk was one of the last English counties to have a railway system, according to the *Historical Atlas of Norfolk*. The first Norfolk line to be established, in 1844, was the Yarmouth and Norwich Railway, followed by the Norfolk Railway between Norwich and Brandon in 1845. By around 1850 the major towns of Norwich, Yarmouth, Fakenham and Lowestoft were linked, the lines spreading out from Thorpe station in Norwich, but the north Norfolk coast remained unconnected. By 1862 all the lines then serving Norfolk had merged to become the Great Eastern Railway. In the 1870s independent railways were built from King's Lynn to Fakenham and from Yarmouth to North Walsham, eventually joining at Melton Constable and extending to Norwich and Cromer. These lines formed the Midland and Great Northern Joint Railway. In order to compete, the Great Eastern Railway, in a joint venture between themselves and M&GNJR called the Norfolk and Suffolk Joint Railways, extended and improved their own network to the coast. This included the line between North Walsham and Mundesley, and eventually on to Cromer, which passed through Knapton and Paston. The station was called Paston and Knapton, as it served both villages, and was opened in 1898 for passengers and freight. During its lifetime the station was important not only for passenger traffic but as a vital hub for trade and agriculture in the area.

Josiah Bane (1882–1972) left school at twelve in 1894 and quite soon *'bought my first dickey off old Waterfield* [a horse dealer in North Walsham]. *At that time the railway was being built between North Walsham and Mundesley.'*

Not only did Jo Bane see a 'dickey' – donkey – as vital for his living at that time, but the railway, which would transform the life of Knapton and its area, was already under construction. Furthermore, Jo Bane was to see the railway open, and close, in his own lifetime.

Renie Miller (Morris) (b. 1921) lived with her family near the station and remembers: *'We children used to love waving as the train passed by. At certain holiday times there would be so many carriages taking families to the beach, food all packed up (in newspaper in those days). I remember you could hardly find a space to sit down on Mundesley beach.'*

John Capes (b. 1930) recalls this particular service. He writes: *'There was an express train along the line. On summer Saturdays a special holiday train, which I think may have been called either the Holiday Coast Express or the Norfolk Coast Express, would come through at about midday heading for Cromer. This would have started at Norwich and consisted of about eight carriages pulled by a large mainline locomotive. On several occasions I remember seeing one of the streamline locomotives on it. I think it ran in the early fifties, but it may have also run in the thirties.'*

Leslie Coe (b. 1922) writes that when he was born his father Elijah Coe was a porter at Knapton station, a job he got when he returned from France after the First World War. Leslie continues: *'As time passed, my father came to be the station master, so it was our*

*home until he sadly passed away in 1951. During that period I had
another brother, Ronald, born in 1923, and a sister Doris, born in 1930,
both born in the Station House.*

'*My memories of living at the station in the 1920s and 1930s are
wonderful as it was a very busy station – two goods trains and sixteen
passenger trains a day, except Sundays. Almost every farmer in the area
used the goods yards and cattle pens to send their products to various parts
of the country, sugar beet to Cantley, grain to the flour mills and cattle
to markets. On the incoming side there were house bricks, cement, timber
and road stone, which was collected by steam engine wagons that were
often left parked overnight in the goods yard. Coal was delivered for Mr
Tribberts, which he weighed into hundredweight bags for delivery to his
customers. Mr Allen from Trunch used to bring churns of milk by pony
and cart to go on to the train. Also, the guard on the last train had to put
out the oil lamps on the station platform during the dark nights.*

'*On the passenger side, lots of people from the villages used the
train to travel to North Walsham, Norwich, Mundesley, Yarmouth
and Cromer, and of course other destinations as well. One thing I must
mention is that at times a special train with an engine and only one
coach would come through the station carrying a patient to the sanatorium at Mundesley.*' [This may have been because tuberculosis was
considered to be not only infectious but also contagious, or possibly
because the sanatorium was popular with prosperous and in some
cases very well known people, who could have afforded to charter
a train.]

'*At the entrance to the passenger yard was what we called the Green
Lane. Often, gypsies with one or two horse-drawn caravans used to
park for a few days and would get elder branches from the lane and
make clothes pegs to sell in the villages, often a rabbit as well. They
also used to collect water from our house as we had a pump from an
underground well.*

'*My brothers and I used to cut up old wooden railway sleepers to
make sticks for house fires, which we used to sell in penny bundles. I also
remember an engine that derailed on the points at the entrance to the
goods yard, which was put back on the line by using manual lifting jacks.*

Also, in those days a plate layers' hut was in the goods yard and during the summer months gangs of men with scythes would cut all the grass on the railway banks and burn it when it was dry. To assist in the task we pegged our goats on the banks to eat the grass.'

Leslie Coe's memory of Knapton station as a hub of economic activity was corroborated by Philip Almey (1935–2011). In particular, he recalled the vital role of the station in agricultural trade of all kinds. In the 1930s my grandfather (and Philip's great-uncle), Walter Watts, would from time to time charter a goods train to bring cattle in to Knapton station. Walter Watts went on occasion to Ireland to buy cattle and also to Leicester and York, accompanied by my father, Jack Watts. The cattle would be bought for farmers in the Knapton area: Norman May in Knapton, his brother Arthur in Trunch, Mr Purdy in Paston, John Owles in Witton and the Hayletts in Bacton. From Knapton station the cattle would be driven on foot to their destination, a matter of a very few miles. Philip also recalls that sacks for farm use, for grain at threshing times and for animal feed, pulp and chaff, could be hired from the railway, marked LNER (London and North Eastern Railway as it was called until nationalisation in 1948). They would then be used to convey grain to Gimingham Mill, for example, and much irritation was expressed if they were not returned from the mill in good time and in good order so that they could be taken back to the station and the deposit claimed back.

Gordon Harrison (b. 1942), who lived at Knapton station where his father was station master between 1949 and 1960, also has very happy memories of his boyhood at the station. He writes: *'Living at the station was one of the greatest adventures any boy of seven could ask for. I had my own pitch and putt course in the station yard. It was a bit stony but was great fun. My bedroom overlooked the platform, but I seldom heard the trains as I got so used to them. The first six years at Knapton were the days of steam trains. They were the best years for any railway enthusiast; the smell of a mixture of steam and smoke beats any other smell.*

'The station buildings consisted of a large waiting room and a small waiting room, which was called the ladies' waiting room. There was a

ticket office, a porters' room, or lamp room, which smelled of paraffin, a coal shed and outside toilets. An old railway box wagon in the yard was used as a cycle shed. Inside was a weighing machine used for weighing large parcels, and it also stored the wood for the fires in the waiting room.

'The station house consisted of kitchen, two downstairs living rooms and three bedrooms, but no bathroom: you washed at the kitchen sink. In a little courtyard outside there were the toilet and coal shed. There was no electricity while I lived there, and water was pumped to a tank in the roof of the house before you could get running water and this served all the station.

'At the bottom of the goods yard was the platelayers' hut – they were the men who looked after the line – which housed all the tools they used for line maintenance in the Knapton section, also a fire and plenty of coal.'

Interestingly, Gordon Harrison, who is writing about a period only twenty years after that described by Leslie Coe, says: *'Across the other side of the yard were some old cattle pens; they were rotten and covered with weeds as they had not been used for years.'* By that time, of course, cattle were being transported in cattle floats by road. There was less demand for store cattle in any case. These changes are described in the chapter on agriculture.

Gordon continues his description of the station during his time there. *'The gardens on the platform were planted with red, blue and white flowers. Large stones were used for the borders; they were whitewashed regularly, usually at the same time as the white line on the platform. My father won many prizes for the best kept station.*

'There was also a coal yard. The coalman was Jack Lark, who lived at Edingthorpe. I would help him shovel coal out of the trucks and sometimes hold the sacks while he filled them. Mr Gooch from Bacton also had coal delivered by rail. Several builders had bricks delivered and some farmers had fertiliser come in by the wagon-load. In the winter, during the sugar beet season, the yard would be ankle deep in mud.

'Across the other side of the railway line there was a small piece of land that went with who ever lived in the house. We had chickens and rabbits and grew whatever we liked on the rest. A bridge crossed over the line at one end of the platform. The track from this went across the fields and came out opposite the shop in Knapton Street.'

John Capes (b. 1930) lived with his family in Paston. He writes: *'In the 1930s and 1940s the carriages were always pulled by the locomotive, so at North Walsham and Mundesley the locomotive would have to be run round the carriages to get to what was then going to be the front of the train. I think it was some time in the early 1950s that the couplings between the locomotives and carriages were adapted so that a push-and-pull system could be operated.*

'During the 1930s, 1940s and I think 1950s there were two regular guards on the trains. Mr Shreeve was thin-faced and small, but always had a smile on his face and was always ready to help. Mr Hoarse was the opposite, round-faced, big, inclined to be surly and not very helpful. Tickets could not be bought at the station and had to be obtained on the train from the guards. They came round the carriages with a rack that held pre-printed tickets for most of the likely destinations required, but if you were going elsewhere they had to go back to the guards' van to see if they had an appropriate ticket there, or they would have to write one out. There was a date-stamping device on the end of the rack. The tickets were of card, about one inch by two inches in size, and green in colour.

'In a typically British way, the train locally was dubbed "The Mundesley Express", but its progress was far from fast. It was not exactly slow; a better description would be sedate, as it chugged along at a nice even speed … Although it went at a steady pace, it gave the two villages served by the station a very useful service. We had something that nearby villages like Trunch, Edingthorpe and Bacton did not have: good access to other parts of the country. One way we could get to Cromer, but the other way we could go to North Walsham and on to Norwich, Ipswich and London. At North Walsham we could change stations and use the former M&GN line to go one way to Stalham and Great Yarmouth, and the other way to Aylsham, King's Lynn and Peterborough, and then on to the Midlands or the north of the country.'

Willie Puncher recounts that at least fourteen farms shipped beet from the station during the 1940s and 1950s. John Capes also recalls the vital role played by the railway in the sugar beet harvest: *'The beet all had to be shipped off to the factory at Cantley. Then the station was a hive of activity from early morning until late afternoon.*

To get empty trucks into the goods yard and full ones out the goods train would spend quite a while huffing and puffing up and down, shunting the trucks round the sidings, and now the trains were much bigger, with probably a dozen or more trucks at a time.

'*In the 1930s, 1940s, and early 1950s, quite a lot of horse-drawn farm wagons were still being used by the farms to transport beet and other things to and from the station. I can relate mainly to the Paston farms. Although there was a tractor on Purdy's farm, horse-drawn wagons were still being used in the harvest field and for taking beet to the station into the early 1950s.*

'*Paston Hall Farm was a bit different. It was owned by the East Anglian Real Property Company, which had its headquarters at Cantley and was associated with the sugar factory there. Up to the start of the war their beet were transported to Cantley by a haulage firm called Robinson's. We would often see them loading up near field gateways. On the outbreak of war petrol was rationed and the lorries could no longer be used, so the farm had to start taking beet to the station. They still had horses and sometimes used them with trolleys, and probably used tractors if they had sufficient fuel and if they could be spared from other tasks, like ploughing.*

'*A problem that occurred during the war was the shortage of goods trucks for transporting goods round the country. This was especially true of trucks for sugar beet as they were of the type also used for wartime essentials such as ammunition. So sometimes the transport of beet would be delayed for several days because of the shortage of trucks. I well remember my dad coming back into the house after he had been out in the evening and saying, "So-and-so says they will have a truck at the station tomorrow so they can get some more beet away." As dad was a builder's labourer he had to glean information about the farms from the other men in the village.*'

Until I was nine we lived near Knapton station and used the train regularly to go to Mundesley, North Walsham, Cromer and North Walsham. My mother, who was married in 1932, had happy memories of going to North Walsham by train on market day (Thursday) with her mother-in-law and sisters-in-law. They would order groceries, which would later be delivered by van, look round the dress shops London-Edwards, Loades and Fullers, and have a discreet look at the proceedings in the cattle market behind the Cross Keys public house. It had to be a discreet look because neither my grandfather nor father would have welcomed their obvious presence in what they considered to be a male preserve. There were women farmers who attended, but they were regarded as fellow professionals and not as embarrassing onlookers. My aunts may well have contributed to this view of their presence as they always dressed up for market day. One aunt appeared once, and only once, in a striking, yellow dress and hat, which caused one wit to ask if anyone had seen a lemon rolling round the market. The outfit was never worn again.

The station was always busy on Thursdays for journeys to North Walsham and on Saturdays for journeys to Norwich for shopping and the cattle market. Norwich was the gateway to a much more extensive rail network, especially to London. On one occasion, famous locally, someone got on to the London train by mistake, instead of the North Walsham one, and was conveyed to Liverpool Street. On his eventual and relieved return to Knapton, it was reported that he said, 'There were a hell of a lot of people in London. It must have been market day with them.'

The train was very much valued in bad weather, and particularly during the Great Snow in 1947. The line was not open for the whole of the Snow; indeed, a train was stuck for two weeks between Paston and Mundesley, opposite Poplar Farm where Philip Almey lived with his family. But when a train could get through it was used to capacity.

The line was used by secondary-school children travelling to the schools in North Walsham. The pupils could take the train, with a train pass, or cycle. Many chose to cycle, even though it was between four and five miles, as you got a cycle allowance each term, which was useful cash to have. Children would stream through the town to their various schools when the trains arrived, and stream back in the afternoon. The Cromer train, which went direct via Gunton rather than around the coast, was known as the Plum because of its distinctive cream and plum livery. Looking back, I do not think other passengers would have very much enjoyed our noisy, exuberant company. Mercifully for them, our journeys were short.

The line's demise is laconically related by Gordon Harrison: *'Execution came in 1964 under the infamous Dr Beeching, whose axe severed a branch that was arguably making a profit, and in spite of local objections, although not from the Erpingham District Council. The last passenger train was on 4 October 1964, the last freight on 28 December. The track was lifted in haste and all was gone by June 1965.'*

Even so, the line did not go without a campaign against its closure. In Knapton the protest was led by Miss Isabel Montford, mentioned elsewhere in this book as one of the Sunday School teachers. She had in her youth been governess to the children of the Kaiser of Germany and a nurse in Egypt during the First World War. She had clearly retained an excellent memory of how things should be done. Her campaign instructions, which were displayed on notice boards and given out at meetings in Knapton, were as follows:

PROPOSED RAILWAY CLOSURE
Further information
Individuals are asked to write letters in duplicate, or two similar letters, of HARDSHIPS that would be entailed should the railway line to Mundesley be closed. One copy of each letter to be sent to the Clerk of the Norfolk County Council, Council Offices, Thorpe Road, Norwich NOR 47A, not later than by Monday 16 September 1963 (in time for further consideration by a second meeting of the Norfolk County Council).

The other copy of each letter, or similar letter, to be sent (if not already sent) to the Secretary of the Eastern Area Transport Users' Consultative Committee, 47 Glisson Road, Cambridge, as soon as possible, but not later than by Monday 30 September.

If desired, letters can be brought or sent to Miss I. Montford, Ecclesburn, Cross Roads, Knapton, N. Walsham, by 14 September and she will post them in bulk to the above addresses.

Enquiries if any to Miss I. Montford.

6 September 1963

Alas, the campaign failed, like so many others across the country, before the bulldozers of Dr Beeching.

Photo 13 is a copy of the last railway timetable for the line. The small print states prophetically: 'Train services shown in this timetable are subject to alteration or cancellation at short notice.'

We have already seen that the station was built to serve the villages of Knapton and Paston, and that the stop was called Paston and Knapton. In fact, its position was very inconvenient for many in Knapton. As John Capes (b. 1930) writes, many villagers used the bus instead: *In the 1930s, 1940s and 1950s the bus service that ran through Paston and Knapton was Eastern Counties service number 9. The main Eastern Counties depot was at the bus station in Surrey Street, Norwich, but they also had a small depot in Mundesley. This was near the Coronation Hall on Cromer Road and probably held three or four buses.*

'*The number 9 service served many villages in a long route from Happisburgh round to Norwich. Starting from the country end, the buses would start alternately from Happisburgh or Bacton, and then go to Paston, Mundesley, Gimingham Pound, Trunch Crown, Knapton Green, Swafield and into North Walsham ... then on through Westwick Arch (demolished in 1981) and on to Scottow. I understand that before the construction of Coltishall airfield just before the war, it then went on to Coltishall, and into Norwich on the North Walsham Road. When the road it used was closed because of the airfield the route was changed to go via Tunstead, Wroxham and Rackheath, and into the city on Sprowston Road. Then through Magdalen Street, Tombland, Castle Meadow and I think up St Stephen's and along Queen's Road, to go into the top of the bus station. Quite a long journey for anyone from Happisburgh, but they saw plenty of villages.*

'*The disadvantage for many people in Knapton was that it did not go into the centre of the village because of the route going from Trunch and then on to Swafield to get easily into North Walsham. So I think that people living near the bottom of The Street were more inclined to use the train. The same thing happened at Gimingham, where the bus didn't actually go near any houses at all but just went round the corner near the Pound, and Gimingham didn't have a railway!*

'The buses used were the old-fashioned double-deckers with an open platform at the rear for getting on and off. This could be rather draughty for people sitting downstairs near the back of the bus. Stairs curved up to the upper deck from the platform and under the stairs was a compartment for luggage. In those days buses were manned by a driver and a conductor, and the latter would be based on the platform at the rear and go round the bus collecting fares and issuing tickets ...

'Two of the drivers from Mundesley that I can remember are a Mr Bassingthwaite, who lived opposite the Coronation Hall, and Clifford Smith, who lived along Trunch Road. As the route went past his bungalow Clifford would sometimes stop there for a few minutes, presumably to pay a quick visit to the toilet or have a cup of tea!'

Shirley Wright (Conquest) (b. 1938) used bus and train to get to Norwich. She writes: *'There were two public transport services from Knapton. The Eastern Counties bus service (Number 9) would run from Happisburgh to Norwich bus station roughly about a two-hourly service. The last bus into Knapton would be just after 10 p.m., but there was a later one on Saturday. The first bus would arrive in Knapton at 7.15 a.m. This information is very clear in my memory as for a year, when I was fifteen years old, I had to catch the 7.15 a.m. bus to Norwich, to go to the Norwich City College, and arrive back in Knapton at 5.45 p.m. Quite a long and tedious journey and very cold in winter. It was always a red double-decker bus, and I would usually travel upstairs. The train station was at the other end of the village from our house. When I eventually worked in Norwich I used the train, but I left my bicycle at a house in The Street in Knapton (at Tom and Ena Coe's) and then walked across the fields to the station.'*

Ruth Steward (Matthew) (b. 1943) recalls a school bus journey (after the closure of the station at Knapton) in the snow: *'Starling's coaches were used to transport children to the schools in North Walsham. One winter the bus got stuck in the snow on the Bacton hills. As fast as the driver dug a wheel out, the boys would follow him and fill it full of snow again, until they were made to clear the wheels. We were very late that night!'*

Both Shirley and Ruth recall bicycles with some affection. Shirley writes: *'In addition to studying and working in Norwich, I worked for a time in North Walsham. I used to cycle there, and always cycled to Mundesley. I did not have my first bicycle until I was twelve years old and of course it was second-hand. There was a bicycle shop in the Mundesley Road in North Walsham called Hedges and I remember buying my first new bicycle at sixteen when I started work, and paid 7s 6d each week for goodness knows how long. It was a green racing model of a well-known make, and I thought it was great and gave it some TLC for quite a long time. The only long-distance journey was a trip by coach to London with the school, which was always something to look forward to.'*

Ruth writes: *'I learned to ride a bike in the loke at Church Farm. What fun! I soon found I was capable and then I told mum, and not before. We used to cycle for what seemed like miles, especially in the school holidays, as long as we were home for meals. Later we were able to cycle to the shops at North Walsham, to Trunch for music lessons (in 1950), Mundesley for bread and to have the accumulator charged when we had a radio.'*

Ruth was certainly a capable cyclist. I never was, despite the fact that I cycled all the time, and especially backwards and forwards to school in North Walsham from the age of eleven. I would occasionally take the train from Mundesley, our nearest station when I was at secondary school, but I much preferred to cycle and enjoyed travelling through the countryside at all times of year, watching the changes of the seasons. Skilled, however, I never became, and most weeks were marked by some incident, usually me falling off because I was engrossed in the crops, the wild flowers or talking to another cyclist. Shirley writes of Hedges, the cycle shop in North Walsham. I was a regular customer at Griffins, the cycle shop opposite my school, where I was to be found most weeks having my handlebars turned the right way round again or some scrape or another on the bike attended to.

Cars and motorcycles, from being very scarce at the beginning of the period, were in very nearly universal use by the end. At the turn of the century car ownership was limited to the rector, the doctor, Miss Robinson (her Lanchester), some farmers and my own grandfather, who needed his car for his work as a cattle dealer. This did not mean that he abandoned his horse and cart; that was used for local journeys and for transporting small loads, like one pig or one calf. He never quite learned to drive – which is fortunate, since many of his deals were conducted after market in public houses and he would certainly not have been in a fit state to drive home. On these occasions, George Miller – father of Renie, Nancy and Michael, all contributors to this book, and also of Molly and Derek, and a neighbour of my grandparents – would do the driving. My father was an excellent driver, but never had to pass a driving test as the tests were only introduced in 1933, by which time he would have been driving for at least thirteen years. My mother not only had to pass the test, but took three goes to manage it.

With the war came petrol rationing, so cars on our roads were not numerous, with the result that collecting car numbers was a favourite hobby and we would gather at the crossroads to spot cars. Another result was that many of us retain in our heads to this day the car numbers of the few cars there were. Mr Prichard, the rector's car number was CPW 440; my grandfather's car was AVF 348; and my father's first car, a small Ford, was BNG 20. The fact that there were so few cars on the road, and that they were for the most part known locally, served my family well when in 1947 a large number of chickens were stolen from land owned by my father, about a mile from Knapton. The fish and chip man, Mr Ward, recalled having seen an unfamiliar car driving round the neighbourhood just before the theft. He noted the number on the inside wall of his fish and chip van. He then washed down the inside of the van, but fortunately remembered the number. This was given to the police, who traced the vehicle to a house in the East End of London, where the thieves were living alongside the stolen chickens. They were prosecuted and appeared before the North Walsham magistrates, chaired by Miss Robinson. The chickens were returned – although as my father said, 'They never were any good after that' – and the thieves given a hefty fine and made to surrender their vehicle. They later turned out to be related to some people living in Mundesley.

A journey by road was an event, as June Wild (b. 1951) illustrates in the following account: *'When I was about six to eight months old, in 1951, I had my first trip out of Norfolk from Knapton to St Albans in Hertfordshire to see my father, Henry Wild, who was in Hill End Hospital, part of St Bartholomew's Hospital in London. It was a building with very long corridors that the doctors would cycle to get from one end to the other! My aunt Lily and uncle Jack came from Wymondham to be at Knapton for 8 a.m. to take my mother and me, and my great aunt Lena in my uncle's blue Morris van. He tied the pram, with me in it, securely inside the van. There were also bus seats put in the back that had come from an old Eastern Counties double-decker bus. We left Knapton at 8.30 a.m. There were no motorways or A-roads as we have today, and when we arrived my uncle had a well-deserved rest. We left to come home about 3.30 p.m. and stopped near Baldock for the adults to have a meal, and got back into Norfolk about 6 p.m. The speed limit for the van was 30 miles an hour, but my uncle has told me he did go over it a bit!'*

Barbara Wilkins (Fawkes) (1930–2009) wrote of a car journey with her father-in-law, Herbert Fawkes: *'I drove an Austin 7 car and was taking my father-in-law Herbert to Norwich one Saturday. We were several minutes into the journey when I thought I could smell something. I said, "Father, are you burning?" He said, "No, gel, of course not!" I said, "Are you sure, because I can smell burning?" He put his hand in his pocket and realised his pipe was still alight. We stopped quickly and he jumped out of the car to put out the fire in his pocket. He was a tall man who always wore a trilby and smoked a pipe. We did make sure that for future journeys the pipe was extinguished properly before we started off.'*

The accounts in the jobs chapter below of Barbara's grandchildren, Chris and Sadie Risebrow, and Paul Turner illustrate how the demise of public transport for Knapton and villages like it meant that, for young people like them, car ownership and a move to a town for cheaper housing became the only means of economic and social survival by the end of the twentieth century.

FIVE

HOW WE LIVED

This chapter begins with a section on food and its preparation. It continues with accounts on housework, clothes and shopping, and health.

A number of interesting points arise from what contributors wrote about food. Many emphasised the vital importance of nourishing food for people doing hard physical jobs who had to get around on foot or by bicycle. The maxim of waste-not-want-not loomed large, and until around 1950 the accounts record surprisingly little difference in what people ate and the range of choice they had, and how the food was prepared. Home-grown vegetables and fruit, locally produced meat including rabbits and game, locally caught fish – fresh and smoked, including all kinds of shellfish – eggs, milk and cheese, home-baked cakes, home-baked bread until the 1920s, and all kinds of wild food: all these are lovingly described in all the written accounts. In that period, while the types of foods available did not vary a huge amount, there were significant differences between the diets of the least well-off and the slightly better-off. Some of these differences were eroded by the special circumstances of the Second World War and food rationing described in the chapter on war.

The introduction of school dinners as a result of the 1944 Education Act also eased life for some families, since dinners were free for children from less well-off homes.

After 1948, when electricity came to Knapton and food could be refrigerated and therefore kept for longer, and even more importantly when during the 1960s supermarkets began to open and more people got cars, diets became much more varied.

Making ends meet was a constant struggle for the least well off – those on the lowest wages and/or with large families, or where the breadwinner was sick or disabled. My father, Jack Watts, who was born in 1903 and who came from a long line of reasonably comfortably off cattle dealers, talked about the poorest children he knew at school being so hungry that they would eat raw mangolds pulled from the field.

Josiah Bane (1882–1972) wrote: *'There were eight of us children. Father was a farm worker and earned 10s a week. Times were hard ... I well remember going to Knapton Hall for soup they made for the poor of the parish. Old Grimes lived there then. We'd take the biggest boiler we could find. Many a time we had to share an egg and a herring between two ... The gypsies used to camp up Green Lane. I'd be up there like a shot as I always had a good feed with them. I tasted hedgehog they'd caught, rolled in wet clay and baked. When it was cooked the whole skin came off clean as a whistle.*

Alfred Yaxley (1900–74) remembers his mother, one of the thirteen children of a team-man working at Thurton near Norwich, telling him that *'the children would go to the Hall* [at Thurton] *for soup and even tea dregs'.* This is corroborated by Anne Markham (Stubley), writing elsewhere in this book of her experience in domestic service during the 1930s, when stock would be made available for people in the village if they wanted it. Alfred also writes of sharing an egg or a herring and of his mother sliding out *'a few coppers from the children's money box to buy bloaters. I suppose mother was one of the best of money managers. There just wasn't enough of it to go around.'* He continues: *'Our family consisted of mother and father and five children. We lived plainly and always seemed to have enough to eat and I can honestly say I never went hungry. Of course we had meat but not very much of it and I don't suppose we missed it much. Why should we when we could have those delicious Norfolk dumplings and gravy? The flavour of the meat was in the gravy. My father always grew plenty of vegetables and a good plateful of dumplings and vegetables was a meal in itself. There always seemed to be plenty of fruit in season (except strawberries) and mother used to make immense fruit tarts. Rhubarb was our favourite ... Pea soup made from split peas was another favourite, and many times in the winter we had porridge for tea. Some people might scoff at that, but I loved it: put plenty of Golden Syrup on it and nothing was better for growing boys. Another food we had, mostly for breakfast, was a concoction mother called pepper and salt broth. It just consisted of bread broken into a basin, a dab of butter, pepper and salt, and boiling water poured over it; poor stuff you say, but I liked it. I had a great-uncle, a farm worker, and he had a basin of this every working day of his life. Cocoa poured over broken bread was another standby. Cocoa sop, my mother called it. We even had tea sop at times and, of course, bread and milk. Milk was a penny a pint fetched from one farm or another. Most housewives baked their own bread, although bakers' carts did come into the village, but bakers' bread was a little bit of a luxury. We children liked it very much for a change, but what could be nicer than little loaves of home-made bread hot from the oven, split in half and a wedge of red "American" cheese stuffed in the middle, a meal fit for a king.'*

Josiah Bane's daughter Queenie Wild (b. 1917) remembers taking her father's lunch to the fields on Wallage's Farm during the harvest in the 1920s: *'I carried it in a basket down the loke beside the farm and would sit with him and the other men while they ate. It would be sandwiches of pork or wild rabbit, a bun or apple. To drink he would have tea in a bottle, no flasks, or homemade ginger beer. Mother would also make dumplings and a meat pudding in a basin for me to take. It did keep warm. The horses were left tied near the gate with their tongues hanging out! Those were the days.'*

Renie Miller (Morris) (b. 1921) writes of her mother cooking on an oil stove with an oven over the top. Even when electricity came her mother preferred her old system. Renie writes: *'I remember fish etc. being delivered once a week from a Mr Clarke from Trimingham – such as live crabs, shrimps, cockles, mussels, winkles and whole cod in those days. Also, from the local lads with their small boats at Mundesley, fresh herring, twenty for a shilling. Mother used to thread them on a cane stick to dry first, as they were too fresh to cook straight away, she said. I remember the poor crabs screaming when they were put into boiling water to cook. Shrimps mother stirred with a red hot poker to turn brown. No fridge. Mother kept the milk cool by placing it in a pail of cold water; also jellies to set in the pantry, which was very cold like the rest of the house.'*

Nancy Miller (Lynch) (b. 1932), eleven years younger than her sister, has similar memories: '*Our house did not have a kitchen, neither did we have electricity or mains water. Water was drawn from a well which was shared by four or five other families and our food was covered in butter muslin and stored in a large, cool pantry. We basically lived off the land. My father would shoot rabbits, hares and pigeons for food and during the year would keep chickens, which provided us with a regular supply of eggs and the occasional meal. He also kept a goose, which seemed to spend its time enjoying itself by chasing us round the garden. It wasn't quite so happy though when it appeared on the table for Xmas lunch. Hooray! Our food was always fresh. Nothing was wasted. If any milk went sour it was put in muslin and hung outside to make cream cheese.*'

Barbara Wilkins (Fawkes) (1930–2009) had the good fortune to have a mother who had been a professional cook at Hevingham Hall: '*All our food was carefully planned, from the usual country pies made from rabbit, hare and pheasant, to beef, chicken and vegetable stews made with vegetables from the garden with good Norfolk dumplings. Fruit pies were made with the fruit that was in season at the time, which could be blackberries, gooseberries, blackcurrants or raspberries. These fruits were also used along with strawberries to make jam. When mother baked she never actually got out scales to weigh the ingredients for pastry or cakes. When asked for recipes she would say so many handfuls of this or that. All cakes were home-made because it was so much cheaper and meant there was a constant supply to pack up for my father, as being outside walking with the horses all day meant he had a good hearty appetite, as did all the men and women who worked on the farm.*'

Olive Wild (Webster) (b. 1919) experienced rather different eating patterns when she went into service with the Purdy family at Green Farm, Paston, in 1935: '*The day started with lighting the oil lamps, fire and cooking range, and filling the water tank beside the oven. Then we had to light the fire in the dining room and lay the table ready for breakfast. The family had a cooked breakfast every morning at 8 a.m. After breakfast we all had to meet in the hall for morning prayers. It was a hot lunch every day except Monday, which was cold. At 4.30 p.m. sandwiches of jam or honey and cake were got ready for tea.*

Miss Mary Purdy would bake the cakes. After washing up the tea things the vegetables were prepared for dinner at 7.30. The meat when cooked would be taken into the dining room to be carved by Mr Purdy senior. Our meat was taken back into the kitchen.'

My own family, the Watts – who lived in Knapton Street – were cattle dealers. My grandfather, Walter Watts, was born in 1881 and died suddenly during the Second World War in 1943. His father, George Watts, and as far as I know his father too, had been cattle dealers. My father, born in 1903, was also a cattle dealer and went on attending cattle markets, and dealing, until he was ninety-two. In today's world it is hard to place cattle dealers on the social spectrum, as the trade in the form my family practised it has disappeared. In the context of the village, however, the family was regarded as comfortably off, and although income varied a great deal from week to week there was always money for good food. My father recounted that his father, Walter, would buy joints of beef for all the family when a deal had gone well, or perhaps a box of bloaters or a box of oranges to be shared round. My grandmother, Edith, who had been in service as a lady's maid to the Shaw family at Scottow Hall, was a good if frugal cook. While there was no shortage of food, there was certainly no waste either. Leaving food on the plate was not an option. Like many other families, they would have a joint of meat on a Sunday, to be followed by cold meat on Monday, shepherd's pie on Tuesday, rissoles on Wednesday, and perhaps sausages on Thursday, fish on Friday. Also, like most other women at that time, my grandmother would bake on Fridays: Norfolk shortcakes, jam tarts, fruit pies, fruit cakes, sausage rolls, all to be put in tins and consumed during the week. She was a fanatically house-proud woman.

Despite the fact that she had a range and wall oven in the kitchen, she did all her cooking on paraffin stoves in a shed outside, where she also stored crocks of dripping on a high shelf. Her six children, including my father, used to recount with glee how on one occasion she upset the contents of one of the crocks over her own head.

My mother, Bertha Watts (née Clover) (1911–2006) had a very different approach to food. She was born in Sheffield, where her parents owned a wholesale greengrocer business. Before her marriage she worked for her uncle and aunt, who kept the Royal Hotel in Mundesley. She had therefore experienced a life where shops were open at all hours and where exotic and foreign food such as polony and various kinds of Jewish food, every kind of fruit and vegetable, and ready cooked food like hot pork sandwiches were available. Her own mother cooked dishes like savoury pudding with meat, hitherto unknown in Knapton, as she never tired of pointing out to her in-laws. At the Royal Hotel she learned a great deal from the cooks, and she became an excellent cook herself. One can only imagine how she first learned to cope with cooking on an oil stove, with no running water. I never heard her complain about it, but she did once let a Primus stove smoke out her newly decorated kitchen and my father was so furious (he had painted the kitchen) that he insisted she wash it all down herself with no help from him. Since she was still telling this story in her nineties, we can assume that the hurt ran deep.

Kathleen Johnson (Suckling) (b. 1936) wrote: *'In the 1940s and 1950s our diet was very basic. This was partly due to shortages of ingredients during and after the war. Also, nobody was very affluent. With larger families and men working on the fields, meals needed to be high calorie and inexpensive. Before electricity came to Knapton, cooking was mostly carried out on basic coal ranges and oil stoves. My aunt had a coal range, and in dull, still weather the oven barely warmed up and on a brisk, windy day was more like a char grill! A few people had a Primus stove for faster boiling.*

'My strongest memories are of various pans perched on top of the Valor oil stove; wonderfully crisp roast potatoes cooked in a lidded oval tin; deliciously light steamed puddings in a steamer atop a saucepan; and tasty beef stews in a double saucepan. My own absolute favourite was a frying pan of home-grown tomatoes, sometimes enhanced with leftover gravy. Bread and milk was a very popular breakfast and supper dish. Hot milk was poured over crumbled bread and sweet-

ened with a little sugar. During and after the war a cooked breakfast was considered essential. After the war I always had fried bacon, fried egg and fried bread for breakfast, and usually a bowl of cereal (Farmers' Glory cornflakes or Puffed Wheat). Toast, the staple of breakfasts today, just was not on the menu. Once the open fire had been lighted and the embers started glowing red, making toast with a long handled fork was a treat for tea time, especially if the toast was spread with dripping.'

'The main meals, usually eaten at midday, were basically as we eat today with less meat and more vegetables.'

Ivy Burlingham (Austin) (b. 1933) told Kathleen that she still remembered her own mother's home-made meat pies. As her family had to carry all their water from Knapton Hall – a distance of at least 200 yards – and food was cooked on a coal range with an oven in the wall, feeding the family was not an easy task. Her father had an allotment and a large garden so there was always a plentiful supply of fresh vegetables.

Kathleen Johnson captures the enjoyment of fresh fish and shell fish: *'As a few fishing boats operated out of Mundesley we were able to get really fresh fish. A visit to Mrs Strong for crab still evokes memories of hot summer days. We would eat it with salad and bread and butter for tea. We used to go shrimping at low tide. We would push the nets through the shallow pools and tip the shrimps into a bucket. The shrimps were boiled, and then began the slow and tedious task of shelling them. It was all worth while as the resulting pile of pink flesh had the most delicate, moist flavour imaginable.*

'Autumn brought another treat. The local boats went out to catch longshore herring. We would eagerly wait the boats' return and buy some of the fresh catch, thirteen fish for a shilling. When we got them home the fish would be gutted, heads removed and the scales scraped off. Sometimes my mother opened them and rolled them in oatmeal before frying, but more often they were fried whole in a pre-heated pan dusted with salt. The salt drew out the oil and gave a wonderful crisp skin to the fish, which were just served with bread and butter. Nothing could have been more tasty.

'Desserts were often milk puddings, as these were easier to produce with the cooking facilities available, or stewed fruit and custard. Steamed suet and sponge puddings and apple pie were served for Sundays or special occasions. Other fruit puddings were cobbler with a scone topping or charlotte, which had a layer of breadcrumbs dotted with butter and sprinkled with sugar and then baked until golden and crispy.

'My very favourite sweet was apple snow. Apple was cooked to a pulp, sweetened and left to get cold. Just before serving, one or two egg whites were stiffly whisked and folded into the apples. Delicious! Interestingly, apple crumble (and cole slaw), was introduced by American servicemen and their families. [There were a number of US air bases in Norfolk in the 1940s, 1950s and 1960s.] *Even in the 1957* Good Housekeeping *recipe book, apple crumble was called Canadian Fruit Pie.'*

I was born in 1940. Food in our house was important. Waste of any kind was not permitted and my father had very strong likes and dislikes. During and after the war my mother, like most other women in Knapton, made huge quantities of jam and bottled and preserved fruit and vegetables. Surplus eggs were kept in isinglass (a gelatine-like substance used to preserve whole eggs in their shells). If a pig was killed by us or by a neighbour or relative, every part was used and eaten. My father was particularly fond of chitterlings (pigs' intestines), which he cleaned meticulously and which my mother subsequently boiled, sliced and then fried. Pigs' fry (a mixture of offal with the caul), oxtail, beef pudding and pork cheese (a pork brawn) were all regulars made from the cheaper cuts of meat. My mother usually cooked at teatime, as my father was out all day at the various cattle markets that surrounded Knapton. He always had some livestock to feed, so we ate around 5.30 p.m. Food was cooked fresh. Meat, cheese, butter and lard were kept in a perforated metal meat safe in the larder. Milk was kept fresh in a milk cooler, an earthenware container standing in a bowl of water. Although electricity came to Knapton in 1948, very few people had a refrigerator until much later.

Certain tinned goods were regularly eaten: Heinz tomato soup, for example, Heinz beans, sardines and pilchards, and sometimes tinned peaches. Some things were regarded, rightly, as a great treat: duck eggs, the occasional pheasant or wild duck, and toast made in front of the fire with a toasting fork, spread with dripping and pepper and salt, a wonderful Sunday tea. New potatoes and peas were eagerly anticipated in the spring and the first tastings savoured and discussed. I remember a friend inviting me to visit her family 'when we've got new potatoes and peas in the garden'. That was in 1952. I can also remember my father saying at the end of winter how much he would savour 'some green food when it comes'. The first longshore herrings in the autumn were also greatly prized. Father loved all shellfish and smoked fish, including sprats. The preparation of food, with no running water, was not simple, but we were used to it. Ready meals were unknown, apart from fish and chips, which arrived once or twice a week in Mr Ward's van.

Entertaining was very simple. People were much more likely to be invited to tea rather than lunch (unless they were family). For tea guests, ham, egg or sardine sandwiches would be provided, with fresh celery in a tall glass vase and plenty of salt to put on it, and perhaps tinned peaches with evaporated milk and home-made cake. People were often invited in the evening, when sherry or whisky would be offered with, for example, cream crackers and cheese, followed by fruit cake, and at Christmas a mince pie. My family professed to believe that to eat a mince pie promised a merry month in the following year. On one occasion, an uncle by marriage ate no fewer than ten, on the grounds that to refuse one would bring bad luck.

We drank tea and cocoa. Coffee in the 1940s and early 1950s was Camp coffee from a bottle. But my piano teacher Miss Twaddell offered ground coffee in this period, a quite different drink, I found. At the end of the 1940s Nescafé came in, as did coffee bars. A coffee bar even arrived in Mundesley and we used to congregate there on Sunday afternoons. My mother made fresh lemonade in the summer. In the early 1950s a very popular brand of fizzy drinks, Corona, became available at the village shop. Pam Dixon (Garnham) (b. 1935) remembers delivering Corona round the village with her father, who owned the shop, and collecting the empty bottles.

Children's parties were memorable in that in addition to sandwiches, often made with meat or ham paste or sandwich spread (a great favourite), there would be jelly and blancmange, pink or chocolate, in the shape of a rabbit. Because in the early post-war years sugar was rationed, anything with sugar in it was considered a great treat, like iced biscuits or iced cakes. Bought cakes were frowned upon.

The earliest accounts in this book recount that at the start of our period bread was made at home, although when it began to be delivered to the villages baker's bread was sometimes eaten as a treat. Deliveries of bread were certainly routine by the late 1920s and 1930s. However, I do remember bread being rationed in 1946, something which had not happened throughout the war. Peter Hennessy in *Never Again* writes: '*An especially sharp blow to public morale came in the summer of 1946 when bread was rationed … It lasted two years and almost everybody, including the official historian of the Ministry of Food, now thinks it was unnecessary … It was, however, introduced for remarkably altruistic reasons – to help alleviate famine in Asia and defeated Germany … There was uproar; from millers, from housewives and from the Conservative Opposition who went to town on the inevitable anomalies of the scheme.*' There was certainly uproar locally, and I still remember being with my mother outside Gedge's bakery in Mundesley in the middle of a crowd of furious, shouting women. I also remember our elderly neighbour asking us round to taste bread she had made in the light of the crisis. It was delicious: a milk roll, baked golden brown.

Shirley Wright (Conquest) (b.1938) remembers her mother using a wall oven, '*very difficult to gauge the temperature but we would nearly always have shortcakes*'. She adds: '*We had no running water and had to fetch water from a well and a pump for use by the twelve tenants of the council houses on the green in Knapton. No electricity when I was small, using oil lamps that consisted of a delicate mantle and wick, which would burn the oil, usually leaving a mark on the ceiling. There was also a stock of candles in the cupboard which would be used in the bedrooms. Surviving without catching the house on fire was amazing and of course coal fires and wood which our family would go to gather in the hedges and lanes, helped to keep the fires going.'*

Ruth Steward (Matthew) (b. 1943), writing about her earliest memories in the 1940s and 1950s, reinforces the point that food and how it was cooked had changed very little for the past sixty or seventy years: *'Our main meals were from garden produce in season. We all loved new potatoes, but cabbage was not such a favourite. Toast and dripping in the winter months – bread came from Mundesley – also fresh fish, herring, crab and smoked haddock. I can remember having my first kipper when I stayed in the school house with the Johnson family, late May or early June 1949. My dad had a share of an allotment as well as a large garden, so vegetables in season were plentiful, also raspberries, strawberries, currants, red and black, and apples. Spare eggs in the autumn were put in isinglass to use when hens went off the lay. We also had two goats, Betty and Dimple, for milk, until it was delivered in the village by Twiggs of Mundesley. Shortcakes were a favourite: flour, lard, sultanas or currants, mixed with egg and milk or just milk, cooked on a flat tin. I must not forget jam-making, all varieties when the fruit was available, especially blackberry, which we picked from the hedgerows.'*

June Wild (b. 1951) recalls in her family home at 3 Crossroads a wall oven on one side of the fireplace and a copper on the other, although she never knew them in use. Her mother used a paraffin oven with rings on top. Water had to be fetched from the well yard behind the cottage. When water came to Knapton in 1958, she remembers the well being filled in.

Interestingly, the welfare measures introduced by the Liberal Government in 1906 included free school meals for the children of large families. However, school meals were not universally available until the implementation of the 1944 Education Act. This stated in clause 49: 'Regulations made by the Minister shall impose upon local education authorities the duty of providing milk, meals and other refreshment for pupils in attendance at schools.' It added that the regulations should make provision 'as to the manner in which and the persons by whom the expense of providing such milk, meals or refreshment is to be defrayed'. At Knapton School meals were provided before this, as recalled by Roy Fawkes (b. 1932), who left Knapton School in 1946: *School dinners started when Mrs Johnson (the head teacher) asked the children who walked from Swafield and Trunch to bring a potato each to bake on the open fire in the big room so that they had something to eat at midday. Then she started cooking on oil stoves with steamers and ovens for a few pence a day. Then the older girls cooked the dinners as part of cookery lessons. In the end, any of the children could stay, not just those who walked in every morning from the other villages. All the cooking was done in the classroom during the lessons; the boys had to put covers over the desks at lunchtime and then had to wash up afterwards.'*

I started at Knapton School in 1945, and I think it was a little after that when what had been the boys' entrance and cloakroom was converted into a very simple kitchen, with a sink and cabinets for crockery and cutlery. Here Miss Townshend, aunt of Pam and Babs Dixon, would pour out milk into beakers for playtime and dish up the meals, which by then were delivered daily by van from a central kitchen at Bacton School. It is interesting that no one, in recalling their memories of their Knapton lives, has a bad word to say about school dinners. For many large families the meals must have been a godsend. There is no doubt that they were nourishing and varied. They were not improved by their van journey from Bacton in their metal containers, but everyone loved the steamed puddings and stews. I also remember quantities of raw carrot and cabbage salad to go with slices of corned beef and baked potatoes, and an extraordinary purple jelly, exactly the colour of methylated spirit, from which I was convinced it was made. We ate at our desks, which we covered with oil cloths. Then we cleared away and Miss Townshend would wash up. Afternoon lessons, especially when the windows and doors were closed in winter, were redolent of whatever we had at dinner time, not so good when it had been fish.

It is obvious from what the contributors wrote about food that the growing, procuring, preparation and cooking of food was very consuming of time and labour, especially as Knapton had electricity only in 1948 and mains water only in 1958.

The writers quoted above describe without exception a world where a good deal of food was home-grown and consumed (and eagerly anticipated) according to the season. They also describe the cooking processes, in a coal-fired range, on the hob, in a wall oven or using a paraffin-fuelled primus stove. All of this was almost incredibly time consuming. Collecting and chopping wood and kindling, the visits of the coalman, storing and hefting coal and wood indoors, ordering and buying paraffin from the hardware store or local garage, the constant trimming of wicks and servicing the lamps and stoves – all of this had to be done. So did the cleaning that accompanied cooking on an open fire, and smoking paraffin stoves and lamps. Kathleen Johnson (Suckling) (b. 1936) describes what was involved in providing light: *'Lighting was supplied by paraffin lamps with a tall glass chimney. The wicks had to be carefully trimmed and even so they were known to smoke. Later on we had a Tilley lamp, which gave out a much better light. These lamps had to be primed by methylated spirits and then pumped up to force the paraffin vapour up to the mantle to be burnt. These lamps gave a gentle hiss all the time they were in use. We had a Tilley radiant heater and a Primus stove, which both worked on the same principle. It was possible to buy a Tilley storm lantern, which could be taken outside.'*

Spring cleaning, with a change of curtains for the summer, was essential after a closed-up winter of cooking smells and smoke. Thus housework, washing and cleaning were also extremely time- and energy-consuming. Without the vacuum cleaner and a hot water supply, not to mention detergent and washing-up liquid, cleaning and laundering were hard labour and everyone was expected to help.

I was eight when electricity came to Knapton, and the foreman of the team that brought it was billeted on us. He was called Walter and came from Ipswich. Strangely, I can recall more about him and the dramatic scenes in the village as the poles and transformers were put up than I can of what must have been an extraordinary change, from candle light to electric light. This may have been partly because to start with everyone was extremely frugal in the number of power points and appliances they had. Nancy Miller writes elsewhere that her mother continued to prefer her old oil stove and oven, even though she had an electric cooker. My mother may have taken the same view. It is certainly the case that to the end of her life in 2006 she continued to use the saucepans and two-bar electric fire she had acquired in 1948, from which I assume that they were not over-used.

The writers also describe, in a matter-of-fact way, a world without running water. They describe the arrangements they had at home which invariably involved a shared well or pump, and bringing the water for the day into the house or wash house. Even in Miss Robinson's house, water had to be pumped up to a tank before it could be used, as Olive Wild recounts elsewhere in this book. Outside lavatories were the norm, with pots used at night. Although Knapton is now on the mains water supply, it is still not on the sewer.

We shared a pump with our neighbours, Mr and Mrs Wright. It was about 75 yards from the house and each morning my father would fill three pails with water, which he brought up to the house to last for the day. They were kept beside the sink with a dipping can beside them. If hot water was required it had to be heated on the Primus stove in a large saucepan. We had a washhouse down the yard, next to the outside lavatory, with a copper for boiling clothes.

I never remember my mother using the copper. Instead she would boil clothes and tea towels in a large pan on the Primus stove, using soft water from a tank that stood against the wall of the house, and which was usually full of dead butterflies and petals from a large clematis that overhung it. The kitchen would be filled with soap-scented steam, and the smell would transfer to the living room on wet days when the wash had to be dried in front of the fire. She did send sheets and towels to the laundry in North Walsham, as did many people. As a girl in Sheffield, and even while she lived in Mundesley at the Royal Hotel, she had had the luxury of running water, and yet I never remember her complaining about the lack of it. There was no detergent either, until the early 1950s. People used Fairy soap, washing soda and soap powder like Rinso and Persil. Washing soda was used for washing up and Vim for scouring pans, which were often black with soot from having been used on an open fire or hob.

None of the other writers describe disputes between people sharing wells or pumps, but my father had a blazing row with our neighbour Mr Wright about the use of water from the shared pump. Mr Wright had complained that my father had used water drawn from the pump to water tomatoes. My father objected violently to this criticism and told Mr Wright so in very colourful terms. The row caused bad feeling, which lasted until we left that house, and it is surprising, given the absolutely vital importance of the water supply, that no one else has recorded similar disputes.

Josephine Langham (Hourahane) (b. 1936), who was an evacuee living in the School House towards the end of the war, writes with feeling: *'Housework was all hard labour. Sweeping, dusting, cleaning, washing: all were labour intensive. I still have the original Ewbank carpet sweeper from the School House. It was considered very modern; now sixty years old at least. Needless to say, I do now have a vacuum cleaner. Monday morning was always wash-day and Miss Townshend used to help. Friday was baking day for a week's supply of cakes: Eccles cakes, rock buns, bakewells, three monkeys chocolate cake.'*

Barbara Dixon (Jarvis) (b. 1938) describes the routine in the Dixon household: *'I remember each day of the week was set aside for different jobs to do.*

'Mondays was always washday. I lived in the Shop House in Knapton Street. We had a large yard with buildings around it, and one of these was the wash house. In the corner of it was a copper made with a brick surround, and underneath a fire had to be lit to heat the water. I had to fill the copper before it was lit with soft rainwater from a large tank that stood against the house. The rain water came off the roof into the tank. When the water was really hot some was taken out and put

into a metal tub where we washed the clothes. A washboard stood to one side of the tub, and we scrubbed really dirty clothes against the board with a scrubbing brush. The whites were then put into the copper to boil to make them really white, and we prodded them with a large pole like a giant rolling pin. Once they had had a good boil, they were taken out and rinsed, and then put through a wood mangle to get most of the water out. If it was fine, they were then pegged on the line to dry.

'Tuesday was ironing day. The flat irons were heated on the open fire or on top of the oil stoves. We had two irons. While you were using one the other was getting hot. Once they were hot, you slipped a little bracket over the bottom of the iron so as not to dirty the clothes. The ironing was done on the kitchen table with a blanket under the sheet so we did not burn the table.

'Wednesday was baking day. We had two ovens, one in the dining room which had a coal fire to one side. As you banked up the fire it heated the oven. The other one was in the kitchen, a large metal box about four feet long and two feet high. It stood on tall legs with two double oil burners underneath to heat it. Mum Dixon baked some wonderful cakes in this oven. We also had six oil burners, where we could cook vegetables or boil a kettle if you did not have an open fire alight. Every week after baking and cooking it was my job to clear the wicks of the oil burners to make sure they burnt evenly, and of course I had to keep them filled with paraffin.

'On Thursdays the downstairs rooms were given an extra clean, although every day we used a brush and dustpan to clean the floors. We also had to dust every day, but on Thursdays it was more on a grand scale. We also cleaned all the downstairs windows, inside and out.

'On Fridays the upstairs windows were cleaned inside and out, and it was also bedroom day. The sheets were changed on the beds ready to wash on Monday. The bedroom floors had lino. I first had to brush up all the dust, then mop the floors and then polish them, but not under the rugs in case you slipped over.'

Shirley Wright (Conquest) (b. 1938) also remembers the same washday routine and comments: *'What a hard job compared with now, and it would take a whole day to get it done.'* Undoubtedly true, and it had to be done with washing soap, not detergents, which did not appear until the early 1950s.

In the Steward household, Ruth Steward (Matthew) (b. 1943) also recalls the grind of washday, which in her family was Saturday, *'no doubt so we had clean clothes for the start of the week'*. When it was wet, all the washing had to be hung round the fire to dry. All the family had to help with the chores, upstairs and downstairs, and she remembers her brother Eric dusting under the beds pretending he was a goalkeeper, diving down with his duster in hand. *'Spring cleaning was always done in the Easter holidays: more hands to take part. Small furniture was removed from each room to make the task easier. Walls and ceilings were brushed down, beds were stripped, bed bases and springs were brushed, head boards polished, also wardrobes and chests of drawers. Rentokil was used if the dreaded woodworm was active.'*

There was no set baking day in this household. *'Baking days were as and when needed. Fruit pies, stewed fruit, jam roly-poly, shortcakes, buns, sponges and fruit cakes were made. These were stored in the pantry. Bought cakes were a treat.'*

Pearl Hicks (Eves) (b. 1951) has two brothers, David and Chris. She remembers: *'When we were children we were not allowed out to play on a Saturday morning until we had helped with the housework. We had carpets in the centre of the rooms and our job was to polish the edges of the wooden floors. Spring cleaning was a big event. Everything from each room in turn was emptied out, mats were hung on the linen line and beaten with a carpet beater, each mattress was turned over, curtains washed, windows and woodwork scrubbed or polished.'*

June Wild (b. 1951) recalls: *'When it was time for spring cleaning, my mother would take down the front room curtains and put up lighter ones for the summer. The others, which were thicker and heavier, would be washed and put away until the winter, when they were put up again. Carpets got a good beating on the linen line. As we had an open fire, no spring cleaning would be started until the chimney sweep had been.'*

The relative isolation of communities like Knapton meant that food shopping was done very locally or food was delivered. Knapton had a shop throughout the period covered by this book, until it closed in the 1980s. Pam Dixon writes that she closed the shop in 1981. It was re-opened for a few years after that by the Bishop-Leggatt family.

North Walsham, about four and a half miles away, was the main shopping centre for people from Knapton, although some things were purchased in Mundesley. Both could be reached by train and bus, and also easily by bicycle. Market day was on a Thursday in North Walsham, which was for much of the twentieth century a flourishing market town that could provide most goods and services. There were, during the 1940s and 1950s, two independent chemists, one of which was also an optician; a Boots store; dry cleaners; several butchers and two fishmongers; greengrocers; two wool and haberdashery shops,;at least two sweet shops; and an excellent stationers called Leeders. A specially wonderful shop was Randalls in the market square, next to the Cross Keys pub. Basically, it was a hardware store, but it also sold small agricultural items such as chickens' troughs and water fountains, and all the paraphernalia associated with oil lamps, heaters and stoves. It smelled strongly of paraffin and farming and was laid out in aisles bordered by very tall banks of shelves. My father always maintained that you could live inside the store for days without anyone knowing you were there. The staff were all known to everyone, and wore brown overalls, or smocks as they were called. If an unusual item was required, the oldest members of staff would be consulted, as they were likely to know if it was in stock and where on the shelves it might be kept. A search would then be set in train, with long ladders being climbed and moved from aisle to aisle as the quest continued. Great was the rejoicing if the item was eventually run to earth. Bills and cash would whiz through the air on wires from the cash desks to a secret sanctum upstairs, from where change and receipts would whiz back, apparently untouched by human hand. There were two drapers' shops and a general store named Loads, two bicycle shops and a number of banks, which were always particularly busy on market day when the farmers came into town. There were three bakers' shops, one of which, named Fayers, also had a café for tea, coffee and light lunches. The grocers, butchers, bakers and fishmongers all delivered to the surrounding villages, and it was common practice to order groceries on your visit on a Thursday, for them to be delivered the next day.

I can remember going to North Walsham on a Thursday with my mother, usually by train. The town was alive, not least because there was a cattle market on that day. You could hear and smell the cattle, whose floats would be parked behind the market itself. There were a number of market stalls for fruit and vegetables in the market square, but the purpose of the visit was usually to buy fish and meat, any hardware or clothing that might be required, and to visit the grocer, Rusts, to order goods for the forthcoming week. I can remember sitting on a high cane chair next to the counter, my legs scraping uncomfortably against the large biscuit tins on display and sniffing the wonderful combination of bacon, cheese, tea and coffee smells that pervaded the shop. Cheese was cut with a wire cutter, and sugar and dried fruit were expertly packed in twists of strong blue paper. Butter, margarine and lard were cut with a kind of palette knife and wrapped in greaseproof paper. Biscuits (and for a long time after the war, there was only one kind, Lincolns) were put into a brown paper bag. It was always an exciting visit and one eagerly anticipated.

Nancy Miller (Lynch) (b. 1932) writes: *'We didn't need to travel to the shops very often since many of the things we needed were either grown by ourselves or delivered to us. Bread, milk, fish, vegetables and meat were all available from tradesmen who called at the door. When we did go shopping it was normally to North Walsham and we either went on our bikes or by train. The things we bought were flour, sugar, butter etc., all things that my mother could not make. The list was passed to the assistant, the order made up and subsequently delivered to the house.'*

Barbara Dixon (Jarvis) (b. 1938) writes: *'The butcher would deliver two days a week. We had a large box with shelves. The sides, front and back were made of very small mesh so the air could blow in but not flies. The box hung just outside the back door in the porch to keep cool for meat or fish. Our milk was delivered in big urns on the back of a trailer. Mr*

Chamberlain from Mundesley used to stop outside the shop and I would run out with the milk jugs, which he measured the milk into. I can still see Mr Chamberlain to this day.'

Alfred Yaxley (1900–1974) writes about his early childhood tussles with clothing: *'I have never attached much importance to my own clothing. Perhaps this indifferent attitude towards bodily covering stems from my early life. I was fifteen before I had a suit of brand new clothes, bought with my own earnings. Except for occasional items bought at jumble sales, my mother made all my clothes, usually from various garments, male and female, given to her or bought at the aforementioned jumble sales. She was a great "jumbler" even up to the days of her old age …*

'My trousers were all of the knickerbockers type. I never had shorts and I never wore a jersey, or Gansey as they were mostly called. Some boys did, and I always envied them.

'I always had to wear boots. Most children did and shoes were not so popular then. Mostly my boots were made by one or other of the village cobblers, or "shoemakers" as they were called. I always dreaded the day when I was told to go and get measured for a new pair of boots, as I knew what sufferings lay ahead. They were well made and good leather was used, but certainly I never had a pair that didn't take weeks to break in. The leather always seemed to be stiff and heavy, and by the time they got comfortable the toes were getting worn and I would get the inevitable lecture on the wickedness of kicking stones. These home-made boots were, however, bliss compared with a pair of boots bought cheaply for me by mother from another family. They were made of black patent leather, had cloth tops and buttoned up. They were shaped like kidney beans, and although I wore them as much as they could be worn simply because I had no others, they did things to my feet that only Army boots could cure.

'Most of our other requirements in the clothing line were bought from a shop in North Walsham, not directly, but through an agent or representative, or whatever they called themselves in those days. He would travel by bicycle and call every fortnight. He would have a cup of tea, take mother's orders, if she had any, and hand over anything she had ordered. I should explain that these things were bought on what we call

today the Hire Purchase. I don't know what it was called then. Mother would hand over her shilling or whatever she could afford, and would be treated if she was the firm's most important customer.'

John Capes (b. 1930) remembers his grandmother, Libby Wright, buying clothes from Mr Brown the Packman at her home in Knapton: *'Mr Brown came round about once a fortnight, or maybe monthly. He was a big jovial man from North Walsham. He would come marching around the corner of the bungalow to the back door with a large pack under his arm, knock smartly on the door and call out, "Anything today, Mrs Wright?" He would then come into the living room and put his pack on the table.*

'The pack was about two feet long by eighteen inches wide and a foot high, wrapped in an oilcloth type material. He would quickly undo the leather straps around the pack, and open it to reveal the contents.

'In the pack would be vests, skirts, blouses, knickers, petticoats and lisle stockings (no nylons or tights then) for the ladies, and for the men, vests, pants, shirts, pullovers and socks, and of course hankies for both sexes. If something more substantial was required, he would say, "Ah, wait a minute, I've got some in the car," and off he would dash to get the item. Obviously, he could not cope with all sizes in his pack, but he would have a selection from his stock, so sometimes it would be a case of "Sorry, I haven't got that with me today, I'll bring it tomorrow".

'The contents of the pack would vary according to the season. In spring and summer there would be cotton shirts, blouses and skirts, but in autumn he would have woollen and serge things and "long johns" for the men. I think Mr Brown dealt mainly with the working class as his items were mainly plain and practical and reasonably priced. Clothes are not things you buy very often, so on most occasions Granny didn't buy anything, but that didn't deter Mr Brown from saying, "Anything I can tempt you to buy today, Mrs Wright?"

'Payment was on an instalment basis. Granny had a card on which purchases and payments were recorded, and would pay off a regular amount on each visit, probably about a shilling (five pence today), but I think this went up a bit if she bought a more expensive item. Mr Brown must have died in the late 1940s or early 1950s as I can remember that

his daughter had to come round to collect the remainder of the money owing to him.

'If such things as suits, coats, boots and shoes were required, granny and grandad would have to go to North Walsham on the train, although if grandad was going on his own he might have biked. They would probably have dealt with Loades shop at the bottom of the market place.'

Barbara Wilkins (Fawkes) (1930–2009) and her sister Brenda (b. 1941) write: *'Our clothes were all home-made by our mother, who would go into North Walsham by bus or train and stand outside Loades the drapers to study the latest fashions in dresses, skirts and blouses, which would be hanging in the window. She would then buy some material and come home and make patterns out of newspaper. A lot of measuring went on before the final pattern was produced, then mother would make Brenda and me whatever was in fashion at the time at a fraction of what it would have cost in the shop.'*

Their mother had a Singer sewing machine that her mother had bought her when she was twelve years old to make clothes for her younger sisters. *'In those days all shoes had leather soles and our mother used to put tips on the toes and heels to make them last longer. When the soles wore through, Mr Carr up the road used to repair them for us. Our shoes, coats, hats and Wellingtons all came from Loades.'*

Brenda remembers that when she was seven she went with Willie Puncher to a Guy Fawkes bonfire in the village, wearing her brand new gabardine raincoat. Unfortunately, a piece of burning paper got lodged under the belt, and in the dark she did not see it. *'When I got home I had a hole burnt through my new coat. Mother had to patch it. Needless to say, I never went to another bonfire night!'*

Ivy Burlingham (Austin) (b. 1931) remembers going with her younger sister Grace to Sunday School at the chapel at Easter time, wearing Easter bonnets tied with ribbons, dresses and white socks with white or black shoes. In winter they would wear vests and bodices with rubber buttons (Liberty bodices) and socks they had knitted on four needles, black or grey. Ivy adds: *'I had a gold coloured knitted jumper with green cuffs and it was a yarn wool. I hated it because it was big!'* Later she remembers *'much longer skirts (the*

New Look), stockings with seams, wedge-heeled shoes with bows on the front and coats with hoods.'

Nancy Miller (Lynch) (b. 1932) remembers school clothes, blouses and gym slips for the girls, but for Sundays *'we had what we called our Sunday best, which we wore to Sunday School every week. Most of our clothes were bought from a man who sold them from a suitcase and came to the house once a month Occasionally we would shop in North Walsham for clothes but that was considered somewhat as a treat.'*

Shirley Wright (Conquest) writes: *'Starting school in 1943 during the war, I remember that the clothes I wore were mostly second-hand. The winters were very cold and I remember little jumpers and skirts, long socks and wool stockings, always a beige colour and held up by elastic. My sister, who was fifteen years older than me, worked in an ammunitions factory in Hertfordshire, and on one occasion when she came home she bought me a pretty floral cotton summer dress and took me on the back of her bicycle to North Walsham to have my photograph taken. As I got older, at around eleven years old, I had a new winter coat for Christmas. I did not really like it and thought it rather drab, but I had no choice, I had to wear it.*

'Apart from these two items, I cannot remember having anything else new, but I remember always having something special to wear on Sunday, with, of course, white socks. One thing that I vividly remember is my father, who was very much an outdoor person with a love of gardening, knitting me a Fair Isle cardigan. He had never knitted a stitch before. It had a beige background and red diamonds, and blue and dark brown patterns and other colours mixed in. I wore it a lot as it was brightly coloured and I thought he had such patience while knitting it. I think that when I was about fourteen I had a bottle green winter coat, which was originally Kathleen Johnson's, which I wore for a long time. As I got older, about fifteen, I worked in the summer holidays, fruit picking or in a hotel, and got money to buy my own clothes. The first outfit I bought was a cherry red coat with navy accessories. I also bought the then fashionable "jigger" coat, a jacket below the waist on a yoke. Then came the clothes for dances, which I did enjoy wearing: black brocade with a bit of net and sequins etc.

'*Summing it all up, it was a very poor era for most of us during and after the war, but we all shared the same hardship and accepted it.*'

Ruth Steward (Matthew) (b. 1943) was a member of a family of four. She writes: '*As small children we had knitted clothes, as mum was a good knitter and needlewoman. When I started school for winter I wore a jumper, gymslip, three-quarter length grey socks. In summer we wore dresses – mine were mostly hand-downs from my older sister Janet – and short white socks and sandals We had new clothes for the Sunday School anniversary in May. My favourite dress was blue and white check with a white sailor collar. I must have been four when I had it. Three summers later it was too small, and I was very upset at not being able to wear it again.*

'*Our shoes came from the Co-op in North Walsham, and if repairs were needed they went to Mr Mason's cobbler's shop in Trunch. Passing the Eleven Plus meant uniform for school: navy blazer and hat with a badge, green and white striped blouse, navy gym slip, grey socks, and later navy socks became available. A gabardine mac was needed for cold or wet weather. Summer was a green check gingham dress and navy cardigan. For PE we had navy shorts, white T shirts and navy plimsolls. Then there were indoor shoes.*

'*There was a dressing-up cupboard at Knapton School. I can remember one year we dressed up on May Day, the girls as flowers. I was a marigold. We walked round the village and danced on Knapton Green.*

'*I was twelve when I had my first nylon stockings, older than some girls. They were stretchy and fitted so well; they came from Marks and Spencer in Norwich and were for "best" only.*

'*I made a dress at Knapton School. It had small blue flowers on it and was a shift dress. My knitting did leave a bit to be desired at first: "dish cloths", my dad called it. But I went on to knit jumpers and other things. I can remember knitting socks on four needles and turning heels as well as anyone else.*

'*School gym slips and coats were taken to the dry cleaners in Kings Arms Street in North Walsham perhaps once a year.*'

June Wild (b. 1951) also writes of Sunday best clothes: '*In the summer it would be a new dress with a cardigan knitted by my mother, who would also knit all the winter jumpers and cardigans during the year, for herself, dad and me. One coat was kept for Sunday best, for the winter to go to Sunday School in and for visiting relatives, always wrapped up with a wool hat, scarf, gloves or mittens.*

'School uniform at North Walsham Secondary Modern School in the 1960s was a red and white gingham dress for the summer, and for the winter a red V-neck jumper (later a black one), a white blouse and grey skirt. When the mini came in, we would turn the waist band of the skirt over to make it shorter, until a teacher caught you, when it would have to go back to its proper length.

'There were also midi and maxi lengths. Other fashions were hot pants, tank tops and flared trousers, platform shoes and boots, which I did not find very good to walk in.'

Like everyone else, I had hand-me-downs as the staples of my childhood wardrobe, such as it was. When I went to North Walsham High School at the age of eleven, I was particularly galled to have to make a debut in Kathleen Johnson's cast-off school tunic and striped blouses, a baggy, home-knitted, rather bright, navy cardigan, and an outsize blazer bought to last. New items of school uniforms for Norfolk's grammar schools could be bought at Greens outfitters on the Walk in Norwich.

Because my father went each week by car to Norwich market on a Saturday, we often went too. Norwich in the 1940s and 1950s, with the livestock market taking place in the centre, was to us breathtakingly exciting. Many of the farmers and dealers attending the market would take their wives and families, and there was a definite air of being up from the country. I liked to look into the windows of the art shop, Levetons, and a wonderful fur shop with double windows, Brahms.

Jarrolds, the department store still flourishing in Norwich, had an enticing education department, as it was called. I would linger there for ages, looking at the vast range of school stationery, pencil cases, exercise books and folders. We would not usually have lunch, as my mother would cook a meal when we all got home, but we might have coffee and biscuits in one of the department stores. Very occasionally, we would go to the Scotch Tea Rooms, where a curious soup with prunes was served (later identified as Mulligatawny) and a delicious mince with small triangles of fried bread. Sometimes there was time to visit the Castle Museum with its stuffed animals and criminals' death masks in the dungeons. Later, I would take a school friend and we would go to every museum in the city, and visit the Corn Exchange and the covered market in front of the City Hall. At 2 p.m. we would go back to the market, find the car and get in it – it was always, like everyone else's, left unlocked – to wait for my father. His mood for the drive home was heavily dependent on how business had gone and how much of a celebration or drowning of sorrows had ensued. It was sometimes a white-knuckle ride.

On 5 July 1948 the National Health Service came into being. Peter Hennessy in his book *Never Again* hails the NHS as 'one of the finest institutions ever built by anyone anywhere'. That is undoubtedly true, and yet perhaps surprisingly the contributors to this book make little distinction between the medical services they received before 1948 and afterwards.

In *From Dawn to Dusk* Arthur Amis describes the death of his mother in 1925, leaving a family of ten children: *'Edie* [a sister] *was in service at Dr Quaite's in Mundesley. He was the doctor who looked after mum. Dad's doctor was Dr Shepherd of North Walsham and Mundesley. He became the family doctor. I remember dad used to call at the house where Dr Shepherd had his surgery if one of us had a cold. He would give dad a pint and a half of cough mixture and say, "Give them all some. If they haven't got it, it will help." He had two surgeries and a private telephone line from his house in North Walsham to the one in Mundesley. The wires were strung out and attached to trees before poles were put up. He rode a motor cycle. These old family doctors were quite a part of family life.'*

He adds: *Just before mother died, my sister Ellen* [mother of Janet,

Ruth, Eric and Mary Steward] *had to live in a shelter in the garden.*
She was on her back in this shelter for two years. I am not quite sure
what it was, but possibly TB. The shelter was supplied by the Council
and the District Nurse used to come in every day. We all took turns in
looking after her. The shelter revolved so we could turn it round when the
wind was from the wrong direction. Ellen got better, went into service
and had four children.'

Janet Steward (Munro) (b. 1940) writes of her mother Ellen:
'My mother was not always a well person, although it never occurred to
us that there was anything wrong. It wasn't till much later in life we
learned that as a young child she had contracted TB and spent several
years living in a hut in the garden.'

Llewellyn Kirk (b. 1930), who was a neighbour of my great-aunt
and uncle, Adeline and Lou Watts, graphically illustrates a pre-
telephone age. He writes: *'Lou Watts was ill and I rode my bike to*
North Walsham to get his medicine from Lings the Chemists. When I
got back he had died.'

After Lou's death Adeline had a companion/help, Georgie
Hewitt. Georgie was delicate and also had TB, and like Ellen
Steward had a shelter in which she had to sleep at night, even in
the bitter winter of 1947. It was at that time part of the fresh air cure
recommended for the treatment of TB.

Nancy Miller (Lynch) (b. 1932) remembers Dr Miller: *'He was*
a super doctor who came from Mundesley. Our dental health was taken
care of by the school dentist, who would visit the school in a large van
and inspect our teeth. My mother always insisted that we had everything
done that was necessary. We did not have a bathroom at home so on a
Friday night we would bathe in a tin bath in front of the fire. (Bliss!)
This was followed by a spoonful of Syrup of Figs. (Yuck!) My brother
Derek, who sadly passed away in 2008, was rather thin, so he was given
Maltalene, which was quite nice. Mother believed that it was something
good, so she also gave a spoonful to my brother Michael and me.'

Barbara Dixon (Jarvis) (b. 1938) describes an accident in which
Dr Miller came to the rescue: *'One day after spending rather too*
long watching the harvest we knew we would be late. Sister Pam and

I were running home, and I fell and caught my foot in a pothole in the road and took a lump out of my leg. I remember Dr Miller coming to the house. I was sitting on the table in the kitchen, scared stiff, but before he put stitches into my knee he first put one into my doll, Joan. He was really kind and I remember he wore very tiny glasses on the end of his nose.'

Shirley Wright (Conquest) (b. 1938) remembers Dr Miller too: *'Usually when we were ill we called the doctor in as it was difficult to get transport, especially when you felt quite ill. I remember having the usual illnesses as a child, but had a bad spell of whooping cough, which later would give me spells of bronchitis, so I think the doctor saw me quite a lot. At school I was given malt, which I think was usual for most children there. I remember the dentist coming to school in a mobile unit, and I dreaded this. He seemed quite an oldish man, and not very gentle.'*

Janet Steward (Munro) (b. 1940) describes Dr Miller's surgery at St Brannocks on the Cromer Road in Mundesley. *'The waiting room was a large room with a very large, marble fire-surround, and on the mantelpiece were several large mammoth bones, which Dr Miller had found at various times in the Mundesley cliffs. These bones are now on display in the Mundesley Maritime Museum. Dr Hugh was a lovely man. I remember him visiting our house but have no recollection of any of us being ill.'*

Her sister Ruth (Matthew) (b. 1943) does remember the doctor calling because she had measles. She also recalls a visit to Cromer Hospital: *'When I was very small I had to go to Cromer Hospital. I hated this and can remember hiding under the cot when mum left me. We had a nurse visit Knapton School to test us for TB. Both mum and dad had been ill with it in their younger years. As my test was positive, we all had to go as a family to Norwich Hospital for X-rays. Obviously, the result must have been OK as nothing further had to be done. Mrs Turney, who lived in Pond Road in Knapton and whose husband Mr Turney was the optician, was a District Nurse, and I remember her calling to see my brother Eric when he broke his wrist, and also my younger sister Mary when her face was scalded by accidentally running into mum who was carrying a pan of boiling water.'*

June Wild (b. 1951) describes her father going to Mr Turney for an eye test. Mr Turney found something *'not quite right, and sent dad to his doctor, Dr Fee, in North Walsham. This was in 1951. Dad was admitted to the Norfolk and Norwich Hospital on 18 August. On 22 August, he was transferred to Hill End Hospital at St Alban's, which was part of Barts Hospital in London. Two days later he was found to have a brain tumour. It was a worrying time for my mother* [Vera Wild] *as I was only a few weeks old, but she had help and support from all the family who lived in Knapton. People would stop mum and come to the door to ask how dad was. As there was no water laid on, Willie Wild would come and get the water for mum from the well-yard.*

'It was a long way to go to visit, but mum, I and the family did, though I did not go every time. Uncle Jack, dad's brother-in-law, took us. Herbert Hicks took us to Norwich to meet my uncle, so that he did not have to come to Knapton each time. Dad received letters, which he kept, keeping him in touch with the village, and he replied when he was able. Arthur Johnson, Kathleen's father, wrote to him with a detailed report of the new Men's Club meeting. It had not been opened for long. Miss Robinson wrote from Knapton House that she was going to open a fete and that her speech would not be a long one!

'Before the operation, dad would sometimes go down to the hospital workshops: he was a carpenter. On 8 September, uncle Jack picked dad up and brought him home for a few days. He also visited his sisters, who lived the other side of Norwich. He went back to Hill End and had the operation on 14 September, and it was successful. He came out of hospital on 4 October.

'This was followed up by going to Barts for check-ups, which involved various tests, first each year, then every eighteen months, and later two- and then three-yearly intervals, right up to the 1980s. He always kept his brain active, very quick at mental arithmetic, reading, etc., and remained so until the end of his life. Dad died in 2005 aged ninety-three years.'

SIX

JOBS

K*napton Remembered*, the first book on Knapton produced by this group of writers, covered the period 1934 to 1961. That period was chosen because it was the time during which Kathleen (Kitty) Johnson served as the gifted head teacher of Knapton School, where the writers began their school lives. *Knapton Remembered* contains an analysis of the occupations of the writers' parents, and of their own subsequent careers, which is reproduced as Appendix 1.

This book is more ambitious in its scope, both in the length of the period it covers and in the spread of its contributors. Both are illustrated in this chapter, starting with Josiah Bane's memories of work, born in the late nineteenth century, and ending with those of Christopher and Sadie Risebrow and Paul Turner, all born in the early 1970s. The chapter also charts the journey of Knapton from a more or less self-sufficient community to the position at the end of the twentieth century, when it had lost its school, station, shop, carpenter's workshop and blacksmith.

Josiah Bane was born in 1882 into a family of eight. His father was a farm worker and his mother also worked. *'She used to take in washing from gentry in Mundesley and North Walsham. She would fetch it in the old chap's dickey and cart. That's how she found out he went in pubs, as the dickey stopped at pubs he used ... I left school at twelve and my first job was at Church Farm; Pains farmed it then. I was paid one shilling a week for cleaning shoes, knives and forks, milking the cows and clearing out stables. I had my first pipe of baccy there in the stable, blowing the smoke out of the pop hole, but I got caught and got a hiding off the old chap, but that didn't stop me when I could get hold of some. It couldn't have cost much as mother took most of my money. I soon left there and went to John Walpole's at Edingthorpe and got 5s for a seven-day week feeding bullocks.*

At that time the railway was being built between North Walsham and Mundesley.

'*The only time I left Knapton was to work at Felixstowe on the sea front from Cobbles Wall to the the Fletcher's public house. It was hard work barrowing shingle from the beach. When I came back I helped to make the road from Mundesley to Trimingham breaking stones with a hammer. After that I went back to bullock feeding. On market day we had to drive them from Norwich, calling at different farms on the way, sometimes leaving them somewhere for the night and carrying on the next day ... The General Strike was a bad time. My brother Tom went to America and my sister Eliza to Canada.*'

Alfred Yaxley (1900–1974) left school at fourteen, and then went back because he had no job to go to. But in April or May 1914 he was offered a job by the farmer and auctioneer for whom he had worked part-time when he was still at school. '*Taken in the whole, it wasn't an unhappy period in my working life. My first job was weeding corn in the company of my great-uncle and another man. My equipment consisted of a spud, a sort of miniature Dutch hoe on a shaft, and a sack tied around my middle in such a way that it had an opening like a kangaroo's pouch. Docks had to be pulled up by the roots and put in the pouch, and then emptied on the hedgerow at each end of the field. Thistles had to be cut with the spud and left to die. Walking up a knee-high field of corn all day might seem monotonous but it wasn't hard work, and I don't remember being bored. My companions were not talkative and neither was I, so we got along very well. It was lovely calm, sunny weather, the skylarks were singing, and to a boy starting out to earn his own living, all seemed right with the world. I can't remember what my wages were, probably five or six shillings a week. I was to be a general dogsbody, spending my time at farm work when needed, and the rest of the time in the yard or the garden. Sometimes the farm work would entail driving a horse roll, a job which I liked very much even if it was a bit hard on my clothes, which got very dusty in dry weather. Later on in the season I had to lead the horse pulling the horse hoe. This was used to hoe between the rows of root crops. The horse was led, as the man steering the machine had to keep his attention on the hoes, which were set as close*

*as possible to the rows of plants. It would have been easy to cut up plants
if his eyes wandered.'*

Alfred Yaxley finally became a gardener for Mrs Lee at Footpath
Cottage in Paston. More descriptions of his early career working
on the farm are included in the chapter on agriculture above. He
is also mentioned by Marjorie Schamp in her account of service at
Mrs Lee's house.

My father Jack Watts (1903–99) was born into a family of
cattle dealers. His father Walter and grandfather George are
both recorded in *Kelly's Directories* as 'farmers and cattle dealers',
although any farming they did was more to do with fattening stock
or keeping it until it could be sold on than with arable production.
For these purposes they would rent land, sometimes locally, but also
on the marshes bordering the Norfolk Broads.

Jack was the second child in a family of six. He was born in a
cottage in Knapton Street and the family moved further down The
Street to Verbena Cottage later on. He attended Knapton School
and at twelve years old took the School Leaving Certificate so that
he could start work with his father. His younger brother Leslie was
apprenticed to a carpenter; his sister Mollie was apprenticed as a
dressmaker at Cubitts, the general store in North Walsham; and
his sister Babs worked in a nursing home. Ivy, the eldest sister, left
home as soon as she could for London where she lived for most of
the rest of her long life. Trixie, the youngest, stayed at home until
she married.

The profession, if it can be so called, of cattle dealing has more
or less completely died out now. But when my father started work
with his father in about 1915, the cattle dealer exerted considerable
influence in the farming community, and was able to make a good
if rather precarious living, attending local markets and buying and
selling cattle for farmers who might not have the time or connections to buy for themselves. A strong nerve, good judgement of
livestock on the hoof and quick wits were necessary attributes.
My great-grandfather George was known as 'Wits Watts'.
Communication and knowledge were all. Early photographs show

my grandfather in his pony and trap, but the family were among the first in Knapton to have a car and a telephone, both essential for the job. Given that many transactions took place in market pubs after the sales were over, a good head for drink was also required. George Miller, father of the Renie, Nancy and Michael quoted in this book and also of Molly and Derek, lived next door to Verbena Cottage, and worked with my grandfather and father, driving them back from market when the pub deals had been too much for safety on the road, among other things.

The local markets were at Acle on Mondays, Stalham on Tuesdays, Norwich or Bury St Edmunds on Wednesdays, North Walsham on Thursdays, Aylsham on Fridays and Norwich on Saturdays. My father remembered cattle being driven from Norwich cattle market to Martineau Lane, the site now of Norfolk County Hall, where they were kept overnight before being loaded on to trains. He also remembered driving cattle home on foot the twenty miles from Norwich. Overnight lairage was provided at Crostwight, roughly halfway. To buy cattle, he would go by train (and boat) with my grandfather, and after the latter's death, with colleagues, as far afield as York, Leicester and even Ireland. Some people in Knapton remember my grand-father hiring trucks on a goods train to bring cattle back, probably from York.

My father regularly fell out with his father, since both had hot tempers. On one occasion, my father left home and went to the Britannia Barracks in Norwich to join the Army. He was just being handed the King's Shilling when my grandfather arrived, mopping his head, to persuade him to change his mind. My father did so, but got his chance again when war broke out, subsequently joining the Marines. He was stationed in Deal throughout his time, but was called upon to drive equipment all over the country. What he saw as ludicrous Army practices exasperated him but he enjoyed getting away from Norfolk, and often spoke with pride of his 'years under canvas'. He did not speak until the end of his life of the horrific job he had to do disposing of corpses after the incident at Slapton

Sands in Devon when hundreds of American servicemen lost their lives in an exercise that went disastrously wrong.

In 1943 his father Walter Watts died. The death was recorded by Renie Miller: *'During the war my father helped a cattle dealer, Walter Watts. Our family and his family were very close, and they were good to us. We then lived at the bottom of The Street quite near them. One day, my dad was with Walter Watts in a bullock yard in Wallage's Loke (at the White House Farm in Knapton), looking at some cattle. The yard had just been strawed out and so clean. Walter Watts dropped down dead. All the cattle stood round in a ring, looking on as if they all knew. Jack Watts had to come home then to carry on the business.'*

He did come home for a period, but was frequently recalled during the rest of the war.

To the end of his life my father was a man of few words, but I know that he valued beyond price the freedom his job gave him. He enjoyed being on the road, using his wits and pulling off deals. He kept chickens, pigs and a few store animals from time to time, and brought some of the first Charolais cattle to be seen in Norfolk: he was enormously proud of them. He was respected for his integrity within the farming community in Norfolk, but regretted the early end to his formal education. He continued dealing until he was ninety-two.

The profession of cattle dealing died at about the same time, though its decline had begun at the beginning of the twentieth century. The *Kelly's Directory* for Norfolk of 1892 lists 183 cattle dealers spread evenly throughout the county, as were the cattle markets. The dealers would accept commissions from farmers, landowners, and others to buy cattle at the markets, or from individuals wishing to sell, and arrange for the cattle to be driven to markets or to the buyer. The role of the drover needed skill and knowledge of cattle and road routes was crucial. My grandfather's preferred drover was a distant cousin, always known as Smock. Obviously the distance cattle could walk in a day, or with overnight lairage in two days, from any given market or train station accounted for the geographical spread of cattle markets, and indeed of cattle dealers who in 1892 would themselves be travelling by horse and cart.

By 1922 *Kelly's Directory* for Norfolk lists forty-three cattle dealers, – a number of factors having brought about this change. One was that, as is explained in the chapter on agriculture, fewer cattle were being kept in Norfolk. Another is that by that time dealers were travelling by car and taking their commissions by telephone; their influence and knowledge, upon which their living depended were not limited by their proximity to their most local cattle markets. The advent of regular cattle price reports on the radio and in the newspaper again enabled more farmers to do without the middle man or cattle dealer, and the 1933 *Kelly's Directory* shows the numbers shrinking again to just thirty-one.

Our next five contributions record another work activity which has almost disappeared: domestic service. The accounts of life below stairs from Archie Wright, Anne Stubley, Bertha Watts, Olive Webster and Marjorie Schamp are given in chronological order, and the period they cover ranges from c. 1919 to the outbreak of the Second World War.

Archie Wright (1904–95) was born at the Post Office Cottages, in Knapton. *'There were twelve in our family and I was the ninth. My father was road foreman for Erpingham District Council and a thatcher. We had lived under Robinsons* [the Robinson family of Knapton House owned these cottages] *but they had a new gardener come and they wanted the Knapton cottage for him so we had to move to Gimingham. We lived in the Master's House of the old Gimingham workhouse in the Pump Yard. I left school in July 1917 and worked on a farm until 1919, when the war was over.*

'My sisters, Violet, Alice, Edie and Norah were all in private service and used to come home and say what a wonderful life it was. It made me want to go in too. Violet was undercook at Haywards, the pickle people, in London. Alice was cook for the Countess de Clare in London, Edie

worked for Sir James Porter, a wood merchant in Norwich and finished up as cook, and Norah was housemaid and lady's maid at Langley Hall. They all got their jobs through the school or through the parson. My mother used to do a lot of washing for the big houses in Mundesley and had contacts there. Nearly all of us had to move away to get a living. One brother went mining in north-east England, two went to Canada, one was in the Battle of Jutland, and was never the same again: he died in Thorpe [a psychiatric hospital near Norwich].

'I started in a private school at Suffield Park near Cromer, as house-boy. We had gas there and in the morning I had to light the ranges and look after the boiler, and help with the vegetables, wash up greasy plates which I hated, all for 12s a week and my keep.'

After a short time at the school Archie left, packed a tin trunk with his belongings, got a one-way ticket to Liverpool Street, and made his way to where one of his sisters was living. *'She only had two rooms for her and her husband and the two children, although they lived well: he was a butcher's assistant. She had an old bed chair in the kitchen and we pulled the tin trunk up to that, and fixed me up a bed with some cushions.*

'I was walking up past Harrod's a day or two after I got to my sister's, looking for Ennismore Gardens where I had been told there was a job. Outside Harrod's there was a huge commissionaire, in a marvel-lous uniform and covered with medals and ribbons. I went up to him and said, in my Norfolk accent, "Excuse me sir, but can you tell me where I can find Ennismore Gardens?" To my surprise, this very dignified and splendid man burst out laughing, and said in an accent at least as broad as mine, "And do your father keep a dickey, bor?"

'I replied, "Yes, that he do, and he keep that chained up with a bit of rope."

[To this day, this is an exchange used by a Norfolk-born person who happens to meet another outside the county.]

'It turned out, of course, that the commissionaire was from Norfolk, and he told me it was like a real breath of fresh air to hear his native tongue coming from me. All the time I was in London, I never heard of a Norfolk person out of a job.'

Certainly Archie was no exception to his own rule. His first job in London was as a delivery boy for Sainsbury's, and then as a general helper at the YMCA in Euston Square. Thinking that he had had enough experience to try service, he went to the Regency Bureau in Duke Street, St James's, from where he was directed to a job as a hall boy in Green Street, off Park Lane, in the household of a Major Holden. He worked in the pantry under the butler. *The boiler was really the main thing. That water had to be hot in the mornings, and I had to take tea to the footman, scrub the marble front door step, clean the brass knocker and bell, then get washed and set the breakfast table in the servants' hall. We had breakfast at 8 a.m.*

I never lived so well in my life ... There was the butler, a footman, a lady's maid, head housemaid and housemaid, cook and kitchen maid ... The Major had a radio set in his lounge and he did a lot of entertaining in that kind of world: Beaverbrook, Josie Collins, Gladys Cooper and Lady Diana Cooper, a very elegant lady. He had two Rolls Royces. He was a stock broker and private banker, and a founder member of the Embassy Club where Ambrose had his band, and sometimes Ambrose would come to the house. He married one of the daughters of Mrs Kate Meyrick. I met her and she was a very charming woman. Opposite our house was the house of the Duke and Duchess of Sutherland. When the Duchess went shopping she had a special car: it was petrol electric, like a square box with a tiller. The Duke had his own railway carriage for when they went to Scotland.

I was known by my second name there, William, as it was thought to be more suitable. One day the butler said, "William, there is a treat today, dumplings for dinner." I was ever so pleased, as I hadn't had a dumpling since I left Norfolk. I had to get the dish of salt beef from the wicket, it was a great big joint, all surrounded with little carrots, new potatoes and onions, and then I had to go back for some more vegetables. "Where are the dumplings?" I wondered. Well, imagine my surprise: they were already round the meat, tiny little old things about as big as a shilling. I said, "My mother used to make them as big as your head", and they all burst out laughing, although cook was a bit indignant.

I had to sleep out at that place and because I wanted to sleep in I got a job in Melton Mowbray, at Saxilby Park, with a Captain Forrester who had been Master of the Quorn. I had to look after his riding boots and habit, and wait at table. I only stayed there for the cubbing season. It was very hard work indeed, boning up the boots and cleaning the habits. They always had to be perfect for the next day …

'My next place was at Brasted Place near Westerham in Kent, with the Urquharts. The lady stood six feet tall; she had been a Gibson Girl and she used to follow me about with her eyes, and I used to colour up.

'I left after six months because they were cutting down on staff, but it was a very busy place. They also had a house in Kensington and during the season you never got any sleep.

'My next place was 35 Eaton Place with Sir Robert Lisle, one of the syrup people. At least it had been his household: he'd dropped down dead at polo at Hurlingham just before I went there. There was a butler, a first footman, three in the kitchen, four in the pantry, two lady's maids, a head housemaid with two or three under her, a cook housekeeper and, when Sir Robert was alive, a French chef and a valet. In the household there was the lady, her widowed daughter and Robert, Diana and John, her children.

'I had to do the silver and act as personal servant to the lady. I had to go about in the car with her and do jobs for her lady's maid. While I was there, Miss Diana was presented at court by her mother. Miss Diana had a gramophone and sometimes when I was passing through the ballroom she would say, "Come on Arthur, have a waltz." (They called me Arthur there.) We had a Daimler that had been built for the Kaiser of Germany. He never had it because of the war and funnily enough it stands today in the museum at Sandringham, where I've seen it.

'I had to go to Buckingham Palace when Miss Diana was presented, sitting in front with the chauffeur with a cocked hat on. When the car was stopped in the Mall, two people looked in and laughed. They were my sisters!

'This was in 1921, and it was the first court and season since the war. My people had a box at Covent Garden and went every week. I used to have to as well, and got to know a lot of operas that way. During the season we were lucky if we got six hours' sleep a night, but it was a pleasure to do it and we lived so well. I lived like a lord, and that's when my education started.

'I used to have to valet Mr Robert, put out his loose change, gloves, shoes and so on, and bring his breakfast tray. Our breakfast was a huge

marvellous meal. We had to get the trays ready for the ladies and after that the cook housekeeper went up to get her orders for the day. The butler had the menu first for the table settings and wines, and my orders came at 11 a.m. She would say perhaps, "The galleries this morning" or "Dress shops". At 12.15 we had our lunch. Then I had to change into my footman's uniform for their lunch at 1 p.m. We used to have to hand round vegetables in dishes with hot water in the base, and we did not wear gloves.

'Once we had to go to a wedding at Holland Park House. It was so huge it even had its own nine-hole golf course in the garden. The wedding itself was at Brompton Oratory. Lord Lonsdale was in the car next to ours and, as he got out, two footmen started to argue and then fell to scrapping. Lord L. watched them and then said to me "5 to 4 on the little one".

'He had a Daimler built out of yellow wood built like a horse box.

'My last place was in Herefordshire, with the Hon. Charles Bateman Hanbury, but I wasn't there long. I came home then. For ages my mother had been writing to me begging me to.

'I worked nine years in a hotel in Cromer, then at the Eighteenth Hole in West Runton till the war. Then after going into the Army, I went to Erpingham Horseshoes then to Alby Horseshoes, and I also had my own milk round.'

Anne Markham (later Stubley) (1907–90) also writes about domestic service: *'Personally I have nothing but praise for the system and regret very much the passing of it. Why servants were looked down upon as they were was always a mystery, as are we not all servants in one way or another? In good situations girls were trained, well clothed and fed, and with so much choice of jobs – why did they stay in bad conditions? I started as temporary kitchen maid at the Hall on the estate where we lived, six weeks while the other girl recovered from a bad scald. The lady of the house was a bit of a meany. I had only to cook for a staff of six. Each Wednesday each of us was doled out half a pound of farm butter, one pound of jam, a quarter of tea and a half pound of sugar. Milk came from the Home Farm in a churn. Imagine setting a table with six plates of butter, six jars of jam: it was rather like the three bears, "Who's been eating my jam or butter?"*

'It was winter time so rabbits were plentiful and staff had them every day. After my stint there I must have been quite an authority on ways to disguise a rabbit, so much so the lady said the staff meals were more appetising than theirs. Incidentally, the Squire always had his tea in the Servants' Hall. It was the only place he could get a decent cup of tea and doorsteps of bread and butter instead of wafer thin. Mind you, he also had his allowance of tea, butter and sugar. I was asked to stay on, but my father said a firm no.

'Then came four happy years with an old lady of the old school, to whom I will always be grateful, a super cook and manager in every aspect, and a great sense of humour. My parents died within six months of each other, so rather than stay with relations, domestic service seemed the answer, which was a wise decision.

'My first post lasted thirteen years. It began as cook to a family, house in Norfolk, flat in London. The elderly husband worked in town and spent his weekends in Norfolk. His young wife spent practically all her time in London, so it was not long before I had to take over as there were two teenagers at boarding school who came home for the holidays. They became my family, getting them out of scrapes and acting as buffer between the parents. Then came a crisis. The husband died. No money, only the house, an attractive one, so it was decided to turn it into a guest house. No money for staff, so the lady had to work for the first time in her life. We had lots of laughs. It paid off and quite soon we had a successful business and a staff. There were all sorts and conditions of visitors, like the Russian who left a £2 tip, big money in those days, for his first taste of roast beef. Then the war came and the house had to be closed.

'While waiting to be called up for the WRNS (after being accepted), I took a temporary post with a wealthy bachelor, who lived with an older sister and a niece. There was also a houseful of evacuees, mostly from the East End. Unfortunately this was considered to be my war effort, so the Navy was not for me. But perhaps trying to teach the mums how to housekeep and cook and discipline their children did some good. I finally left to get married and on my last day my employer said, "If your marriage doesn't work out, drop everything and come back to us." He died six months later, so no escape route!

'Now some details. First, dress. It was mostly blue print for mornings, with long white aprons; black for the afternoons, with frilly aprons. Either a blue check or hessian half apron for dirty work. When the wealthy bachelor interviewed me he said, "Do the staff have to go round looking like magpies?" so I got patterns of material and he chose a pretty red for winter and blue for the summer. The clothes were made to measure and very smart, with light stockings and brown shoes instead of black.

'Gardeners. War was always being waged between them and the cooks. They like to see their rows of vegetables growing till the peas are like bullets and the new potatoes unscrapable. It reaches the point where the employers have to choose: a new cook or a new gardener. The cooks always win.

'But not all gardeners are like this. One dear old man in Somerset always made the staff a buttonhole for their afternoons off and a posy on their birthday.

'Chauffeurs are another problem. If they live in they usually valet the boss and if they live out they can't always be found when wanted. As a housekeeper one of the perks was to have the car for shopping. It was great telling the driver where to go.

'Dinner parties. What wonderful events they were, a beautifully set table, wonderful food, plenty of hard work and then the guests in evening dress, and then when it was all over, how good a hunk of bread and cheese and a cup of cocoa tasted.

'Food. It always amazes me now how people managed to get through so much food. For breakfast they had porridge, bacon and egg, fish and cold ham, etc. Lunch was soup and a made-up dish or cold meat, usually a choice of sweet or cheese. Afternoon tea was sandwiches, scones and a variety of cakes, and an ordinary dinner was at least four courses – then at 10 p.m. the drinks trolley with snacks, etc.

'In a well run household even the staff lived well. And one always had to have good stock in hand for anyone in the village who cared to come for it, and bowls of dripping, such as we never see today.

'Time off. So much has been said on this subject and a lot of it is true, but if a girl lived a long way off, what with no bus service, cinema, etc., there was not much to do with time off. Quite often they would work, *and then have a night off in lieu, and there was always something going on – cards, sewing etc.*

'Money. Wages were paid monthly, as maids were engaged monthly, notice either side being the same. Housekeeping money was usually paid weekly. All books and expenditure had to be produced, sometimes each item gone into, but in one situation, a glance at the total, a cheque, a list of forthcoming dinners and lunches, and then a glass of sherry! Happy days.

'Nursery. Dedicated women who had the care of the children of the wealthy from birth practically 'til boarding school. The children hardly saw their parents. Young girls who started out as nursemaids often landed up in very good jobs. Friction between nursery and kitchen was an occupational hazard, with cook and nanny heads of their own departments, but it usually worked out.

'I for one have no regrets at being part of Upstairs Downstairs. *It is unfortunate that there are so few people left in these days who could afford this way of life, and those who can haven't a clue as to how or what to do.'*

Anne Stubley did not get her chance to join the WRNS, but her son William spent his career in the Royal Navy, which must have afforded her great satisfaction.

My mother Bertha Watts (née Clover, 1911–2006) describes a different kind of domestic work, in a seaside hotel in Mundesley, where she met my father Jack Watts. *'I was a town girl born and bred, and lived in the heart of an industrial city* [Sheffield]. *I always had a feeling for the country, so when a letter arrived for my mother from her sister-in-law, who owned a seaside hotel in Norfolk, asking if I could go and help out, I was very anxious to go.*

'I was then sixteen and off I went on the long train journey to the east coast. I was met at the station by my uncle, who drove me round the village of Mundesley on the way to the hotel (the Royal), and said "That's it, that's the village." From the busy streets of Sheffield to this tiny place, it was nearly past belief, and I remember thinking, "What shall I do with my spare time?" I needn't have worried – I never got any!

'It all started very pleasantly with a little light work, as the hotel was fully staffed. I found out that this happened each year. The hotel was

adequately staffed at the beginning of each season, but as it progressed they all left. My aunt was an absolute tartar to work for, so by the time the season actually started the staff consisted of me and a little old lady who worked as kitchen maid.

'My day commenced at 6 a.m. and in the summer I was lucky to be in bed by 11 p.m. It went something like this: up at 6 a.m. to dust bar, office, snug and smoking room; see all was clean and tidy. Then up to the still room for breakfast, see the tables in the dining room were OK; up to change to act as waitress in dining room. Serve, clear away, wash up and reset tables for lunch. Up to the bedrooms to help with beds. Wipe the washstands (tables with jugs of water and bowls), dust the rooms, clean bathrooms, etc. Down again as waitress for lunch, also helping with salads, etc. Fly down to the bar if drinks were required in dining room; clear, wash up and set up for dinner. Have my own lunch; polish glasses used in the bar. Be ready to prepare and serve afternoon tea if required. Again wash up. Prepare dining room for dinner. In between tea and dinner cans of hot water were carried up to the guests' rooms as of course there were no washbasins and taps in the bedrooms. After dinner, which usually took between one and a half and two hours, the usual washing up and laying up the breakfast tables. Tea towels were always washed and everything left tidy. By this time it would be between 9 and 10 p.m., when I had to go into the bar and help to serve, wash glasses, empty ash trays and wipe tables. Then I used to fall into bed. The next moment, it seemed, it was morning. How I used to wish I could wake up once during the night, just to feel the comfort of bed.

'My off-duty time was 3 p.m. to 8 p.m. on Tuesdays, and occasionally an hour or two on Sunday afternoons. This was exploitation as I see it now, but I managed to have a great deal of fun. Our easiest time was from the end of September to the end of the year. I loved that time. There was always a huge roaring fire in the bar which we used as a sitting room on winter afternoons, accompanied by the family pets: an old parrot and a ferocious old dog named Boxer [who, as Photo 14 illustrates, was not a Boxer at all] of which I never completely lost my fear. Also on winter afternoons, I was free to walk into the village and along the sea front, nearly always shopping for my aunt.

'Those halcyon days were of short duration. In the New Year spring cleaning started. We started on the furthest bedroom on the top floor and worked solidly down. Day after day this went on, and we were jolly glad to rub and polish to keep warm as it was bitterly cold in the rooms which faced north, overlooking the sea. However, the cold did come to an end eventually.

'Quite often my uncle and aunt would go off out and leave me, at the tender age of seventeen, in charge. I do not think this was very safe, although Boxer Dog was supposed to be on guard. One day, a commercial traveller came in for a meal, and I gave him salmon mayonnaise. I proudly reported this to my aunt on her return, and she said, "I am glad you remembered the salmon in the refrigerator." I dared hardly tell her that I had forgotten the fresh salmon and had opened a tin!

'Time went by, but breaking point came one early summer Saturday afternoon when I faced the debris left by a party of seventy who had enjoyed a high tea. Instead of clearing it all up I went to my room and wrote to my mother telling her I would be coming home. I posted it, and then told my aunt what I had done. She then got help to clear all the remains of the high tea, but too late – I went home. My mother was very indignant at the way I had been exploited and wrote to my aunt giving her point of view in very explicit terms!'

Bertha Clover says that she 'had fun', despite the long hours and exploitation. Later on in life, she would tell stories of what went on in the bar in the evenings. She would play the piano, and the local boys (of whom my father was one) would gather round and sing along. Her uncle regularly got merry and would dance with high kicks aimed at the light in the ceiling. The local miller Norman Larter would tell long stories which everyone knew by heart, especially the punch-lines, with which they all joined in. When she dusted the bar in the mornings, she would sometimes taste all the liqueurs, which helped pass the time, as she said. She was enormously interested in clothes and the way she looked, and her clothes, bought in Sheffield, must have been something of a local talking point.

After her dramatic exit from the Royal she did various jobs back in Sheffield, but was eventually persuaded to return to Mundesley, where she got to know Jack Watts and married him in February 1932.

Olive Wild (b. 1919) went into service at fourteen when she left school in 1933. *I was a day girl at Mundesley. Then at sixteen I went to work for the Purdy family at Paston Green as a housemaid and lived in, where the cook and I shared a bedroom in the attic. There was one chest of drawers for the two of us and one wash basin. We had our own towel and flannel. We had to be up and dressed before 6 a.m.*

'*The day started with lighting the oil lamps, fire and cooking range, and filling the water tank beside the oven. Then light the fire in the dining room and lay the table for breakfast. At 7 a.m. the enamel jugs were filled with hot water taken from the side of the cooker and taken upstairs for the ladies, Mr Purdy senior and junior to wash. Refill the water tank ready for washing up. The family had a cooked breakfast every morning at 8 a.m. After breakfast we all had to meet in the hall for morning prayers. Then we started our own work.*

'*I did the washing up, then scrubbed the passage floors and scullery where there was a stone sink, no hot water. Then prepared the vegetables. After washing up the lunch things I would change into afternoon clothes and then clean the silver. When visitors came, like Miss Robinson, they would put their card on a silver tray and wait while it was taken in to the family, and then the visitor would be announced. Tea of sandwiches and cake were served. Daughter Miss Mary Purdy would bake the cakes.*

'*After dinner I would do the washing up, fill stone hot water bottles and put in the beds and turn back the covers. (To this day, I still turn back my own bed covers in the same way!) Then go back in the kitchen for a cup of cocoa, then we had to be in bed by 9.30, which we were ready for!*

'*I had one half day a week off in the middle of the week, and Sunday afternoon and evening off every other week. Two weeks holiday after you had worked for a year. My wage was 5s a week.*'

Marjorie Bane (later Schamp) (1924–97) went most unwillingly into service. She wrote: '*It was summer 1938 when I left school at the age of fourteen. I remember going home one afternoon and outside our house was a large black car. I didn't know it then but my future was being decided at that moment, for inside was my future employer Mrs*

Lee and my cousin Alfred Yaxley, who was her chauffeur/handyman. Mother told me I was starting as housemaid at Footpath House, Paston, as soon as school finished.

'I was shattered. For as long as I can remember I had wanted to be a nurse. I cried, pleaded, stormed and a lot more, but to no avail.

'I presented myself one Monday morning at 7 a.m., having cycled there on my own. The cook (May Saunders) and the parlour maid (Ethel Howell) took me under their wings and fitted me out in a blue cotton dress and a large white apron, also a sacking apron for dirty work. For afternoons I was given a black dress and a small white fancy apron and cap to match. The cap had black velvet ribbon threaded through it. I remember them saying I was such a little thing they didn't think I could do the work. I must say at this point that although I hated the work and thought they were all very ancient they really did look after me, and Mrs Lee told them to feed me up.

'My first job when I arrived at 7 a.m. was to do the fire places. Then I would grind the coffee beans. I enjoyed that and loved one to suck. I then had to help the parlour maid with all the cleaning duties. There was a lot of polishing to be done and Cook made the beeswax in a pot on the stove. Silver and brass also had to be cleaned. On the stairs and in the hall and landing were animal heads of all descriptions that had been shot on safari by Mrs Lee and her late husband. They gave me the creeps when I had to go up in the evenings to turn down the beds and in winter to put in a brass warming pan. The maids' rooms were at one side of the house with separate staircase. They also had a separate sitting room next to the kitchen. The floor covering in the kitchen was cork of some kind and I had to clean it with milk, which seemed a wicked waste to me. I had to learn to wait on table for dinner parties and answer the door to visitors. Mending of linen and darning clothes had to be done in the afternoons.

'I had one afternoon and every other Sunday afternoon off. As I lived out I had to cycle home around 8 p.m., and pretty scared I was at times. My wage when I started was 5s a week and when I left it had gone up to 10s. The vicarage was across the road and my friend was housemaid there so we could wave to each other with dusters. While doing all the

vegetables and piles of washing up for cook I learned quite a lot about cooking. Mrs Lee came into the kitchen every morning after breakfast and arranged the menus with cook. The amount of food consumed annoyed me; even when war came it did not seem to make a lot of differ-ence. The parlour maid had a separate pantry for the dining room, silver, china, glass and wines, also a sink for washing up.

'Before Christmas, the big cases began arriving from Harrod's and other large London stores. It was like a treasure trove and I could not believe my eyes: whole hams, jars of ginger and other goodies of all descriptions.

'The coming of the war brightened our lives, as the Army had a searchlight at the end of the road and the officers used the bath and sitting room.

'One day when I was on my own, Mrs Lee having gone visiting, I thought I would have a nice bath in a real bath with running water. (All we had at home was a tin bath in front of the fire.) I was having a nice soak when I heard the car coming up the drive. It was lucky for me that Mrs Lee was a very large lady with bad legs and took a long time to get out of the car ...

'I left Footpath House when I was called up for National Service and joined the Civil Nursing Reserve. Although I had not enjoyed being in service, I'm sure it was good for me and helped me in later years.'

Henry Wild (1911–2005), father of June Wild, left Knapton School in 1925. He began his working life by selling groceries and greengrocery goods from a pony and trap, travelling round the neighbouring villages. One customer he used to call on would open the door with a Bible in his hand and start preaching at him.

In September 1926 he became an apprentice carpenter with Billy Small at his carpenter's shop opposite the blacksmith's in Knapton Street, and remained there for two and a half years. Mr Small was also a wheelwright and undertaker. There were a few tricky moments, according to June Wild, when a coffin would have to be taken to the home of the deceased, and when quite often a window had to be removed to get the coffin into the bedroom. It would then have to be lowered down with the body in it.

Whenever work was short Henry would 'job about', cycling each day to wherever work could be found or going into lodgings if necessary. He worked on the building of Mundesley Holiday Camp in 1932, and when it was completed in 1933 he went with the same firm to build another, in Deal in Kent. He could get back to Norfolk on most weekends by travelling with the wood lorry and then had to make his way back to Knapton, doing the same journey in reverse on Monday aboard the lorry loaded with wood returning to Deal.

From 1935 to 1941, and again after the war, he worked for Bertie Gotts, builders in Mundesley, as a carpenter. Before going into the Army in the war, he also worked on repairs to bomber buildings and on the construction of RAF camps. From 1967 to 1976, when he retired, he worked for Frank Gray of Paston, but continued to do bits and pieces of carpentry work right up to his death in 2005, aged ninety-three.

Henry's wife, Vera Rouse (later Wild) (1914–2000), mother of June, was born in the Swan Public House in Long Stratton, Norfolk, where her father Russell Rouse was the licensee. When he went into the Army in the First World War, his wife and children had to move out of the Swan and went to live with his mother at Woodton, and later Silver Green, Hempnall, in South Norfolk. After the war the family moved to Mundesley, where Russell became a porter at the Manor Hotel. In later years he became the roadman in Knapton and died in 1946, aged sixty-two.

Vera left Mundesley School at fourteen and for a while did seasonal work at a small drapery shop on Mundesley seafront. She then went into domestic service at Paston with Mr and Mrs Scott, who lived opposite the church, until they moved to Bacton. After a short period Vera went to work at Manor Cottage for Mrs Bloomfield, a widow. Although Vera lived in Mundesley, she had to live in at this job, getting some time off on Sundays and a half day or evening off on Tuesday and Thursday. She worked there until her marriage to Henry Wild in 1939, but continued to work as cleaner, including cleaning the Parish Room and Men's Club at Knapton.

Renie Miller (b. 1921) writes illuminatingly of the hard employment conditions for some farm workers. *'My father George Miller moved around his job quite often to other farms and other cottages. First of all our family lived in a farm cottage in Hall Lane. While we lived there I can remember our next door neighbour was turned out of his home. Everything was put out on the garden in front of their home as he had lost his job. It must have been Michaelmas Time, about October, a time, in my days, that farm workers dreaded.'*

When Renie left school, she went to work at Rusts Grocery Shop in North Walsham. *'I can remember saving hard for some time, and bought my first coat for 9s 6d, then later on a pair of black patent shoes for 13s from Stead and Simpsons.'*

Leslie Coe (b. 1922) lived at Knapton station, where his father Elijah Coe was station master. He writes: *'My father at the time of my birth was a porter at the station. As I got older I learned how he got the job at the station. It was when he returned from France after the end of the First World War, and on being demobbed, he went to the station to travel to North Walsham to register at the dole office for work. I understand that the station master said to him, "Hello, it's nice to see you again, where are you going?" My father told him he was going to town to register for work so the station master said, "There is a job going as a porter if you want it." My father accepted it, so it was the beginning of my many happy years round the station. As time passed, my father came to be Station Master, so it was our home until he sadly passed away in 1951.*

'When I was a teenager, when the shooting season started, I went beating in the woods and fields on the Paston estate owned by the Mack family. Usually I was given a pheasant, a hare and a few pence for a day's work. During the harvest, when the sheaves of corn were ready for stacking, they were loaded onto horse-drawn wagons and I sometimes used to ride a horse and shout, "Hold yer!" before moving off. Then after it was all gathered in I used to go gleaning to take the odd bits of straw home for our chickens.

'Next job was potato picking. During the summer months I used to cycle to Mundesley Golf Club to act as a caddie and often would do two or three rounds a day, earning as much as 3s, and of course the iron clubs had to be cleaned with emery paper.

'After I left school I went to work for Mr Larter at the grocery and provision shop by the Manor Hotel in Mundesley, and I often had to go out on a trade bike to deliver to his customers. I worked there until I was seventeen and as the Second World War was imminent I decided to join the RAF, as my brother Thomas along with other lads from the village were territorials in the Royal Norfolk Regiment. So on 7 June 1939 I travelled to London by train, and after passing education and medical tests in the Strand I was sent to West Drayton, where I was sworn in and received the King's Shilling.

'So it was the beginning of my career of almost thirty years serving around the country and in various parts of the world. After my basic training I was posted to Cranwell and was there on 3 September when war was declared. After moving to different units I was posted to the Middle East in 1941 and had quite a long journey to Port Suez [sic]. Eventually I ended up with the Desert Air Force. After El Alamein, when we had driven the enemy from that area, I was posted to the Canal Zone and was stationed at RAF Fayed. On the camp was a small church which I used to attend. We decided we needed a bell for the small tower, so I wrote to Miss Robinson at Knapton House and asked if she could give me the address of the bell foundry which a few years earlier had retuned Knapton church bells. At one time I used to ring bell No. 3 in a peel of five. She wrote back and said she had a ship's bell at Knapton House, which we could have if we wanted it, and that she would send it to us, which she did. When I left to come home in 1945 it was hanging proudly in the tower.

'As things changed politically in that area I have no idea of what happened to that bell. I was confirmed in Cairo Cathedral during my years in Egypt.'

June Wild (b. 1951) writes: 'When I left school in 1966 I did a hairdressing apprenticeship in a salon. To begin with there was a lot of running about with making coffee and tea for the clients, sweeping up hair and passing rollers, pins etc. to the stylists, putting ladies under the dryer and getting them out, and making sure the shampoo bottles were filled up. The trolleys with the rollers were kept tidy and ready for the next client, plus many more tasks we had to do to help the stylists.

'*Our hands were often in water with the shampooing. I used a lot of hand cream! One busy afternoon a lady came in – she had not been in before – and I was asked to shampoo her hair at the forward basin. She put her head down and I was about to put the hose on her hair when she pulled off a wig to reveal only a few strands of hair. I cannot remember what the stylist did for her.*

'*We watched and learned from the stylists. After school girls would come in to be models for the apprentices to practise on. This was when ladies had shampoo and sets, with a lot of backcombing to create a beehive look. They would come in at the same time each week. We were especially busy on Fridays and Saturdays, and before Christmas and New Year. It took about an hour for a shampoo and set, more if the hair was cut as well. Perms took about two hours and some extremely strong-smelling lotions were used. Hair colours varied in time, depending on what was to be done. I enjoyed putting in blonde highlights. A cap was put on the head, like a swimming cap but with very small holes in it through which you would pull small strands of hair to be bleached.*

'*Our backs and legs used to ache with standing all day, but we were always told to keep changing our shoes and it did help.*'

Richard Wild remembers that in the 1950s most people were involved in farm work in one way or another, but as farm jobs began to reduce in number because of mechanisation people worked at the Bacton Gas Terminal or in factories in North Walsham. Others, like Richard himself, became bricklayers, plumbers, car mechanics, coach drivers, gardeners and carpenters.

Ruth Steward (Matthew) (b. 1943) remembers the Knapton roadman during the same period: Tommy Coe, who kept verges tidy and cleared gulleys. Some of the women helped at the hotel which was opened in Knapton Hall in 1957, did domestic work or worked in North Walsham in the laundry, the egg-packing station or the canning factory. Ruth adds: '*In the summer, from the age of nine, I went fruit and broad bean picking. This gave me pocket money to buy clothes and things for the high school when I went there. I never thought of it as a chore, but being grown up.*'

Appendix 1 illustrates the very wide range of occupations

undertaken by the children who were at Knapton School between the 1930s and 1960s. This range is in sharp contrast to the strong agricultural and local bias of their parents' occupations.

The children of Linda Fawkes (Risebrow) (b. 1950–) and her sister Rene (Turner) (b. 1952) represent the next generation. Christopher, Linda's son, was born in 1972. When he left North Walsham High School at sixteen, he joined a Youth Training Scheme and was placed at Roys of Wroxham, a very well known department store in the Broads area. He writes: *'I have had jobs in the surrounding area, but I've never been out of work. I work for Roys now. Once I passed my driving test, grandad lent me the money for my first car, so thanks to grandad I became independently mobile. I live in North Walsham and have done since 1996, when I bought a house. Unfortunately I couldn't afford to buy a property in Knapton or I would have stayed in the village.'*

His sister Sadie also left North Walsham High School at sixteen, in 1990. She joined a Youth Training Scheme to study horticulture at Easton College, near Norwich. *'With the help of grandad Ronnie, I passed my driving test, then grandad's loan helped me to buy my first car. This was a great help as YTS placed me at Meales of Stalham (about eight miles from Knapton), where they grew tomatoes in greenhouses, and I was required to go into work at 3 a.m. to pick the tomatoes as it was too hot to pick them later in the day. I have since worked at HL foods (in North Walsham) until they closed, then I went to work at Norwich Airport, cleaning planes and delivering the meals to the plane ready for the turnaround. We weren't given much time but everything came together. I now work at Trend Marine at Catfield as a polisher of stainless steel for luxury Sunseeker yachts. I live in North Walsham as I couldn't afford a property in Knapton, but you never know – one day if I win the lottery I may be able to live back in Knapton again.'*

Rene's son Paul was born in 1970. He too joined a YTS course on leaving North Walsham High School and was sent to North Norfolk District Council for an interview to train as a printer. *'I started there in November 1986 and attended Norwich City College one day a week, where I obtained my City and Guilds in Lithographic*

Printing. As part of the course I did a project on lifeboat coxswain Henry Blogg. One of my then colleagues saw it and 10,000 copies were printed and donated to sell in the Cromer Lifeboat Shop. Grandad bought a Morris Marina which he used to take me out in when I was learning to drive. I still work at the North Norfolk District Council in the print room today.'

Interestingly all three of these young people undertook further training on leaving school. All three have had to be able to drive and have a car in order to be employed, and all three have had to move to the local town to be able to afford housing. The employment opportunities and job satisfaction they have had are perhaps better than those enjoyed by their parents and grandparents. Perhaps what they and their forbears demonstrate best is that one kind of limitation is often replaced by another.

SEVEN

NATIONAL SERVICE

The 1944 Education Act introduced sweeping reforms and improvements in the education system, transforming the life chances of many. But it was another kind of education, near-compulsory, which affected the lives and aspirations of many more young men than were influenced by educational change pure and simple, and this was National Service.

The National Service (Armed Forces) Act 1939 made all able men between eighteen and forty-one liable for conscription directly into the armed forces. Men aged twenty to twenty-three were required to register in October 1939, the start of a long-drawn out process of registration by age group which saw 41-year-olds registering only in June 1941.

At the end of the Second World War National Service continued. The National Service Act 1947, due to come into force in 1949, initially required a period of one year to be served in the armed forces, but the Cold War, the Malaya emergency and various financial crises brought about the National Service Amendment Act 1948, which extended the period of service to eighteen months. Later, because of the Korean War, it was further extended to two years, which remained until the last intake of National Servicemen in 1960. Between 1945 and 1963 more than two million were called up, exposing young men from all walks of life to contact with a far greater variety of people than they would otherwise have had; to travel, in some cases overseas; and to a taste of military discipline.

Two contributors to this book, John Capes (b. 1930) and Roy Fawkes (b. 1932) have written about their experience of National Service.

John attended the Paston Grammar School in North Walsham, where he was a member of the Army Cadet Force. He was working as an accounts clerk with Eastern Electricity in November 1948 when he was summoned to Norwich for an interview for National Service, having opted for the Army. His call-up papers arrived the following February. *'I was to report by 0900 hours on a Monday in March to the Seventh Selection Regiment, Royal Corps of Signals at Catterick Camp, North Yorkshire. There was a rail travel warrant to Richmond, the nearest town ... I decided to travel overnight so on the Sunday afternoon I went to Paston and Knapton Railway Station ... From Norwich I had decided to go via Ely and March to Peterborough, and get a mainline train from there rather than going down to London ... It was just getting light when we arrived at Richmond. Lined up in the station yard were about a dozen three-ton Army trucks. Standing by each one was an NCO, mainly corporals, shouting out the name of the appropriate regiment. I and quite a number of others quickly found the truck for Seventh Selection Regiment and climbed aboard. If you couldn't get a seat it was a case of standing and holding on to the bars that supported the tarpaulin that formed the sides and roof. So I arrived at Catterick which would be my base for the next nine months.'*

It has not been possible to do full justice here to John's wonderfully detailed account of his time in National Service; there is only space in this book for some of the highlights, which follow.

Not surprisingly for one accustomed to plenty of sport and having to walk or cycle everywhere, John found some of the physical activities included in the initial training, such as route marches, quite easy. *'About three miles to start with, then four, and the Corporal was always telling us we would have to do five miles in an hour in the final week of initial training. This was just up my street. I had always been good at walking and running. I think my legs had been strengthened by all the running around the fields I had done in my youth. I often walked to my grandparents at Knapton and did longer walks from Paston around Edingthorpe and Bacton, or along the cliffs to Mundesley.*

'But what happened on the marches was quite coincidental. On the parade ground at the start of each march we formed a long line with the smallest at the left and tallest at the right. Being only 5 ft 5 in tall, I was usually at, or near the left end. I think it was on the third march

that I happened to be at the end. We then did a right turn and marched forwards into the standard three ranks, which meant that I was at the front of the rightmost rank, and that's the one that sets the pace. So it was, "By the right, quick march, and I want a good pace, Capes!" Off we went and he got his good pace, but it was not to the liking of some of the squad, and I took a bit of stick in the barrack room that evening.'

After initial training, which John did not find *'as bad for me as it was for most of the others, because I had covered much of it in the cadets at school,'* he was told that he was to train as a radio mechanic. *'This was rather good, as it was the highest paid trade in the Signals, and if I qualified it would mean an extra shilling a day. Training to be a radio mechanic meant going back to school! There was a morning parade and roll-call, and then it was into the classroom, here called Lecture Room. No more drill but still a bit of spit and polish to keep up a smart appearance. The course lasted twenty weeks, and there were about twenty people in each group. As far as I can remember, I think everyone in our group had been to either a grammar school or private school. Most of us had passed School Certificate (equivalent to GCSE), a few had Higher School Certificates (A-levels), and one or two had university degrees.*

'We started with simple things we had done at school: electricity, electrical circuits, switches and similar things. From about the third week we were into radio waves and layers in the atmosphere that reflect them around, then types of aerials. Each week we had a test to see how much we had absorbed; if we got below a certain mark (60 per cent, I think it was) we were held back and made to repeat the week. I managed to keep above the minimum mark each week.'

This training was, however, unexpectedly interrupted. *'In June 1949 there was a strike by the London dockers. Soon after the strike started there were rumours around the barracks that the Army would be called in ... Then it was announced on a special morning parade that the government had decided to put troops onto the docks and we would be going down to near London later that day ... We had about two or three hours to clean equipment and pack the essentials for a long stay if necessary ... My recollection is that we left the barracks in lorries in late morning and then left Richmond in a special train at about midday.*

We arrived at a disused war-time camp at Purfleet in Essex during the evening. We were allocated to the area on the north side of the river between Tower Bridge and London Bridge, which in those days was a mass of warehouses and dockside cranes. We were then split into groups to deal with different ships. There were about twenty in our group and we would be loading general cargo into a ship of about 5,000 tons, which was going to the Middle and Far East.'

Four of the group who had had previous office experience, including John, were selected to become tally clerks, whose job was to measure each item and record the dimensions and weight, the sender's details, the destination and any distinguishing marks. John writes: *'My memory is of the items being wheeled out of the warehouse with sack-barrows or on handcarts. On the dockside they were loaded into large nets, which were then lifted over to the ship by crane and down into the hold. As the drivers were on strike the cranes were operated by Royal Engineers. As far as I remember, the stevedores who packed the goods into the hold were luckily not on strike, as packing loose items into the holds was a job requiring considerable expertise. There were groups of dockers standing around the dockside and an incident I remember very vividly happened on the second or third day. One of them stepped forward and pointed out that the way things were being put into the net was dangerous. His colleagues immediately pulled him back and remonstrated with him for giving advice,. He tried to hold his ground but was shouted down; their attitude was, "Let them do it their way, and they'll soon find out if they are doing it wrong."*

'Nothing like that happened again. So we carried on – to the docks in the morning, loading the ship, mid-morning break, loading the ship, back to camp in the evening. Although we were there for probably two weeks, we didn't finish loading the ship.'

Once he had successfully completed his radio mechanic training, John was asked if he had any preference for where he would like to be posted. *'I put down East Africa or the Far East with the idea of going as far as possible at His Majesty's expense. Then came the final briefing and announcement of postings: "Capes – North-West Europe." This meant the British Army of the Rhine in Germany.'*

He travelled by troopship to the Hook of Holland, and from there by train across Holland and Germany. He was struck by his first sight of war damage at Essen. *'Essen was a big pile of rubble. From the station there was not a complete building in sight: the odd wall here, the skeleton of a building there, but predominantly rubble and more rubble. There were no station buildings, just platforms pock-marked with signs of bomb craters. They had just been filled in with earth so were clearly visible. I had seen bomb damage in Norwich and London, but nothing to compare with this and this was four years after the end of the war.'*

His main posting in Germany was to Dortmund (Photo 15). There he joined F Troop Signals attached to the 40th Field Regiment, Royal Artillery. *'I soon realised that life at Dortmund was going to be fairly easy ... We were all now fully trained and were over there to work, but we were certainly not overburdened with it, and a lot of the time there was a shortage of things to do ... What does an Army do in peacetime? Practise, practise and more practise, it seems. The Artillery did a lot of that but there was not a lot we could do.'*

Eventually he *'did more and more with batteries, and this meant more liaison with the Artillery. Each battery had a signals sergeant who was responsible for the smooth running of communications, and there was already a good rapport between them and us. This actually improved as I made a point of going over to see them about once a fortnight, or if I knew they had been out on manoeuvres, to see if there was anything that needed doing.'*

John did take the opportunity to visit Dortmund. *'There was a fairly good tram service into the centre, on which we had free travel ... The MP for the city was a Communist and on occasion Communist rallies were held in the city. For these we were advised to go in groups of at least three, preferably more. Only once did I see one of these rallies, but it is something I have never forgotten. The city square was a mass of people and we crept along the edge. A speech was being made from the Rathaus balcony; behind the speaker was a huge portrait of Stalin and along the front of the balcony was a large banner saying (in German): "JOE FOR THE NEXT FÜHRER."*

'To cater for those who did not want to go home there were several leave centres in various parts of the country … The popular one, which was quite near us, was at the Moehne See. This was the large lake formed by the Moehne Dam that was the subject of the Dambusters raid in May 1943. I went there at least three times, once for a whole week and at least twice for long weekends. We lounged on the shore, some went swimming and we went boating. Some of us walked down to the bottom of the dam and looking up could see the large V shape of the new concrete that had been inserted to repair the damage of the bombing.

'I was due for demob in early September 1950, but the Korean War had started on 25 June and by August rumours were flying around that National Service would be extended by six months to provide more manpower for the Services. Nothing was announced by the time I was due to come back, so back I came to Pocklington in North Yorkshire in late August. Then the extension was announced, but the question then was which Demob Group would be held for the extra six months. I was in Group 248 and we were held for an extra fortnight while a decision was made. Then came the announcement: Group 249 and beyond would be held for the extra six months. I would be going home.'

John continued in the Territorial Army for a further four years after his demob. He concludes: *'Some time in the last year I was promoted to Lance Corporal. Thus ended my Army career.'*

Roy Fawkes' National Service experience was in the RAF, following an apprenticeship at Hannant's Garage in North Walsham, which he had started on leaving Knapton School at fourteen. He writes: *'On 20 February 1950 I got the first train from Knapton station and travelled all day to get to Padgate, near Warrington. We went cross-country and there were several changes on the way. At each station more young lads joined the train. At Warrington any young lad with a suitcase was sent to the RAF trucks just like a load of sheep, for the final part of the journey to Padgate. There were so many RAF police about there was no chance of escape. This was quite late in the evening. When we arrived at Padgate, our first meal was cheese and potato pie; it was the strongest cheese I have ever tasted (and I haven't had one since).*

'Next day, after a medical, I became 2462023 Fawkes RG Airman

2nd class. We were kitted out and about three days later we were on parade, and everyone's names were called out except mine and another chap's. His name was Ken Barwick and he came from Aylsham (about ten miles from Knapton). All the others – about 150 of them – were posted off to another camp for square-bashing.

'Ken and I were moved to another part of the camp to join 100 or so recruits – all ex-apprentices (so we found out) and all different trades. We were all older than the first group because our call-up had been deferred to allow us to finish our apprenticeships in Civvy Street. We then had eight weeks' square-bashing at Padgate, spit and polish, everything. After passing-out parade we were given one week's leave, and then we went on to RAF Weeton, near Blackpool.

Just four of us went to Weeton, which was the RAF motor training school for drivers and motor mechanics. The RAF were short of motor mechanics at that time, so they gave us a trade test straight away and anything we failed on we would have a short refresher course. (The normal course was six months.) On the morning of the test, the officer in charge said, "None of you will pass because you can't fill in any of the necessary forms." My examiner was not in the RAF – he was a civvy – and after my test, about two and a half hours, I asked if I had passed. He said he couldn't tell me, but not to worry about it. The following day I had to see the officer in charge again: I had passed the test and he wasn't very pleased about that! The other three had to take some more training on certain subjects.

'I spent the next week or so waiting for a posting to a regular station, and most of that time I spent on Blackpool beach – though I couldn't do much as I had no money: only 18s a week.

'I got my posting to RAF Honington (near Bury St Edmunds in Suffolk), 94MU part of 42 Group. What a difference from Padgate! A pre-war permanent base, brick-built living accommodation with hot water showers, baths, central heating, while Padgate had old wooden huts, hot water once a week for a bath. This was pure luxury.

'Our working day was from 8 a.m. to 5 p.m. with one hour for lunch, but still some spit and polish, guard duty, fire duty and duty fitter. The work was easy. I had just finished five and a half years at Hannant's

Garage in North Walsham. Most of the chaps at Honington were National Service recruits and not really interested in what they were doing. Only the corporals and sergeants were regular RAF.

'One day Starling, the officer in charge, came and said they had a problem with some high-ranking officer who was due to make his annual inspection, and there was something wrong with the staff car. (I had noticed the sergeants and one of the corporals playing with it for two or three days with no success.) In desperation he had come to talk to me. I asked for a test drive and we went off. I found the fault. I said it was the rear axle. Starling said it had been put in new just before I had joined the unit. I just said, "Rear axle." He then said: "What can we do? We can't get a replacement in time." I said: "You've got the old one, let's make one out of two." There was then a long discussion between Starling and the NCOs. They said it couldn't be done. I said we'd done it all the time in Civvy Street. The officer said to me, "Can you do it?" I said I could, but I would need some help. He said I could go ahead. By now it was lunchtime and I had till the next morning to get it right. Corporal Smith said he would help me, but he added, "I hope you know what you're doing, because I've never done anything like this before." I just said, "Trust me," and we worked all afternoon and all through the night. At midnight Starling brought us supper and beer from the officers' mess. We finished and tested the car by 8 a.m.

'The next morning Starling was the first one in. "How's it going?" was all he said. We said we'd finished and everything was OK. I went with Starling for another test run. Then along came the sergeant and he said, "Well, you boys had better get some rest, see you after lunch." Starling then asked us into his office. This was a Wednesday, and he made out two passes, and said, "See you Monday morning." The sergeant was not impressed. From then on the only jobs I got were the ones nobody wanted or couldn't do.

'Shortly after that I was marched into the CO's office. I wondered what could be wrong now, but I was introduced to the Group Engineering Officer 42 Group. He had a Riley car and someone had overhauled the engine (an ex-Rolls Royce fitter!), and it wouldn't start. Could I help? I said yes, and he said the car had got this and got that, and I said they *all work the same. I spent several evenings taking the car apart with the help of the chap who had worked on it first. I pressed the starter: the battery was flat. Next night, with a good battery, the engine started first time. If you could have seen his face, it was a picture, he was so relieved. He said he wasn't allowed to pay me, but if I wanted anything, he would help if he could. I said that I wanted a posting to Hockering near Dereham, about 25 miles from Knapton. He said, "That's easy, I will arrange it straight away." And so to RAF Hockering, and what a difference: Nissen huts made from corrugated iron, hot in summer, cold in winter, bucket toilets – but no parades, no guard duties, no fire duties. All I had to do was make sure the cars, trucks, cranes, fire engine and ambulances were serviceable all the time.*

'We had just three officers on the unit. I looked after their private cars as well but that was unofficial. I finished on 20 February 1952.

'When I joined the RAF it was for eighteen months. Then the government added six months, so in the end I served for two years. I can't say I really enjoyed National Service, but I met all sorts of different types of people. I wouldn't have wanted to have missed the experience. You learn so much when you are in the armed services. It is regrettable that we have lost National Service, as the comradeship and discipline you learn give you a good grounding for life in general.'

EIGHT

POLITICS

One of my earliest memories is of the announcement of the 1945 General Election result. Election Day itself had been on 5 July but the result was not announced until three weeks later on 26 July, as time had to be allowed for the votes of the many service people abroad to be counted.

When at around tea time the result came through on the wireless, people in Knapton went out into The Street, calling to one another over their gates, saying either 'We've won' or 'They've won' according to their political persuasion. Gloom descended on our household and I asked what had happened. 'They've got rid of Mr Churchill,' I was told. For a child of five, as I was then, and brought up during a war to believe that Mr Churchill was invincible (he had after all beaten Hitler), this was unimaginable. For a time I genuinely wondered if we had after all not won the war, despite the VE celebrations and the barn dance at Mr May's farm. Who were 'they', these people so much more powerful than Hitler, and even than Mr Churchill himself, who had got rid of him?

In fact, the result of the 1945 election should not have been a surprise to anyone. Opinion polls conducted by Gallup from 1942 onwards revealed that the electorate were preoccupied with the need for housing, for full employment and for social security once the war was over – all issues on which the Labour Party was campaigning. In the end, Gallup correctly predicted the election result to within a single percentage point. Despite that, Mr Churchill told the King the day before the result was announced that he expected to win by between thirty and eighty seats.

What really was surprising on 26 July 1945 was that so many people in Knapton revealed their political colours in public as the election results were being announced. Strange as it may now seem, the way you voted was regarded by many at that time as your business, despite the fact that in many cases it must have been very obvious. This was true even in some activist families. Janet Steward (Munro) (b. 1940) writes: *'Politics was a secret business when I was growing up, and it would have been quite wrong to ask anyone who they were going to vote for. However, it wasn't much of a secret in our family, as we were very strong Labour. In those days I really believed that chapel people were Labour and Church of England people were Conservative. Both my parents were on the committee of the North Norfolk Labour Party, mum's brother Arthur Amis being Political Agent to Bert Hazell, then Labour Member of Parliament for North Norfolk.'*

In our household my parents always voted Conservative, though my mother out of a much stronger conviction than my father, who certainly believed – and held the belief to the end of his life – that all politicians were knaves and fools into the bargain. Neither of them would have dreamed of putting up a Conservative poster, delivering election leaflets or even giving lifts to the polls on election day, at least partly because of an extreme reluctance to show their colours publicly. Like the Steward family, and many others in Knapton, they believed that the way you voted was very much your own business. My mother had been brought up in the strongly socialist atmosphere of early twentieth-century Sheffield, where her father ran a small wholesale fruit business. Her sister married a Communist union activist and, although his views softened towards the end of his life, my maternal grandfather totally opposed everything his son-in-law believed in. This did not make for comfortable family relations on that side of the family.

Even so, politics were often discussed in our house, mostly in very critical terms and regardless of the colour of the government of the time. It was generally assumed, not without reason, that rural issues and in particular agricultural interests were ignored by whoever was in power. Union activities were disapproved of and my father would often describe someone as 'a union man', and not admiringly. The Budget was routinely dreaded, mostly because of what it would do to petrol and cigarette prices.

The Civics lessons we had in the third year at secondary school gave us a reasonable grounding in the way democracy worked at local and national level, and as a result I was always intrigued by the drama of General Elections, keeping a careful count of seat losses and gains with the help of charts in the *Eastern Daily Press*. I was certainly fascinated by the glamour of politics and the fame and lifestyles of the top politicians. Most of all, however, I was impressed by the fact that they were apparently prepared to expose themselves to the risk of public defeat and humiliation by standing for election at all. I could not imagine putting myself in that position. But I was also – and I continue to be – fascinated by the power of the ballot box, which had done what Hitler could not do: 'get rid of Mr Churchill.'

It is not surprising that as a child I expected Conservative candidates to be defeated in elections. In all the General Elections between 1945 and 1970 the Labour candidate won the North Norfolk seat. In fact, from 1885 to the present day, the seat has been held by a Liberal or Labour member for seventy-seven years, and by a Conservative/Independent or Conservative for forty-nine years. Those bald figures conceal the seemingly monolithic hold of Labour on the seat in the 1940s, 1950s and 1960s, followed by a seemingly equally unassailable Conservative majority from 1970 until 2001, when Norman Lamb at his third attempt narrowly won it for the Liberal Democrats from David Prior, the sitting Conservative. The seat remains Liberal Democrat and Norman Lamb now has a strong following in North Norfolk.

The figures also conceal one of the most interesting features of North Norfolk politics, namely the historical link, illustrated by the careers of Edwin Gooch, Bert Hazell and Arthur Amis among many others, between the Agricultural Workers' Union, the Labour Party and in some cases Primitive Methodism. Obviously as the number of agricultural workers declined so did their voting power. The fortunes of agriculture affected Norfolk politics, as they did its economic and social development.

John Capes (b. 1930) like Janet Steward came from a political family. His parents were also political activists and he has clear memories of Labour's victory in 1945 and of the Labour Party organisation on the ground. *'The election which really stands out is that in 1945. After Churchill had rallied the country during the war years I think that there was a general expectation that the Tories would win, but the general mood in the country was obviously different and of course there was a landslide Labour victory. At that election Edwin Gooch won Northern Norfolk for Labour … My father was in the Army – a case of "last in, last out" – so was not active in local politics and I was too young to vote.*

'The Paston and Knapton Labour Party must have been formed sometime between the 1945 and 1950 elections, as my father was a founder member and I think he was probably one of the prime movers in setting it up. I think at the time there was a general move by the Labour Party to get branches established across the country.

'Jack Leeder of Knapton was the chairman, and my father was the secretary, with committee members from each village. From Paston there was Bill Plant and from Knapton one of the Wild brothers. I can very clearly remember Edwin Gooch coming to our house on several occasions to see how things were going locally, and he probably visited Jack Leeder as well. He usually arrived on a Sunday morning and was accompanied by another man, who presumably was the agent. I can remember a Mr and Mrs Lubbock from either Cromer or Sheringham going round the district holding social evenings. I think they would come to the Paston reading room probably twice a year, usually in spring and autumn. I would have thought they would also have gone to Knapton. I also remember my mum and dad going to a Labour Party event one Saturday evening at Cromer. Presumably there would have been a coach going round to pick people up as we didn't have a car and it wasn't easy getting to Cromer and back by train in the evening. I think this was almost certainly in the winter of 1950–51. What I don't know is how long the local party lasted, I cannot even remember if it was still in existence when I got married in 1963.'

The extracts from Arthur Amis's autobiography below make it clear that the local party would have been very much alive at that time, and for many years to come.

There was certainly a Conservative counterpart to this Labour Party organisation in Knapton, supported by Miss Robinson, Major and Mrs Wilkinson, and others. In the run-up to elections, posters would be put up, cars would be organised to give lifts to the polling station and a rota of tellers would be put in place. Since my family would not under any circumstances have got involved I am not sure how active it was between elections, but I can recall being asked to do a turn of duty outside the polling station at Knapton School at the 1966 General Election, when Bert Hazell, who had taken over from Edwin Gooch following the latter's death in 1964, beat the Conservative candidate Ralph Howell by 737 votes. In 1970, Ralph Howell won the seat with a majority of 4,684 and it remained strongly Conservative until 2001.

Arthur Amis (1905–2000, see Photo 16) was uncle of Janet, Eric, Ruth and Mary Steward, and although he lived in Trunch he attended Knapton School for a time, and also worked in Knapton for a period. In his remarkable career he encapsulated the links between the Agricultural Workers' Union, the Labour Party and the Methodist church, and describes them in his autobiography *From Dawn to Dusk*, printed in 1992 by M.F. Barnwell of Aylsham, Norfolk. He writes of a life-changing decision he made in 1958, after nearly forty years working on the land: '*I was a member of the Agricultural Workers' Union and also of the Labour Party, and the job of Secretary-Agent of the North Norfolk Labour Party was offered to me. I knew this would mean a great financial improvement for my family and me. I talked it all over with Harold* [Hicks, his employer] *who quite understood. He said he did not mind and I gave only a fortnight's notice instead of the usual month. In June 1958 I left the land which had been my life for about forty years.*

'*I now had a job in party political organisation which was a totally different way of life from anything I had done before. North Norfolk had a Labour MP, Edwin Gooch, who lived at Wymondham* [south of Norwich]. *As well as being a Member of Parliament he was President of the Agricultural Workers' Union. As for myself, I had no office. The North Norfolk Labour Party had no office either ... I had a shed which*

I turned into an office. I got the phone laid on and appointed my wife as an unpaid clerk. My car was not very reliable, but I got about with it. I was able to get some local parties together and the work increased rather rapidly. I had to ask the executive to let me engage a secretary. That made things easier, but I knew full well that if an election came up I should need a far larger place.

'In the spring of 1959 I was directed by the National Party to a by-election in South West Norfolk, caused by the death of the MP Sidney Dye. He was killed driving his car to the station during a frosty spell when his car skidded. This was a real tragedy for the Labour movement as he was brilliant, a good constituency member. The new candidate was Albert Hilton, a Union organiser. I had to go to Dereham for three weeks … and I came home every weekend. This was indeed a new experience and a good education. I learned a lot from the agent there. Canvassing was something I had never done. When I got started it was something like a milk-round; I had many cups of tea. In any case, canvassing for a political party was a real testing ground. One came across all sorts of people, some who shared the same political views and others who definitely did not. Some wanted to talk and there were those with real problems. Others wanted to discuss nothing and they included those who were not at all interested.

'I shall not dwell on my reasons for joining the Labour Party. My early life as the son of an agricultural worker made me anxious to do what I could to improve the conditions of farm labourers. I knew what poverty their families had to endure. At times I have seen my mother in tears when there was no money in the house and not much food. At an early age I was determined that things were going to be better. That is why I joined the Union; that is why I turned to the Labour Party. The 1923 farm workers' strike was a real eye-opener as to what the farmers, and indeed the whole country, thought of those who worked on the land. "Yes, during a war we must grow all the food we can and you can have a little more money while we do so. But in peacetime, we are all right, Jack." The strike was to prevent a starvation wage being reduced to poverty level. That grand old pioneer, George Edwards, cycled hundreds of miles at that time to encourage the men. I know that the whole episode

had a lasting impression on my life and the experience stood me in good stead in my new job. I was very fortunate.

'I could contact Edwin Gooch, the MP for North Norfolk, at any time – and this was quite often. So many of the working folk needed advice. As Union President, too, Edwin was a great help, as were the Union organisers Jack Boddy, Jack Lambley and Jack Wilson. All too many requests concerned tied cottages. These were a curse to farm workers. I would venture to say that a great number of them who had taken a tied house wished they had never done so. In some cases there was no choice.

'At the election in 1959 I engaged an assistant, Mr R. Risebrow, who was invaluable to me. The National Union of Agricultural Workers sent down some organisers. These all took oversight of various areas. I laid down one condition: that I was not prepared for any election work on Sundays, although I knew my colleagues in other constituencies did. I was a Methodist preacher and I would not have it, and I am still against a lot of unnecessary work on Sundays. My upbringing as a Christian stood me in good stead all the years I worked as a party agent, and I hope and believe that I am respected for my stand on this. We won the election. Mr Gooch was returned as member for North Norfolk.'

One of Arthur Amis's aims during his time as Labour Agent in North Norfolk was to provide the party with offices. After a long campaign, with twenty-two local parties contributing, the offices in North Walsham were declared open in 1961, by the Rt Hon. Hugh Gaitskell. Many years later, Arthur wrote: *'As I write this my heart is full … After fewer than thirty years these fine headquarters are no more. I am not now officially connected with the party, but my loyalties remain. The opening ceremony will live in my memory until the end … It is ironic that just across the road stood the Angel Hotel where on 6 July 1906, George Edwards had founded the Agricultural Workers' Union. As for Edwin Gooch, he was George Edwards' agent when that grand old man first was elected to Parliament so many years ago. Edwin himself was elected in 1945, and again in 1950, 1951, 1955 and 1959, a great record.'*

During the 1959 Parliament, Edwin Gooch announced that he would not fight the next election but, sadly, before that election was called he died on 2 August 1964 and a successor had to be found. At a meeting at the Norwich Labour Club, Bert Hazell was chosen as the prospective Labour Parliamentary candidate for North Norfolk. Arthur Amis wrote, *'This I was extremely pleased about, as here was another National Union of Agricultural Workers man. Like me, he was caught up in the 1923 farm workers' strike.'*

Among many other public offices, Hazell became a National Union of Agricultural Workers Organiser, first in Essex and then in Yorkshire. He was elected as MP for North Norfolk in October 1964 and in 1966 he became President of the National Union of Agricultural Workers.

Arthur Amis describes the political change which overtook North Norfolk in the 1960s: *'In 1964 Bert had polled 19,360 to the Tory's 19,307 and there was a recount. In 1966 Bert won by 20,796 to 20,059, with a slightly increased but still very slender majority. By this time, Norfolk was becoming a well-sought-after area; the political complexion completely changed. What had been a Labour stronghold is now a Tory fortress. In 1970 we lost the election and that is it.'* Ralph Howell, the Conservative candidate, took the seat in 1970 with a majority of 4,684.

During his time as Agent, Arthur met many senior Labour politicians including Shirley Williams, George Thomas (later Lord Tonypandy), Sir Elwyn Jones, Harold Wilson and George Brown. *'All in all they were twelve years of hard work,'* he reflected, *'but well worth it. I never regret taking on the job.'*

Arthur Amis writes of the role of Sir George Edwards, a towering figure in the development of the Labour Party and the trades union movement. Interestingly, Sir George also had connections with Knapton. His granddaughter Stella married Roger Dixon, who was born in Knapton and is extensively quoted in this book. Stella's father Noel Edwards, himself a distinguished local government politician, wrote the biography of Sir George entitled *Ploughboy's Progress*.

George Edwards (Photo 17) was born into extreme poverty in 1850 and began work at the age of six, scaring crows. He became a devout Methodist and lay preacher, and began his career as an agitator (not an insult in the context of the day) at a meeting in Alby near Aylsham in June 1872 called to found a branch of Joseph Arch's National Agricultural Labourers' Union in the village. In 1906 he founded the Eastern Counties Agricultural Labourers' and Small Holders' Union in the Angel Hotel, North Walsham. This Union eventually became the Agricultural Trades Section of the Transport and General Workers' Union. He played an important role in local government, not least on the Norfolk County Council, and in a 1920 by-election was elected to Parliament as MP for South Norfolk. He lost the seat in 1922, but his election was a triumph for him and for the organised farm workers who supported him. He played a vital role in the Norfolk strike of farm workers in 1923, which ended in a negotiated settlement, no wage cuts and the survival of the union. He was knighted in 1930 and died in 1933. A memorial to him was unveiled in Fakenham Cemetery in 1935 by Edwin Gooch, who had been his Agent in his election campaign in 1920.

A service of remembrance started to be held each year on May Day. Arthur Amis always attended these services, and describes that held in 1949: *As a member of the National Union of Agricultural Workers and as a Methodist preacher, I was invited to take part in a Sunday May Day service at the graveside of Sir George Edwards. This was a very special occasion; the Prime Minister, the Right Honourable Clement Attlee, was to be chief speaker … I stood next to the Prime Minister and read the scripture lesson he had chosen, Ecclesiasticus 44, vv. 1–15: "Let us now praise famous men." What a momentous occasion … I thank God for those grand pioneers, who fought to make conditions better for the poor old folk of the late nineteenth and early twentieth centuries. We should remind ourselves sometimes of what we owe to the stalwarts, who laid the foundation of better times and conditions for those who laboured so hard, and for their successors. I am proud to have known George Edwards and that I have tried, in a small way, to help on the work he started. Of this I am absolutely certain that those Methodists of the early days were able to carry on inspired by a divine strength.'*

But George Edwards had another, even closer, connection with Knapton and its near neighbour Trunch. In 1906 he had become the first direct Labour representative to be elected to the Norfolk County Council, where he became very involved in committees close to his own interests: smallholdings, public health and old-age pensions. He was re-elected to the County Council for the Freebridge Division, King's Lynn, in 1910, strongly supported by James Coe of Castleacre, another Union organiser, and later a county alderman.

In March of that year George Edwards was approached by a group of men from the Trunch area. Reg Groves, in his book *Sharpen the Sickle*, first published in 1949, takes up the tale, calling it 'a preliminary skirmish for the newly formed Eastern counties Agricultural Labourers' and Small Holders' Union.' Groves continues: *'In March the farmers in the Trunch area asked the men to make the usual springtime adjustment of working hours to ten hours a day. The men refused to agree to work the extra hours unless they were given another one shilling a week. The farmers then gave their men a week's notice to leave unless they were prepared to work the ten hours. The men left. Seven farms were involved in the lock-out. George Edwards arranged to attend a special meeting of the Trunch branch on 11 April. Before the meeting he had an unofficial talk with the Secretary of the Sheringham Farmers' Federation and the two men reached an understanding, Edwards promising to get the men back to work on a nine-hour day, and the Federation Secretary promising to stop the farmers bringing in non-union labour, or changing the hours until the union and Federation had been able to meet.'*

The men agreed to return to work on this basis, only to find when they went back to work that the farmers were still insisting on the ten-hour day. Another meeting on 16 April left the men standing out against the farmers' demands and asking for the support of the Union Executive. The Union raised funds to support the men, with an excellent response. Meanwhile the Norwich branch of the Independent Labour Party now turned out to help with the struggle, and one of the meetings was held at Knapton. After a few weeks all the farmers save one, a Mr Bircham of Knapton, agreed to a nine-hour day for the old wage. Mr Bircham was however, under notice to leave his farm. This was Parrs Farm, where eventually Roger Dixon's uncle Dan Dixon and his uncle George Dixon farmed, and where Willie Puncher still farms today. In his capacity as a member of the Norfolk County Council smallholdings committee, George Edwards advised the locked-out men to apply for small holdings, and so great was the demand that when the farm came up for sale George Edwards was able to persuade the committee to buy it. As a result, by the autumn several of the locked-out union members were settled as smallholding tenants on the very farm from which they had been locked out.

Sir George Edwards, Arthur Amis, James Coe and Jack Boddy were very important figures in the development of the Labour movement. All of them also played a key role in local govern-ment, using their position as elected district or county councillors to improve the lot of working people, particularly agricultural workers. Sir George Edwards had a highly influential role in local politics as well as pursuing his national roles of MP and trades union leader. Arthur Amis also valued the experience his role as a councillor gave him. He wrote: *'I have had the privilege of serving as a councillor at parish, district and county levels. I have gained an outlook on life which I never could have had without this experience.'* When he became a county councillor he too was a member of the smallholdings committee and spent a lot of his time on the Social Services committee, thus continuing the tradition forged by his eminent predecessor.

The Norfolk County Council had been one of the first in the country to make use of the further 4,000 acres for use as smallhold-ings. The aim, then as now, was to enable farm workers with the means to establish themselves, and in time to move on to larger holdings. Smallholdings were also seen as a means of providing employment for ex-servicemen after the First World War. The Land Settlement (Facilities) Act of 1919 made available for county councils a fund of £20 million to provide such holdings, and by 1926

Norfolk had spent over £1 million in buying and equipping 13,000
acres of land for 2,400 ex-servicemen. Even as late as the end of the
1970s there was an epic battle within the Norfolk County Council
on whether or not to sell the smallholdings estate. The presence
of the successors to people like Sir George Edwards and Arthur
Amis, soundly backed by the twenty-two farmer members of the
Council, meant that while some land was sold the majority of the
estate was retained to ensure a ladder of opportunity for those who
worked on the land.

Political passions and disputes were certainly not limited to
national or regional matters. John Capes records that *'until about
1950, there was a joint parish council for Paston and Knapton. I cannot
remember my father being on it before the war, but he certainly was
in the late 1940s. I think that Rev. Prichard was the chairman and
Mr Johnson (husband of Kitty Johnson, the head of Knapton School)
was the clerk. The meetings were always held at the School House in
Knapton. At some point, my father and the other Paston members
became a bit incensed at always having to go to Knapton and started
to agitate for a separate council. I remember dad saying something
like, "I don't see why we should always go up there and they always
seem to have the greater say about things." So eventually the Paston
members applied to the District Council to have their own council. I
think this was approved in the early 1950s and the parishes went their
different ways.'*

June Wild, writing about her father, Henry Wild, has an interesting explanation for his enthusiasm for local government at parish
level. She writes: *'While in Plymouth during the war, my father, Henry
Wild, went to a "morale-boosting talk" given by a Captain Thompson,
who was from the Army's Bureau of Current Affairs. The talk was about
democratic government, which he found interesting. He was also interested in the history of the village and had learned a great deal about it
from his grandfather, Charles Wild, who had lived in Knapton from
about 1870. This all helped when he became a parish councillor in 1948.
He retired from Knapton Parish Council fifty-seven years later in 2005,
when family and people from the village met in the Village Hall, and*

Gillian Shephard presented dad with a portrait of himself, on behalf of the parish council and residents of Knapton. This was painted by John Stear of Trunch, and still hangs in the Village Hall.'

My own political career obviously took a somewhat different turn from those of the great figures of the Labour and trades union movements described in this chapter. When I started out in politics I was deeply influenced not only by my own family background of small business and self-employment but also by the national political scene of the late 1970s, dominated as it was by the Winter of Discontent, over-mighty unions and massive economic upheaval, and I entered local and then national politics as a Conservative.

However, as a Norfolk woman I could not fail to have been aware of and impressed by the work of Sir George Edwards and the wrongs he had worked so hard to right, and by the work of his successors like Arthur Amis, whom I had known and respected all my life; James Coe, whose county councillor successor I eventually became in Freebridge, King's Lynn; and Jack Boddy, distinguished Union organiser and EU union representative, who lived in my South West Norfolk constituency. And so it was that towards the end of my career as Member of Parliament for South West Norfolk I in my turn helped to strike a blow against the vile employment conditions – including, incredibly, a reappearance of the infamous tied housing – imposed on migrant workers by unscrupulous employers and gangmasters in the early years of the twenty-first century.

No one living in agricultural areas of Britain around the turn of this century could have been unaware of the large numbers of migrant workers entering the UK at that time to take up employment in agriculture, food processing and manufacturing. The input of these workers was necessary to do work local workers did not wish to do, notably harvesting and processing crops and manual factory work. Some had entered the UK entirely legally, since they were citizens of other EU countries, particularly Portugal. Others were illegal migrant workers, employed in many cases by devious gang masters.

In my South West Norfolk constituency, council officers calcu-
lated that in 2002 there were some 22,000 migrant workers living
and working in the Breckland District Council area alone. The
Labour government claimed to have no idea how many migrant
workers there were in the UK and that it did not matter anyway.
It did matter of course, because those from other EU countries
were entitled to the same employment protection as UK workers,
and many were not getting it. Those here illegally were entitled
to no employment protection at all and so were at the mercy of
unscrupulous employment practices.

The Thetford Citizens' Advice Bureau produced a highly critical report in 2003 describing the working conditions of some of
these workers: the fact that their employment and pay were linked
to living accommodation, often of an appalling standard, and that
they were simply thrown out of their housing if they got sick, with
no means of getting back home or finding another job. All of this
in the Norfolk of Sir George Edwards.

There were reports of house fires in Thetford and King's Lynn,
with up to thirty-eight tenants hot-bedding in a single house. I
took up the cudgels, but was frustrated almost beyond endurance by
the bland denials put out by the Home Secretary, by other ministers
and by the County Council. Norfolk had at the time three Labour
MPs, none of whom supported my cause. They refused point blank
to accept that there was a problem – and worse, implied that my
concerns were motivated by racism. I used every parliamentary
means open to me to raise the problem, putting down questions,
taking part in debates, and as a member of the DEFRA Select
Committee initiating two enquiries into the situation, both of
which were highly critical of the government.

All of this was to no avail, until the truly appalling disaster of the
drowning of more than 120 Chinese cockle pickers in Morecambe
Bay in February 2004, with many of them, as they drowned, talking
on their mobile phones to their families in China because there was
no one they could phone in the UK. It turned out that many had
been illegally employed and as the event was debated in the highly

charged atmosphere of the Commons, even government ministers found their earlier denials of the problem difficult to maintain.

In January that year a Private Member's Bill had been introduced into the House of Commons by the Labour MP Jim Sheridan, and the Gangmasters (Licensing) Bill had its second reading in the Commons on 28 February 2004. Its purpose was to set up a Gangmasters Licensing Authority to operate a licensing scheme for labour providers in agriculture, forestry, horticulture, shellfish gathering, and food and drink processing and packaging.

The Labour government was totally opposed to this Bill (as was the Conservative opposition), and because it was a Private Member's Bill we had no recourse to official briefing. This was provided for us by officials of the Transport and General Workers' Union under the guidance of Jack Dromey. I often wondered at the time what Sir George Edwards would have made of that. Together with the likes of Frank Dobson and Nick Brown, both former Labour Cabinet ministers, I took part in the Bill's proceedings and we relentlessly pursued Alun Michael, the minister in charge. Unfortunately for him, and the Labour government, public opinion was so outraged by the truly terrible deaths in Morecambe Bay that they were obliged to look more kindly on the Bill, and it finally became law on 8 July 2004. It was limited in its scope and could not right all the wrongs, but its existence did lead to the arrest and imprisonment of some of the worst gangmaster offenders.

One of the most treasured tributes I had for my work as an MP and in particular for this whole episode came at that time from Jack Boddy, who told me: 'Well done! I would never have thought a Tory would have stood up for working people as you have done on this issue. I am ashamed that my own party in government did not do so.'

NINE

TIME OFF

Until the early 1960s, Knapton was in many ways, and like many rural villages of its size, largely self-sufficient. That self-sufficiency applied as much to recreation, entertainment and social activities as it did to many aspects of economic life. The lack of easy transport was one reason for this and the fact that the majority of people were employed in and around the village, or a short cycle ride away, was another. Knapton was fortunate in having village leaders like Miss Robinson and the headmistress Mrs Johnson who took it for granted that they should organise or help with all kinds of activities, many of them to raise money for a variety of causes but some just to provide entertainment for the community. It was an accepted part of community life that the majority would lend a hand when there was a village activity on the go.

What went on? Many social events revolved around the church and chapel, some of them money-raising, of course, but enjoyed nevertheless. The church and chapel Sunday School parties, treats and fêtes were mentioned by many contributors as highlights of their year. The school ran fund-raising events, such as beetle drives, although occasions such as schools sports took place during the working day when most parents could not attend.

A Women's Institute was founded in Knapton and Paston in 1921. This meant that the two villages were in the forefront of the establishment of Women's Institutes nationally, as the National Federation of Institutes had been founded in Britain only in 1915 (having come from Canada), and in Norfolk in 1919. Knapton and Paston's initiative may have had something to do with Miss Robinson's leadership. She became the Institute's first president, and held the post until 1967.

From 1969, a Women's Own Club was run under the aegis of

the Methodist Chapel. This is still going strong, whereas the WI, despite efforts to revive it, stopped functioning in the 1980s, not least because of a hike in the membership fees at that time. The chapel also ran a Men's Fellowship.

The Men's Club provided indoor sporting activities for the men and boys of the village. Village socials were held in the Parish Room, and barn dances in Mr May's barn at Church Farm. Whist and beetle drives also took place in the Parish Room, later succeeded by bingo. Barbara Wilkins (Fawkes) (1930–2009) wrote: *'For a number of years in the 1960s I ran a bingo in Knapton Parish Room on a Wednesday evening once a month. On the day of the bingo after finishing work at 1 p.m. I would go to Somerfield's in North Walsham to get the prizes. During the afternoon Henry Wild and I went to the Parish Room where Henry would set out the tables and chairs, while I would get out the cups and saucers for refreshments during the interval and set out the prizes on the stage. Then it was home for a quick dinner and off to Paston to pick up ladies who wanted to support the bingo but had no transport, but I had to be back at the hall with the bingo tickets by the time the supporters arrived. I was also the bingo caller. All proceeds from one bingo would be used to fund the next one.'*

Barbara and her helpers ran these bingo sessions not to raise funds for a cause nor to make a profit, but simply to provide entertainment for people in the village. They were very well supported, despite the fact that this was the 1960s.

For a while in the 1950s there were dancing lessons in the Parish Room, run by Grace and Bob Wright, who lived in The Street. Pam Dixon (Garnham) (b. 1935) also remembers a Joyce and Bob Crisp from Cromer giving dancing lessons in the Village Hall to gramophone records, and holding social evenings there for dancing. *'They also held these evenings in Trunch and Gimingham village halls. I remember cycling in the snow to Gimingham one St Valentine's Day to a dance they organised.'*

Amateur dramatics were a feature of village life throughout the whole period of this book. They usually took place in the Parish Room, but there was at least one open air performance of

A Midsummer Night's Dream in the garden of the Old Hall in the 1930s, organised by the Kiernan family. (According to Roger Dixon, old Mrs Kiernan had been an opera singer and her interest may have influenced activities.)

Occasionally a film, slide show or talk would be put on in the Village Hall. Roger Dixon recalls a film show taking place in the 1930s outside on a summer evening in the drive of Knapton Hall.

From time to time village coach outings would be arranged, to see the tulip fields in Lincolnshire, for example, or to well known seaside resorts or beauty spots a little further afield. Between 1970 and 1976 Linda Risebrow helped organise a Knapton Friendship Club with a varied programme of talks, films and outings.

The village did not have a designated playing field until the mid-1950s when, thanks largely to the efforts of the school headmistress Kathleen Johnson, enough money was raised from sheer local effort and a National Playing Fields Association grant, to provide one next to the Men's Club in Hall Lane.

June Wild (Wild) (b. 1951) writes: *'The field runs down the side of the Men's Club, where swings and bars for the children were provided. It was of course large enough for football and cricket to be played, and there was a gate from the school playground, so that the children could use it at playtimes. The grand opening was performed in 1956 by Sir Edmund Bacon, Lord Lieutenant of Norfolk, who was also President of the Norfolk branch of the National Playing Fields Association. There were sideshows and stalls, although as usual macs and umbrellas were very much in evidence.'* June also recalls extremely popular football matches being played on the field, where the village men would dress up as women and the women as men.

Throughout the period covered by this book, there from time to time a Knapton football team. Before the playing field was provided, home matches were played on the lawn in front of Knapton Hall. Village sports were held on two lawns: the one opposite Knapton Hall and the one opposite White House Farm. Later, of course, they took place on the playing field.

The village itself, and its surrounding fields and woods, was a source of recreation for many people, and their descriptions of walks and games in and around the village are found elsewhere in this book. The family Sunday walk, in particular, was a regular feature of village life.

For young people, the Methodist Chapel ran a Youth Fellowship and Christian Endeavour. In the 1950s Mrs Macmillan, who was at that time living at Knapton Old Hall, ran a Brownie pack. At the same time, Richard Wild joined the first Mundesley Scout Group. Mrs Wilkinson ran a very informal girls' club, mainly for church-goers, but the meetings are remembered affectionately by many.

The year was punctuated by Christmas and Easter, and the other annual celebrations of Shrove Tuesday, Guy Fawkes and Bonfire Night, and the curious rituals of Valentine's Day, described in many of the accounts which follow. I have been unable to find evidence of similar Valentine's Day celebrations in any other English county, and there is a further note about this Norfolk tradition at Appendix 2.

We will begin with the activities of the village children, who in addition to organised games at school, or through clubs, had their own recreations and games, mostly dictated by the seasons or by that strange unwritten law whereby everyone in the playground and at home is suddenly playing marbles or five-stones, or swapping cigarette cards, and the following week, for no particular reason, changing to skipping and pop-guns.

Queenie Bane (Wild) (b. 1917) writes: *At school in the playground the boys would play football and the girls netball. I was shooter. We would also make up other games.*

'We would look forward to Jack Valentine coming on 14 February. There would be a knock on the door and a parcel left, tied with a piece of string, then pulled away. It was dad [Josiah Bane] *doing it! When we did get the parcel indoors inside would be some sweets. When we were young children on Shrove Tuesday our mother would make me and my four sisters small pancakes. Easter Sunday we would each be given an Easter egg, though it would be a small one as they were expen-*

sive. At home on Guy Fawkes Night, dad would have a bonfire, and we would have some fireworks, mainly sparklers. Christmas time, we had a holly tree indoors with a few decorations on it and decorations hung up, some of them paper chains that we had made. In our stockings, Father Christmas would put an orange, a packet of sweets, hankies and socks. I can remember getting a doll and a pair of slippers as Christmas presents. Christmas dinner would be a chicken or cockerel, a home-made Christmas pudding and some crackers to pull.'

Olive Wild (Webster) (b. 1919) remembers: *'In the playground we would play hopscotch and rounders. We had a netball team. I was 'goalie'. We would walk or bike to play against Mundesley and Bacton schools. On Saturdays when I had finished doing what my mother had asked me to do, I could do what I wanted. If fine, I would sometimes go and play in my "house" up the garden (opposite the school – it went with the cottage). My mother had made it. It had no roof but we had broken crockery and an old grate to make a fireplace with. When it was Guy Fawkes time my friend Barbara Farrow and I would dress up in old clothes and go round and knock on people's doors for a penny for the Guy.*

'On 14 February, when it was dark, Jack Valentine would come and knock on the door, and there would be a parcel on the doorstep. The parcel would then be pulled away with a piece of string. This would happen several times and the last time the parcel was left without the string. It was a while before we realised my father was not in the room at the time; he was hiding in the shed.

'Sunday afternoons, winter and summer if fine, I would go for a walk with father and Mr Billy Small (the carpenter) and his daughter Connie. We would walk down to Mundesley, past the sanatorium, on to Trunch, and home about 4 p.m.

'Summertime we had our Sunday School party down at Knapton House, with games on the lawn followed by tea. One of the games was to go into the maze, which had high hedges, and the winner was the person who could find their way out. I mostly was the winner, because I used to watch my father clip the maze hedges with Mr Appleton (the head gardener) who lived down The Grove. I knew my way around!

'*In the New Year, Mrs Anna Wild, known as Widow Wild and later as Granny Wild, would hold a party for her family, and I would be invited up until I left school, as my birthday is on 4 January and her youngest son Victor's was on Boxing Day. My mother and Mrs Wild were friends, as they would bring babies into the world and also help, at the end, to lay bodies out, as they would be kept at home in the coffins until the funeral. The coffins were made by Mr Small and Mrs Small would make the pillows and all the trimmings. My father and I would sit in his workshop in the evening, and I would see him make the coffins.'*

Olive also recalls rather different entertainments being organised by the Brocklehurst family, who lived at Knapton Hall in the 1920s. They hosted tennis parties at the Hall and Olive went with her mother to help prepare the cream teas, with the mouthwatering strawberries being washed, dried, cut up and sprinkled with sugar ready for the guests to add the cream.

Ronald Fawkes (b. 1926), father of Linda Risebrow and Rene Turner, wrote this account of a Guy Fawkes Day when he was at Knapton School, probably in the early 1930s: '*On Saturday, it was Guy Fawkes Day there were a lot of different fireworks. We had two little demons, two jumping jacks and one tadpole, three sky rockets and four chrysanthemum fountains. At school we had about nine little demons and one flying imp. We let off three sky rockets but could not see where they went.*

'*I did not go round Guying, but my brothers did: they got 1s 2d each. I went with Mr Bane (Josiah) to Mundesley. We saw a big fire down by the sanatorium. They had a lot of sky rockets; we saw them very plain. As we got near Mundesley we saw several Guys. They had a turnip which had a candle inside, to use as a lantern or to light their fireworks. When Mr Bane had had his shave, we went down to Alfred Larter's. As we were going there we saw a big bonfire where the fair was, and they let off several rockets. One came down on top of the butcher's shop. It was 10 p.m. when we got home so I had my supper and went to bed.*'

A few weeks' later Ronald was writing: '*Getting ready for Christmas is now coming on. The bakers are getting Christmas cakes ready, and they have got green and red papers in Mr Burton's baker's shop to put the cake stands on. At school we are making calendars. I have made three, one with a dog chasing some kittens up a tree, another with puppies in a barrow and another with a lady on it.*

'I like Christmas, for then we can have snowballs if there is enough snow. The last deep snow we had in Knapton was thirteen years ago this Christmas. We have big puddings to eat and ducks for dinner. I like to hear the bands playing carols; they have been round twice already. Once after the band went away Mr Wright got out his accordion and began to play "Good King Wenceslas", and Mrs Wright sang.'

Shirley Wright (Conquest) (b. 1938) writes: *'At school the games we played in the playground were skipping, which was very popular, and then we tried our skill at ball games by using three balls, and trying to keep them all in the air and, if we got really clever, we would try four balls. We would play hopscotch and noughts and crosses by chalking on the ground, hide and seek, piggy in the middle and many other games outdoors. It was not difficult to find something to do.*

'When I was around eleven or twelve my pastime was collecting photographs of film stars. I used to write to the film studios asking for them. Many including Margaret Lockwood, Ava Gardner, Bob Hope, Alan Ladd and Diana Dors would reply, sending a black-and-white photograph, usually autographed.

'I used to go to the cinema in North Walsham when I was a little older. Village socials and barn dances in Mr May's barn at Church Farm were very popular, and I would always be there. It brought a bit of life to the village, and brought together people who liked to dance. It was a large barn, quite draughty and with a bare concrete floor. Not sure who provided the music but it was great.

'I always helped with the church fête held at Miss Robinson's house, usually in the month of June, and nearly always lovely weather in a beautiful setting. The Methodist fête, always on Whit Monday, was a busy day for the Youth Fellowship team, who would arrive in the morning at Mr May's kitchen and make sandwiches and plate up teas for the afternoon, and then clear up at the end of the day – we all enjoyed it. I belonged to the Christian Endeavour group and Methodist Youth

Fellowship. This was a lovely group of young people doing things together and being guided and supported by Mr and Mrs Herbert Hicks, who did a wonderful job, opening up their house to us all and being so jolly and helping with any problems. They were very happy times for me.'

Ruth Steward (Matthew) (b. 1943) also recalls games in the playground. *'In the summer we played ball games, skipping and many varieties of catch. Boys played marbles; dibble hole was one game. Sometimes the girls were allowed to join in, especially if they had a marble that was wanted by a boy. Sometimes we were allowed to use Mr Guyton's meadow opposite the Parish Room, but some boys climbed through the barbed wire fence, from which they caught ringworm on their necks and this ended our trips for a bit.*

'Valentine's Day holds special memories. Knapton – or is it Norfolk? – is the only place I know where Jack Valentine used to visit, knocking on the door and leaving small parcels: a pencil each, sweets, an exercise book, all greatly appreciated. No one would show themselves. Sometimes boys would play a trick, having a wrapped brick on a piece of string, and when the door opened it was pulled away. This stopped when we had a dog; she soon sniffed them out.

'Christian Endeavour was held on Tuesdays at 6.30 p.m. in the chapel. We sometimes went to rallies, several groups meeting for a special service. On one such night we were going to Swanton Abbott. I went upstairs to change and looking out of the window I saw that the blacksmith's shop was alight. I shouted downstairs and dad went off to help. When I came back from Swanton Abbott later I found Jean Lubbock in my bed. The Lubbocks' house was next to the blacksmith's and was damaged by the fire. The Lubbocks lived next door to us for months while their house was repaired. [A fuller account of the blacksmith's shop fire is given in Chapter 2.]

'In the summer we sometimes went out tracking. A group would leave the chapel first to lay clues and the rest would follow to find them. Sometimes it seemed we went for miles, but we always enjoyed it. We also went carol singing for the National Children's Home. How cold those nights were, often frosty, but enjoyed.

'*The chapel sometimes held concerts or plays in the Parish Room. Christmas plays were a favourite. Everyone seemed to take part. At concerts, "There's a hole in my bucket", "Widdecombe Fair" and other well loved favourites were performed to full houses.*

As children we had a radio but no television (had television been invented then?). We played card games like Old Maid, Donkey and Snap, and later games for older children like Patience and Clock Patience. We also liked Ludo, Snakes and Ladders and other well known games. Bingo had us arguing about who should be caller and often dad had to step in. Reading was high on the agenda. I loved books. We had library books from schools and books for presents. I still have my two dolls. Any other toys were given to "needy others".'

Rene Fawkes (Turner) (b. 1952) also writes of playground games, and describes jacks, which was played by throwing up a small ball and picking up your jacks with the same hand while the ball was in the air. She adds: '*The school had a very long skipping rope and with Mrs Kirk holding one end and one of us the other, we used to see how many we could get skipping together. Then along came the art of French skipping, which called for a length of elastic knotted at one end – you took it in turn to weave your feet in and out of the elastic. There was a dressing up box and we'd dress up, enacting weddings, girls of course playing the parts of bride and groom, bridesmaids and guests.*

'*When Cliff Richard released his first single "Move It", June Wild was seven and I was six. We thought he was the best thing since sliced bread. In our wisdom we thought we'd issue him with an invitation to come and play in Knapton Village Hall. We were so excited at the prospect, we put pen to paper and went halves on the cost of the stamp and sent off our invitation to Winchmore Hill, London. Some weeks later an envelope arrived with an autograph inside. I just cannot think why Cliff never took up our invitation: after all, the Village Hall had always been good enough for our concerts, which were always such fun. Mr Hicks, Mr Stubley, Mr Leeder, Mr Steward, Mr Willie Wild, Mr George Wild, Mr Wright and many others used to dress up and sing. They were great evenings; the whole village was involved.*

'*Away from school there were so many things to do. Mrs Carr at Verbena Cottage used to give me piano lessons. She also formed a choir and we used to meet once a week to practice.*

'*Christian Endeavour run by the Methodist Youth Department was held at the chapel. We used to work towards an Eisteddfod where we exhibited our work, and we also did Bible readings. I still have my certificates for things like scripture examinations, Bible reading and knitting, sewing and drawing. All the villages in the circuit took part and we all used to gather at North Walsham Methodist Chapel to see all the exhibits and see who had won what. A great time was had by all, and because in those days no one seemed to travel very far we all knew one another.*

'*Waiting for Jack Valentine to call on 14 February was exciting in its own way. Aunt Emmy (father's sister, Ursula) would pop in to see us around teatime, then a little later a knock came on the door. It never occurred to us that mum was often missing when Jack Valentine called and put presents on the door step for my sister Linda and me. There would be a baby doll complete with knitted clothes for each of us and after another knock, painting books, crayons and more doll's clothes. This tradition seems to be something confined to Norfolk, as when I have talked to people about the tradition from outside the county they have never heard of it and look what fun they have missed out on. After Linda and I found out about Jack Valentine I can remember going to our gran's one Valentine night with a parcel tied to a piece of string and waiting till she bent down to pick up the parcel, pulling it away, frightening the life out of her.*

'*Guy Fawkes Night was another reason for fun. We used to light fireworks in the garden with Catherine wheels nailed on to the linen post. We would have sparklers to hold. There would be hot dogs with lots of onions and jacket potatoes. Mum and dad used to make it such a special time.*'

There were also more organised games. John Capes (b. 1931), who lived in Paston, remembers football matches between the boys of Knapton and Paston: '*I was certainly playing in these matches by time I went to the Grammar School in September 1942 when I was eleven and probably started a little earlier. All the matches I can remember were played at Knapton, probably because Paston did not have a proper playing field or decent meadow. The games were played on the field at the top of The Street, opposite the Hall ... The matches continued towards the end of the war, as I can remember some of the second lot of evacuees at Paston playing for us, so I suppose that would have been in the winter of 1944–45 ... These were very much ad hoc games, no real organisation someone would come round and say, "Knapton want us to play them next week," or one of us would say, "How about challenging Knapton to another game?", and so somehow a date would be fixed. The games were rather scrappy affairs as usually neither side could raise a full team of eleven and there was quite an age range, going from about eight to fourteen. The Knapton players I can remember were Reggie Smith, Henry Wright, Llewellyn Kirk and I think David Leeder was the goalkeeper.'*

He also recalls that *'immediately after the war, a joint Knapton and Paston club was formed, playing in the North-East Norfolk Primary League. Home matches were played on Mr Wallage's meadow right opposite his farm (White House Farm Lawn), and one of the barns was used as the changing room and for storage of the goal posts.'* John describes an occasion *'at an evening match at Mundesley against their reserve team when the forward line consisted of the five Lubbock brothers* [a Knapton family mentioned elsewhere in this book], *as Aubrey, who was Blakeney's goalkeeper, came over and played at centre forward ... From Paston Richard Hewitt and I were drafted in when we were about sixteen to make up the team if there were not enough adults to play. I think the club only lasted for two or three years because of lack of players, as by the 1947–48 and 1948–49 seasons I was playing for Mundesley Minors (under 18) and also their reserve team ... If I wasn't playing I would often watch the team to give them support and I would sometimes travel to away matches: for instance I can remember going on the coach to Bodham where they were playing in a round of the Norfolk Primary Cup competition.'*

John is describing activities which took place outside the immediate confines of the two villages in the 1940s. Barbara Wilkins

(Fawkes) (1930–2009) recalled attending a Methodist youth club in Mundesley at about the same time. *'My friend Iris Carr and I used to cycle to Raxawa at Mundesley for youth club. Iris's bike had a front light and no back light, and I had a back light with no front light. It was getting dark when we left Mundesley and when we got to the top corner in Knapton someone shouted, "Where are your lights?" We shouted back, "Next to my liver," thinking it was just the local boys. We thought it was funny until we realised it was actually the local policeman. We put a spurt on down Hall Lane I don't think we ever cycled so fast in our lives. There were two cottages on the left hand side. Iris lived in the first one and as she only had a front light she dashed into her yard and turned it off so no one could see her. I had a little further to go as we lived in a cottage in what is now Puncher's farmyard, and managed to get my bike into the shed without being caught. I then had to stay there in the shed for a good ten minutes to steady my breathing before going indoors.'*

Later Barbara and her husband-to-be Ron Fawkes enjoyed going to the speedway in Norwich. Their enthusiasm continued after their marriage and they would take their daughters Linda and Rene when they were old enough. *'We lost Rene in the pits one Saturday night. Ron said she could go and have a look at the motorbikes in the pits which she loved so much. He took her down to the trackside and she only had a few yards to walk to look round the gates from the track into the pits, but instead of coming back, Ron found her, after a very worrying twenty minutes, actually in the pits surrounded by motorbikes and riders. She had a wonderful time even if it did frighten the lives out of us.'*

Special events have stayed long in the collective memory.

The Coronation of Queen Elizabeth II in 1953 was marked by celebrations on the lawn opposite White House Farm on the day after the ceremony, 3 June. It was freezing cold, with rain and a sharp wind. Some said it snowed. A group of people who were children at the time pooled their collective memories. The group included Janet and Ruth Steward (Munro and Matthew), Avril Edwards (Earl), Richard Wild, Jennifer Wild (Lambert) and John Wild. Avril remembers various events on the field and a tea as well in either the

Parish Room or the school. Ruth recalls two teas, one for children and one for adults, and a film show in the Parish Room. Richard and Janet remember that one of the activities set up on the field was an obstacle course for everyone to have a go at. There were hay wagons and straw bales to climb over, stack cloths and pig netting to crawl under and motor tyres to scramble through. Janet remembers her disappointment at having to go and rest, as she was not feeling well, because she had badly wanted to win the obstacle course. Richard recalls a game which involved one person pushing another, holding a pole, in a wheelbarrow and having to get through some kind of hole while avoiding a bucket of water. Failure obviously involved a drenching. All remember receiving a Coronation Mug and from their schools a New Testament, courtesy of the Norfolk Education Committee, inscribed, 'To commemorate the Coronation of Her Majesty Queen Elizabeth II, 2 June 1953.' Janet also received a New Testament from the chapel, inscribed 'Coronation June 1953 for Afternoon Attendance at Methodist Church', and a hymn book inscribed 'The School Hymn Book of the Methodist Church, a memento of the Coronation of Her Majesty Queen Elizabeth II, 2 June 1953.'

The Coronation was a very big event in our lives. Newspaper and newsreel coverage and the wireless more than made up for the lack of television. I am not sure if anyone in Knapton had a television in 1953; we certainly did not. On the day, our family visited an aunt to watch the proceedings on her television, but the experience was somewhat marred by the extremely inadequate quality of the television pictures, and the fact that my aunt, who was prolix to say the least, talked throughout so that we could not hear either. My school, the girls' High School in North Walsham, performed a Coronation Masque, written by a talented member of staff involving many actors, dancers, recorder players, the full school choir and a madrigal choir.

It was performed in the school garden the following month and fortunately the weather by then was perfect. The whole experience is still fresh in my mind, not to mention the words of 'Rose of England' and other gems by Edward German.

There was quite a strong amateur dramatic tradition in Knapton and plays, concerts music halls and nativity plays were put on throughout much of the period covered by this book. The Kiernan family, as has already been mentioned, put on *A Midsummer Night's Dream* in their garden in the 1930s, and also produced a nativity play in the Parish Room. Other events were put on by the Methodist Youth Fellowship. Many people in the village could do a turn: sing, for example, or recite a poem. Mr Leeder, who lived at Stone Cottages, had a fine bass voice and I can recall him reciting 'Gunga Din' on many occasions. There were at least three gifted amateur pianists in Knapton. One was Hilda Turner (wife of George Turner, Miss Robinson's gardener, and born probably about 1910), who frequently played the piano for the WI (alternating with Shirley Wright's mother) and for concerts. A photo of Hilda performing in a dance band is shown as Photo 19. In the 1960s Mrs Carr moved to Knapton and ran a choir, also helping with amateur dramatics.

Roger Dixon (b. 1934) writing in *Knapton Remembered* describes a musical tradition which could have come straight from Thomas Hardy. '*Singing and music played a big part on the life of our family – that is, in the Gee family, my grandmother's people. Every Christmas, we had an enormous party crammed into the cottage where Walter Pardon, the last of the folk singers, lived. He was the last of the family to live there, where they had been since the 1830s. There was a big beam across the middle of what was then the "front room", and the entertainment swung from one side of it to the other. After a song or an item on an instrument (several of them played violin, accordion or flute), suitable refreshment followed, and then there was a call of "Your side o' the baulk", and a person on that side of the room would oblige. In later years, after Peter Bellamy, whom I taught at Fakenham, discovered Walter, one of Walter's records was given that title.* [Peter Bellamy was a well known Norfolk folk singer and musician.] *He kept the big drum of the Knapton band in his shed and there were all sorts of family tales about music-making in the past. One was that the family formed the church band in the reign of William IV in the 1830s, before the Robinson*

1

Knapton crossroads at 'The Candlestick' in the early 1930s. The thatched Village Hall is the building second from the far end of the row.

2

The Street, with the village shop in the foreground.

The church of St Peter and St Paul, Knapton, 2009.

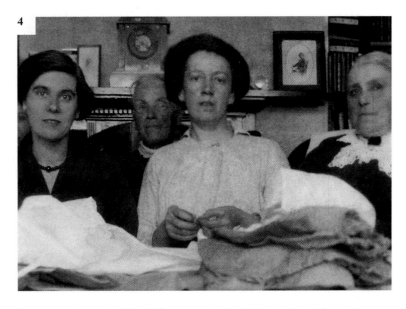

Sewing session at the School House to raise funds for the chapel during the First World War. (See page 26.)

Knapton School, 1919.

Christian Endeavour meeting in the early 1950s. (See page 27.)

7

The Old Hall, 2009.

8

Tennis party at Knapton Hall in the 1920s. (See page 34.)

9

Mr Bussey the blacksmith outside his forge. (See page 37.)

10

Mr. PHILLIP GAZE, Paston, says—"I have used your Manures for the last few years, and have always been satisfied with the results obtained. I used 3 cwt. per acre of your **Special Mangold Manure** without any farm yard, and have an excellent crop of sound Roots. They are of splendid keeping quality."

Advertisement for Hadfield's Special Mangold Manure, with endorsement by Phillip Gaze: 'I have used your Manures for the last few years, and have always been satisfied with the results obtained.' (See page 57.)

11

Adeline Almey on her milk round: 'This is Adeline with her can, / Delivering milk just like a man.' (See page 57.)

12

Bowling for the pig at the fête held to mark the opening of Knapton playing field, June 1956. (See page 163.)

OPPOSITE:

13 The last timetable for Paston and Knapton station, 1962–3. (See page 74.)

14 Bertha Clover (left) with her friend May and Boxer the dog at the Royal Hotel, Mundesley, 1930. (See page 124.)

15 National Service: John Capes in Dortmund, 1950. (See page 139.)

16 Arthur Amis. (See pages 149–53.)

17 Sir George Edwards. (See pages 152–7.)

13

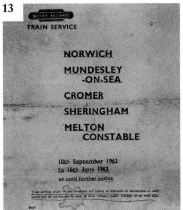

14

15

16

17

18

The Knapton football team during the First World War. (See page 163.)

19

Hilda Turner with the dance band. (See page 174.)

20

Jill Watts with her father Jack, 1942.

family provided the first harmonium for the church. If you have ever read Under the Greenwod Tree, *you will know how the Gees felt about it.'*

In the 1960s Knapton had its own *Black and White Minstrel Show.* Jennifer Wild (Lambert) (b. 1944) writes: *'The* Black and White Minstrel Show *was a television programme on a Sunday night which featured old and popular songs. In the 1960s, we in Knapton had our own Black and White Minstrels. They included myself and my husband Bob, my parents Sidney and Queenie Wild, and my brother Richard. My uncle Willie and cousins John, Malcolm and Keith Wild, and my aunt Marjorie Schamp also took part. Mary Puncher (now Steward) and Pearl Hicks (now Eves) joined in too. We were accompanied at the piano by Mrs Carr, who taught and encouraged us with our singing. Richard remembers singing "Moonlight Bay" solo for the first time, and being glad when it was over.*

'We made all our costumes and Bob blackened the men's faces with grease paint. We performed at Knapton Parish Room, for the 1966 WI birthday party. We also performed in the surrounding villages and old people's homes. Bob remembers singing "Edelweiss" at the Links Hotel, West Runton, with the piano out of tune.

'Mrs Barrett senior, of Swafield Hall, invited us to perform in her lounge, I think it was for the Mothers' Union. She made us very welcome. We were given a bedroom to change in where there was an open fire lit for us. After the show, laid out in the kitchen for us was a buffet consisting of sandwiches, trifles, etc. which we appreciated very much.'

Holidays were not frequently taken in the earlier part of the period covered by this book, for the obvious reason of their cost. Summer in an agricultural community was in any case not a time when people could take time off work. When people did have days off they would, as they put it, 'go out for days'. Coach outings were organised from the village from time to time, as June Wild (Wild) (b. 1951) recalls: *'One coach outing my parents went on before I was born was to Clacton. It was arranged for the employees of Agates, the grocery store in Mundesley, and the coach was then filled up by customers. There were other people on the coach from Knapton, including Dot Wild (Coe) and Ronnie Coe who both worked at Agate's. Mum and dad went on other coach outings from Knapton, one being in about 1948 to, I think, Skegness. There is a photo of them with others standing outside The Crooked House, and a lot of them are wearing seaside hats. I can also remember going on coach trips myself to Yarmouth. These were arranged by Ursula Fawkes and we went to the shows on the piers, and saw Norman Wisdom, Freddie Starr, The Bachelors, Des O'Connor and many more.'*

People would stay with relatives. Pam Dixon (Garnham) (b. 1935) had relatives in Great Malvern and remembers visiting them from time to time.

My mother's relatives, and notably her mother, would come to stay with us from Sheffield. Until my grandmother's death my mother entertained the illusion that her mother loved coming to Norfolk for a break from the grime, noise and bustle of Sheffield. In fact my grandmother, as she walked up our path on her arrival, could usually be heard to say, 'East, west, home's best.' By contrast, I loved going to Sheffield. For one thing everyone spoke quite differently, a fact I found endlessly fascinating. There were different foods, like bread cakes and faggots, and Tizer to drink; there were rattling trams and huge wonderful parks, where the grass and leaves left black stains on your clothes; and of course the kind indulgent relatives with their welcoming houses and huge networks of friends who continually dropped in.

Linda Fawkes (Risebrow) (b. 1950) writes: *'The first family holiday I can remember was a caravan holiday in Felixstowe. Mum had packed the suitcases and Brenda, mum's sister, came too. We had to wait 'til dad got home from work before we could set off for what we thought was a trip to the other end of the earth. By the time we arrived at the caravan park it was dark, and dad had to go searching with a torch for our caravan which was called Mandalay, and which was to be our home for the week. We had a great time playing with all the children on the site and being able to play on the beach and visit towns around Felixstowe.'*

Linda's holiday took place in the 1950s. Richard Wild (b. 1946) remembers two adventurous holidays in the 1960s. The first was with his cousin Michael Self, when they went camping in Michael's black Morris Minor. They went to Scotland, via Bolton-le-Sands, the Lake District and then to various camping sites in Scotland. *'We stopped on camp sites, or just on the side of the road, which would not be allowed today. Near Grasmere we were woken by a farmer herding his sheep alongside our tent, and in another place we were in a hay field and used some of the hay under our ground sheet to make a soft bed. We returned down the east coast, stopping at various places. One of the prettiest places was Robin Hood's Bay. We left there at 8.35 a.m. and arrived back home at 4.45 p.m. on Sunday evening. We had travelled 1,908 miles and we had no breakdowns. The Lake District lived up to its reputation as being wet and windy.'*

A holiday to Norway followed in May 1967, with three cousins, including Michael Self, this time with a white Morris 1,000. They took tents and were struck by the grandeur of the scenery, the fact that there was still snow on the ground in many places, and that the houses, churches and schools were built of wood. Unfortunately for Richard the sea crossing was rough both ways, which put him off cruising for ever.

A number of organisations in and around the village provided a combination of activity, education and recreation.

Mary Puncher (Steward) (b. 1948) writes: *'Knapton was only a small village, but it provided me with lots of hobbies and pastimes. From the age of seven I attended Brownies held weekly at the Old Hall, home of Mrs Macmillan who was the Brown Owl. I was a Fairy and Mary Steward (now Lewis) was an Elf. By the time I was ten I had earned badges for first aid, cooking, sewing, collecting and so on, and had become a Sixer of the Fairies. I can also remember going to the Samson and Hercules Ballroom in Norwich for a Brownie rally. All the Brownies had to hide under toadstool sheets and wait for the commissioners to arrive. When they did, I can remember a voice saying, "Where are all the Brownies?", at which point we emerged very loudly from our toadstools … A big day out for me.*

'At the age of eleven I moved up to Girl Guides. There was no company in Knapton, so I had to bike to Bacton. Then Mrs Macmillan started a

company in Mundesley, so I moved there. Again we were taught lots of skills to help us in later life. I can remember weekend patrol camps in Mrs Macmillan's garden, cooking on open fires and washing outside! We also had week-long patrol camps in Sheringham, Overstrand and one, I think near Woodbridge, in Suffolk.'

Barbara Wilkins (Fawkes) (1930–2009) worked part-time for the Macmillan family from 1957 onwards, and recalled: *'Mrs Macmillan was Brown Owl of the Brownie pack and used to have Brownies camping on the lawn in the summertime, between the tennis courts and the pond. They had a whale of a time. The front hall was used for the Brownies' Christmas pantomime.'*

Richard Wild (b. 1946) joined the first Mundesley Scout Group in the late 1950s. It met in a hut in the garden of the Scout leader, Mr Collins. *'There were about twelve boys split into two patrols. I was in the Peewits; the others were Owls. We learned how to tie knots, make rope bridges, light fires, cook and track, provide first aid, chop wood and of course put up a tent.*

'My first camp was in North Walsham woods. For two days we had thick lumpy porridge cooked in a billy-can, bangers and mash, and bread and jam for tea.

'We also went to Broadstone Warren in Ashdown Forest in East Sussex for a week. We went by train to Forest Row and then by lorry to the camp-site. It had an outdoor swimming pool, a shop and first aid hut. I spent a lot of time in the pool. We also had a day trip to Brighton.

'After the Scouts I joined the Air Scouts, which was run by a Mr Price. We met at Mundesley School and did aircraft recognition and also went on camps. One of these was at RAF Coltishall for a week-end. We did various competitions. One was rifle shooting and one was to free a trapped man from a jeep and carry him on a stretcher to the first aid tent. I am pleased to say we won this. Our prize was a Tilley lamp. We went to the base cinema and saw "Reach for the Sky". I also met Sir Douglas Bader at the base. He had once been stationed at Coltishall.'

The Women's Institute was of great importance in Knapton, from its formation in 1921 right up until its demise in the 1980s.

It served Knapton and Paston, and its founder members in 1921 included Miss Robinson, Miss Leather, Mrs Yaxley, Mrs Hedge, Mrs Pardon, Mrs Dixon (Pamela and Barbara's mother) and Miss Townshend (their aunt). My mother, who came to live in Knapton after her marriage to my father in 1932, joined around that time, and enjoyed everything the WI could provide in terms of company, activity, entertainment and education for almost the whole of her long life. She eventually became president herself and organised the fiftieth anniversary dinner at the Manor Hotel, Mundesley. Three of the founder members, Miss Townshend, Mrs Dixon and Mrs Pardon, were present, together with Mrs Sumner, the immediate past president, my mother, Bertha Watts, and Hilda Turner.

June Wild gives an account of WI activities compiled from their minutes and log books, and from press cuttings:

'Knapton and Paston WI was founded in 1921. Miss Robinson was president for forty-six years, until 1967 when she retired. Mrs Sumner became the new president, followed by Mrs Bertha Watts and Mrs Betty Hammond and others.

Over the years the Knapton and Paston WI won many awards at county competitions, for example first prize for an exhibit of fruit, vegetables and flowering herbs at the WI Produce Exhibition at the Royal Norfolk Show in 1928. They also won awards at the WI Annual Exhibition of Homecrafts and Produce, for a patchwork bedspread, knitted blanket and bowl of flowers, to name a few. In 1948, a Link was formed with a WI in South Africa, and news and correspondence from the Link was a regular feature at the monthly WI meetings. Knapton and Paston sent an embroidered tablecloth to the Link in that first year and in 1971 a member from the Link visited England, and met Knapton and Paston members at the home of Mrs Stubley.

'A look at the programme for meetings in 1935 reveals that for each meeting there was a motto: for example, for February, "None of us know what we can do until we try," and for October, "Some are wise, some are otherwise." The talks ranged from "Feet and their Care" in May, to "Women 500 years ago, from the Paston Letters." There was a competition each month, including "Sausage rolls," in December, and "Best

worked button hole" in September. There was usually a trading stall or pound table, to raise money for a local cause. The meetings opened with the singing of Jerusalem, and closed with a "cooperative tea".

'Activities were extremely varied. Mrs Johnson, the headmistress, organised Keep Fit classes in 1938 and 1939, and in 1939, at the July meeting held in Miss Robinson's garden, the old people of the two villages were entertained by the WI choir and Keep Fit group, and some of the schoolchildren. At an earlier garden meeting the choir sang dressed in costume and acted nursery rhymes and charades. There were many fund-raising activities, whist drives and beetle drives, fêtes and coffee mornings, and on Shrove Tuesday in 1975 a pancake party in the Village Hall.

'Outings were arranged in the summer months. In 1936 the outing was to Felixstowe and Ipswich, in 1956 Woburn Abbey. In 1958 the WI went to Burghley House, in 1968 to Bury St Edmunds and in 1972 to Kew Gardens.

'There were plenty of parties and celebrations. At the thirty-sixth birthday party of the WI in 1957 the WI Skiffle Group made its first appearance. At the fortieth anniversary a one-act play was performed, involving some male performers, and a solo was sung accompanied by Mrs Carr. In 1958, there was a special birthday party for Miss Robinson's eightieth birthday, involving a special tea, wonderful flowers and a birthday cake. The oldest founder members Mrs Hedge and Mrs Yaxley each made a little speech of congratulations. Miss Robinson in her reply thanked the members for giving her such a lovely party and went on to say how grateful she had always been for the loyal support of all the members over the years. She also spoke of the happy atmosphere in the Institute which was so often remarked upon by visiting guests and speakers. And in 1967, when Miss Robinson retired as president, the entertainment was provided by the Knapton Men's Fellowship, with music, songs and sketches.

'I have described some of the local Women's Institute activities and these were very much enjoyed. However, the entrée that membership of the WI gave to county and national causes was and remains one of its strongest features in educating, informing and giving a voice to rural women.

Many members of the Knapton and Paston WI felt that they were part of something big and influential by becoming members. They were right.

'Miss Robinson died in 1968 at the age of eighty-nine. A memorial fund was set up in the village, and it was decided to erect a bus shelter at Knapton Green in her memory. On what would have been her ninetieth birthday flowers were placed on her grave by all WI members, taken from their own gardens.

'Sadly, during the 1980s, Knapton and Paston WI was wound up. There was at the time quite a lot of member unrest at what was regarded as an unreasonable increase in the membership fee. There was a suspicion that too much of the fee went towards supporting the national and county organisation, and despite a number of visits from county executive members, the local membership decided to close down.'

The Women's Own, by contrast, continues to flourish. It is run under the broad aegis of the Methodist Church. There was a branch in Knapton from at least 1969, records reveal, but it is possible that some rather looser arrangements existed before then. The meetings were held monthly in the Methodist school room, and a look at the programme for 1987 reveals that while some meetings were devoted to Easter cake decorations, and Christmas floral decorations, others were addressed by the minister, or discussed such topics as Christian social responsibility, or featured a film on the Holy Land. There was time for fun, even so. There was a Mystery Tour in October and 'Any Questions?' in July. Parties were held, sometimes together with the WI, the Methodist Men's Fellowship and Knapton Men's Club. In 1970 the party goers were entertained by the Aylsham Old Tyme Concert Party and in 1978 by the Mundesley Players.

A quote from the 1976 AGM minutes states that the success of the Women's Own is 'generally the result of hard work, cooperation and loyalty, but above all, our success is the contribution of friendship and fellowship that each and every members makes when attending'.

Another group was set up in the 1960s by Margaret Hicks (wife of Herbert Hicks, the chapel Sunday School superintendent) and

Pam Dixon, now Garnham. This they called the Busy Bees. It was aimed at girls between twelve and fourteen and met at Mrs Hicks' house, The Pines. There were weekly meetings and the girls would sew, knit and make toys. A number of contributors to this book took part, including Pearl Hicks, now Eves, Linda Fawkes, now Risebrow, Rene Fawkes, now Turner, Mary Steward, now Lewis, and Sylvia White, now Minns. Before Christmas they would organise a sale in the chapel school room to sell the things they had made. The proceeds were boosted by selling light refreshments and went for gifts of mainly coal or grocery hampers for pensioners in the village.

Rene Fawkes (Turner) (b. 1952) gives an account of the Knapton Friendship club which began in 1970 with sixteen members: '*It was agreed to pay one shilling each to belong, and at each meeting pay sixpence for tea and biscuits or whatever one felt they could afford. Tea, biscuits and milk were to be given each month.*

'*The programmes for the meetings were very varied, including film shows and games, and in 1971 "Mr Gedge from Barclays Bank came and gave a talk on decimal coins. Each person present received a little bag with three coins in." There was a plan for a Club holiday at Caister Holiday Camp, with the club paying half the expenses. Six members decided to take advantage of the arrangement. Meetings between January and March in 1972 had to be cancelled because of power cuts (the three-day week), but later that year outings were arranged to Yarmouth, Blakeney, Thursford organs, Glandford Shell Museum, Wells, a mystery tour via Blickling Hall, and Mannington Hall.*

'*The Club was clearly very successful with a varied programme of popular events. It held its final meeting in October 1976, with a balance of £61.36 in the bank.*'

There were of course also clubs for men in the village and a brief history of the Knapton Men's Club is given in Chapter 1. Gordon Harrison (b. 1942) describes his own time as a member: '*I joined the club when I was fourteen. It was something to do during the long winter nights, and you were always sure of a nice fire and someone to talk to or play darts or billiards with. I started playing in the billiard and darts teams when I was fifteen, and can remember a lot of the people who were members of the club at that time. Some of them were playing in both teams. There were Willy and John Wild, Eddie Lubbock, Stanley and Billy Wright, Bob Wright, Stacy Buck, Henry Wild, Derek and Michael Miller, and Chalky White, one of my old school teachers during my last year at North Walsham School. Other members included Jack and Tony Leeder, Jack Stubley, Mervyn Fawkes, John Wright, Desmond Hooker and Brian Puncher, and I am sure there were a few more.*

'*Some of the seating at that time had been taken from an old coach, but the club gave you a very comfortable feeling and they were very happy times in my teen years. We used to pay a few pence old money for a game of billiards, and when Henry Wild (father of June Wild) appeared, usually around 9 p.m., he would go immediately to the mantelpiece where we would put the money after playing a game. If he did not think there was enough money there, he would say out loud, "Who hasn't paid?"*

'*On match nights, me being one of the younger members I would be asked by Henry to go with him down to his house, and I would help him carry the tea urn and sandwiches back to the club. Teams in the league during my time were Mundesley, Aylsham, Banningham, Thorpe Market, Southrepps, Itteringham, Alby and Matlaske. For some away games we would travel by coach, usually Starlings of North Walsham.*

'*We would play draughts sometimes and play for money – only pennies. We would get a telling off from Henry. He would say, "If a policeman is standing outside, he will hear the money chinking. We haven't got a gaming licence, and we will get had up."*'

Brian Wild (b. 1941) describes summer games of bowls at the homes of Herbert Hicks in Knapton and his brother Wally's home in Trunch. He recalls there being a bowls team which competed at the Haig club in Mundesley for the British Legion Abraham Cup. He writes: '*Also in the summer on Tuesday afternoons we formed a darts club in the Village Hall, so people from the village could come and play darts, cards or just chat to one another. Unfortunately there were just a few of us: myself, my mother, Queenie, my aunt Marjorie, Violet Thompson, Vera Wild, Eddie Lubbock and his brother Gordon and his wife Connie, and Henry White. We would have a cup of tea and biscuits.*'

Some of the activities of the Chapel Men's Fellowship, counterpart to the Women's Own, are described by Richard Wild (b. 1946): *'We would meet once a month in the autumn, winter and spring in the Methodist Chapel. We started with prayers and then we had guest speakers and slide shows on different topics. It would last about one and a half hours. We also arranged to go on outings to see what and how things were made in factories, like the canning factory in North Walsham and Crane's Trailer Factory. Both of these have now gone. We also went to Laurence Scott's Electro-Motors in Norwich, the* Eastern Daily Press *offices and to RAF Coltishall and Cromer Lifeboat Station. We had evening trips to the Broads, when wives, girlfriends and family members could come.'*

There were of course other forms of entertainment available in North Walsham, which could easily be reached by cycle. During the late 1940s and 1950s we would often cycle to the Regal Cinema in the town for a Saturday matinée, leaving our bikes, unlocked, outside the confectioner's, Paynes, opposite the cinema. Part of the ritual would be to go into the shop before the show to buy Maltesers or Smarties. Another was to have a good look at who was in the back row, and with whom. The North Walsham Regal was on a different film distribution circuit from its counterpart in Cromer, where I went to see Bill Haley and the Comets in *Rock Around The Clock* in the mid-1950s. I was hugely embarrassed by the school friend with me, as she screamed and tore at the seats in her enthusiasm.

During the 1950s there were outdoor square-dancing sessions, with American country music and a caller, and these were extremely popular. Dances took place at The Oaks dance hall in North Walsham on Saturday nights, with a live group. These were very much more interesting in the summer when the town was full of university students, often from Ireland, working at the canning factory or the Bird's Eye freezing factory just outside the town, although we did not lack for young men as there was an RAF camp for National Servicemen at Trimingham, near Mundesley.

For the theatre and classical music we had to get to Norwich, which was impossible except at weekends. Even so, somehow with school groups, overnight stays with aunts and lifts from adults, we managed to get some sort of taste of cultural life, and my life was changed for ever when I heard a performance of Bach's B Minor Mass at St Andrew's Hall in Norwich in 1954. Small wonder that when I got to Oxford I was completely overwhelmed by the rich cultural experience on offer, not least because I could actually get to taste it.

TEN

THE WARS

The period covered by this book encompasses both World Wars. The accounts written by contributors say very little about action in the First World War and, perhaps surprisingly, not much more about action in the Second. We have memories of the start of the Second World War: a wartime wedding, work as a land-girl, the Home Guard, the Knapton 'bomb', memories of evacuees in the village and the voices of two of them, and a first-hand account of military action at the end of the war. Otherwise the memories are domestic ones: the make-do-and mend culture, food rationing, travel restrictions, mines on the beach, the appearance of servicemen – British and American – in the quiet Norfolk countryside, and the sensation that, for the duration of the war, the world was turned upside down. Knapton and Norfolk were never the same again, but the scale of change was not evident except in hindsight.

The county of Norfolk, being so close to occupied Europe, played a key role in the Second World War. In 1939 there were five operational airfields: at Bircham Newton, Feltwell, Marham, Watton and West Raynham. By the end of the war there were thirty-seven. The closest base to Knapton was RAF Coltishall. There were seventeen USAAF airfields in Norfolk. This meant that from our earliest age we were accustomed to seeing American servicemen in our market towns and in Norwich. The construction of the airfields was a massive building project. John Capes's father was involved in work at Coltishall and Norfolk's hitherto quiet roads must have buzzed with construction vehicles of every kind. In 1940 there was considered to be a real possibility of invasion, hence the construction of coastal defences and the barricading and mining of beaches. It must have felt as if Norfolk was in the front line and yet the county was deemed an area safe enough to receive evacuees with

Norwich and Yarmouth being classified as neutral, i.e. in danger of some bombing. Evacuation of this first wave of children began in 1939, as Willie Wild reports (see below), followed by more during the course of 1940. The last wave of evacuation of children from London came in the summer of 1944 when Hitler's flying bombs began to hit London. Josephine Langham and Barbara Dixon, who were part of this evacuation, give their accounts later in this chapter.

The fathers of Kathleen Johnson and Roger Dixon served in the First World War, as did Herbert Fawkes, father of Ronald and Roy Fawkes. His brother later died in the trenches. Knapton's war memorial in the churchyard shows the names of seven men lost in the First World War.

In Arthur Amis's autobiography *From Dawn to Dusk* he writes movingly of a generation lost to Trunch: *'One Sunday evening in chapel, in November 1915, stands out vividly. I shall never forget it. Several young men who had been called up for war service were home on leave. I did not realise that it was before they were to go overseas. Four of them had helped to teach in the chapel Sunday School. I knew them well. It was a sort of prayer-meeting type of service. The chapel was full. One of the hymns was "Stand up, stand up for Jesus". At the end they sang, as I have never heard it sung like that again since, "God be with you until we meet again." Those men's names are on the memorial stone in the churchyard. They never came back. Trunch was never the same. Fourteen lovely men were taken from us. The stone says "Faithful unto death".'*

John Capes (b. 1930) was born in Knapton, where his grand-parents Herbert and Libby Wright lived in The Street, although he and his family lived in Paston. He has the Service Records of two of his great-uncles who were killed on active service in the First World War. He writes that *'the records tell me far more about the two great-uncles I never knew than about their brothers and sisters that I did know'*.

Herbert Capes was born near Aylsham, Norfolk, in 1892. He enlisted in the Norfolk Regiment at Norwich on 12 September 1914, just six weeks after the outbreak of war. He was first posted to Felixstowe, and then on 11 October 1915 to France – presumably, as John Capes writes, *'when the battalion of the Norfolks he was in went* over. At some time he became a transport driver. There is no mention of where he was stationed while in France, probably for security reasons. He was reported missing on 12 August 1916, and his father (as next of kin) was notified of this on 31 August 1916. The final entries on his Service Record state that he is regarded as having died on active service on 12 August 1916, place unknown, and that fact is notified to his family on what appears to be 21 June 1917. Presumably the delay in notification was to ascertain if a body was found anywhere and also to see if he was reported as a prisoner of war. He was awarded the 1914–15 Star, the British War Medal and Victory Medal … These three medals are the ones known as Pip, Squeak and Wilfred, after some famous cartoon characters of the time. As there is no grave Herbert's name is recorded on the Memorial to the Missing of the Somme at Thiepval, near Albert.

'His brother Albert was born in Cawston, Norfolk, in 1893. He enlisted in the Norfolks in December 1915, was put on the Reserve, then mobilised in January 1916 into the Seventh Battalion … He was promoted to Corporal in August 1917. The records do not indicate when he went to France. In both July and September 1917 he had scabies … From 3 to 13 October 1917 he was on leave to the UK – presumably to home. The final entry in his Service Record is that he was regarded as having died on 22 October 1917, place not stated … He was awarded the British War Medal and Victory Medal … As there is no grave Albert's name is recorded on the Memorial Wall at Tyne Cot Cemetery at Zonnebeke, near Ieper in Belgium; this would indicate that he was probably killed in what was officially known as the Third Battle of Ypres which has come to be more commonly known as the Battle of Passchendaele.'

George Dixon (1898–1972), uncle of Roger Dixon, wrote home from Germany to his mother in Knapton on 1 March 1918: 'I was pleased to hear from you and to hear you are well as this leaves me the same. We are having lovely weather here. Yes, I can often picture you at home and wish I was there with you.

'Still all the same, have nothing to grumble at so far, if everything keep the same as it is now and have been, I don't mind being here as far as that go, only it is a long way from home. We get treated better here

*than we do at Woolwich so hope you are comfortable, also father and
don't worry about me. So Cox is home again, he is lucky. I shall have to
tell Bertie* [George's brother and the father of Roger Dixon] *to buck
up and write more to you when I write to him again, he ought to have
more time than me.*

'*Am glad you drive the donkey. Suppose Hubert* [his brother] *very
often go to Walsham … You are lucky to have the hens lay, we can get
plenty of eggs here 5d each if we buy them.*

'*Yes P.* [a man in Knapton] *ought to have joined instead of swank-
ing about … Them sort of people are lucky, can go home when they like,
still roll on if everything go all right I shall have some leave about the
end of May if the war is not over.*

'*Have a good job now, time* [while] *another chap is on leave, am
driving a pair of horses and a waggon, that suit me a treat, tell father
both horses are as big as old Duke he had … when he was on his own.*

'*Well dear mother, I think this is all for this time, hope you write as
much as you can and hope to hear from you soon.*

'*Best love to you and father and all the rest, from your ever loving
son, George.*'

When George came home from the war, he went to work
for Mr Purdy senior at Green Farm, Paston, and proceeded
to do other things, including a stint at the gas works in
Mundesley, as a green-keeper at the Mundesley Golf Course
and as a small-holder in Knapton, taking over his uncle Alfred
Dixon's holding.

By the time of the Second World War many in Knapton were
in the reserved occupation of agriculture, although some enlisted.
Roger Dixon's maternal grandfather lived in the USA and he
remembers the family receiving food parcels from him. Leslie
Watts, father of Brian, Josephine and Patrick, went into the Navy.
His brother, my father Jack Watts, went into the Marines. Tommy
Coe, son of the station master and a roadman by trade, served with
the Royal Norfolks, and his wife made shells at Coopers in King's
Lynn. Herbert Fawkes was a Special Constable. His daughter
Megan served in the WAAFs and his son Ronald was in the Fire

Service. Mrs Johnson, in addition to her full time job as head-mistress of the school, joined the WVS. The fathers of Kathleen Johnson, Willie Puncher, Janet, Ruth, Eric and Mary Steward, William Stubley, Barbara and Brenda Wilkins, and John Wright were in the Home Guard. Others' fathers were in the ARP, including Ivy and Grace Burlingham's father, and Pamela and Barbara Dixon's. The Women's Institute worked at full pelt, led by Miss Robinson, knitting for the troops, making jams and preserves, and collecting salvage. Ministry of Information film shows were staged in the Parish Room. I recall one of a very cross looking Myra Hess performing 'Jesus Joy of Man's Desiring', so cross indeed that I, aged three or four, was moved to ask the whole audience what had made her so angry. No one answered my question, but I knew she was cross because of the War.

Several of the writers of this book describe, variously, a bomb or a mine falling in Knapton in a field along the Mundesley Road, where the crater can still be discerned. I cannot be sure if what Llewellyn Kirk (b. 1930) describes is the same event, but he was certainly an eyewitness to the incident he describes here: '*The plane came down in Knapton. We were in the church choir and the Rev. Prichard was about to finish his sermon when there was an almighty roar and then an explosion. A plane had gone down and exploded in a field halfway down Wallage's Loke (parallel to the Mundesley Road). When the service had finished I got on my bike and went down there. My father and two uncles were already there, also RAF personnel. It was an American trainer aircraft. Two airmen were blown to pieces. There was a doctor and nurse clearing up the remains. I did not fancy food for a day or two after.*'

Philip Almey who lived in Paston can remember shrapnel flying past his back door and getting lodged in a gate from which it was never removed.

The holiday camp on the cliffs between Mundesley and Paston was used by troops. Many people can remember seeing German planes going over to bomb Norwich and seeing the sky reddened by the bombing raids on Yarmouth. Pamela Dixon (Garnham)

(b. 1935) remembers a doodlebug *'one evening when we were walking back from my aunt's at Paston Green to our house next to Paston Village Hall. A flying bomb came right overhead. It crashed somewhere near Norwich.'*

John Capes (b. 1930) writes: *'In 1939 I was eight, but I can remember quite clearly the outbreak of the war. As 3 September was the first Sunday of the month, Sunday School was in the form of a children's service in the Parish Church, starting at 10 a.m. and lasting about half an hour. The Parish Church is some distance from the bottom of Paston Street where I lived, and I probably arrived home at about 11 a.m. I remember dad then saying, "Now I want you two boys to be quiet as Mr Chamberlain is going to speak on the wireless in a few minutes." I think I vaguely knew that there was unease about the situation in Europe , that Germany had invaded Poland a few days earlier and that children were being evacuated from London, which meant that something could happen in this country … We gathered round the wireless to hear what was going to happen. I can remember Mr Chamberlain saying what have now become rather famous words: "Consequently this country is at war with Germany." In rather typical fashion, dad said something like, "That's that then, now we know where we stand," and went off outside to finish his Sunday morning jobs of cleaning the boots and shoes and chopping kindling. A little later he came in to say that he had found a suitable place in the garden to build an air raid shelter.'*

In the event the shelter was never built, as Mr Capes realised that a small village like Paston was unlikely to be bombed.

John Capes continues his account of the war with descriptions of the role of home defence. *'People either volunteered or were appointed to do things. Dad and Charlie Francis, the shopkeeper, became Air Raid Precaution (ARP) wardens. Their main duty was to enforce the blackout. I think they took alternate evenings and if they saw a light showing would sometimes knock on the door to explain where the light was, but probably more usually shouted, "Put that light out!" In winter dad would go out early, but in summer, especially with double summertime, he had to be out quite late … Mr Beck, the Hall Farm steward, became the Special Constable. A Home Guard unit was formed in Paston. Mr Almey from Poplar Farm was the officer … They trained on a Sunday morning.'*

'Soon soldiers became commonplace. The Army took over Mundesley Holiday Camp, the Grand Hotel in Mundesley and Eden Hall children's home in Bacton. We saw them marching around the roads, we saw them creeping along hedges and ditches as they did field training, their lorries often buzzed along the main road through the village. It must have been in summer 1940 that the government was concerned about food supplies and authorised the use of Army lorries to enable the harvest to be brought in quickly. Some were used on Hall Farm, but I don't think Mr Purdy at Green Farm had any. My friends and I used to frequent Hall Farm more as their land was around the village, so that year instead of riding the horses at harvest time we rode in the cabs of the Army lorries.'

John Capes writes of village activities to support the war effort, including National Savings which in Paston were organised by Miss Dunell, sister of Mrs Lee of Footpath House. *'There were special Savings Weeks with specific names. The two I remember were Salute the Soldier Week and Wings for Victory Week … A target was set for each place in proportion to its population, and I think we always achieved our target … During one of these Savings Weeks a prize of a wooden seat was offered, I think, by the Smallburgh istrict Council, as it then was, for the parish in the district raising the most money relative to its population. Paston won the seat and for many years it stood near the crossroads at the top of The Street … On the back of the seat was carved the inscription "Set you here an mardle" – mardle being the Norfolk word for gossip.*

'Mrs Lee herself organised the village children into fund-raising. There was a meeting of most of the children to decide what could be done and what to call the fund – and so the Paston Spitfire Fund was formed.'

A committee of about eight children was appointed, John Capes being one of the younger members. *'We would aim to have Christmas sales of work, an annual concert and an annual fête or garden party.'* The children worked hard, making items for sales of work and running concerts and fêtes, and their efforts were recognised nationally. *'On Sunday evenings there was a programme on the radio … reporting on fundraising around the country, and after each of our events one of the committee would write a letter to the BBC saying how much we had raised. So we all listened eagerly and then there it was: "The children of Paston in Norfolk have raised another £100 from a sale of work for their Spitfire Fund." We were so proud.'*

John Capes, whose father worked on defence projects like gun emplacements in the early part of the war before he was called up in 1943, recalls seeing a German plane *'fairly close. A group of us had just started on the way home from Edingthorpe School on a dull dismal wintry day, in the winter of 1939–40. Then we heard the sound of an aeroplane coming from the North Walsham direction and from its throbbing noise we quickly suspected that it was a German one. Then suddenly it appeared through a gap in the clouds, probably about 500 feet up. We could easily see the Swastika markings and from the silhouettes which had been published in the papers recognised it as a Dornier, a 17, I think. As it was on its own it was probably on some kind of reconnaissance mission or it had got lost.'*

He recalls seeing and hearing bombing raids on Norwich, and a local tragedy at Mundesley. *'One evening the twins Alan and Roy Riley and Ernie Whitworth were playing football near the minefield that had been laid along the cliffs to the north of the village and the ball went over the security fence around the mines. Roy and Ernie climbed over the fence to retrieve the ball and both were killed when one of them stepped on a mine.'*

In 1942 John passed the scholarship and went to the Paston Grammar School in North Walsham, where he joined the Army Cadets in 1944. *'We had uniforms and we were supposed to wear boots. With dad in the Army, mum thought it silly to spend money on boots for me to be used one afternoon a week, something she could ill afford. Luckily grandad Wright had kept a pair of his old work boots … and they fitted me. We paraded on Thursday afternoons and did drill on the playground, or on a piece of ground near the Town [M&GN Station]. We did route marches around the local roads; we learned to shoot on the .22 rifle range. We learned to handle rifles and operate a Bren gun.'*

I was born in January 1940. I do have memories of the war, although they are perforce extremely patchy. But I do recall the fear and worry, transmitted no doubt from my mother who was understandably extremely anxious all the time that my father was away in the Marines. I can remember the sense of desolation when my mother and I watched him, from the back of our house, walk over the fields to the station on his way back to the war. I can remember being given a child's gas mask which seemed to me the stuff of nightmares, shaped as it was like a frog (I thought) and which you had to put over your face and head. The sound of the air raid siren and of aircraft overhead brought a sense of dread. In the back garden was our shelter, which took the form of a grass-covered mound. My mother would not have had the least idea of how to get into it, indeed it might have required a mechanical digger.

Two of my aunts were living in Norwich, which was badly and frequently bombed. Nevertheless, my mother took me to stay with them, for company, and again we had fear-filled nights in the cellar of 100 Constitution Hill, where one of them lived. One husband was in the RAF and the other on a minesweeper. My father's brother Leslie was in the Navy. My eldest aunt's son Ras was a gunner in the RAF. Early in the war he was shot down and killed over Holland. (Years later, a Dutch farm student came to work in Knapton at White House Farm. He came from the village where Ras had been buried in a war grave and sent photographs of it to my aunt. She was overwhelmed, not least by the extraordinary coincidence, but also by gratitude.)

Periodically the fields behind our house were filled with slivers of silver paper, which had been dropped from planes to obscure radar detection. My mother assured me that the paper, which looked to me like Christmas decorations, was in some way poisonous, and should not be touched. The beach at Mundesley was barricaded off to deter invasion and the cliffs adjoining were mined – not that reassuring for fun on the beach! My mother's own family were in Sheffield, so she was also extremely anxious for their welfare. Her sister's husband was in the RAF for the whole of the war, in Italy, and came home only when it was over. Her mother wrote to her every Sunday without fail from Sheffield, and the postman Mr Brighton brought the letter on Mondays, always saying, 'A letter from mum.'

There were other, slightly brighter, memories, although some have been passed down to me. I obviously could not myself remember one of my aunts and my mother giving a lift to a soldier in uniform, one of them steering the car and working the pedals, the other changing the gears. When they asked the soldier what he did in civilian life, he replied, 'I am a London bus driver.' I do remember neighbours killing a pig and home-made sausages being handed over, and going on the back of my mother's bicycle to collect farm butter from Witton, about three miles away. I can also remember us queuing in the Parish Room for the reissue of ration books and the introduction of Woolton Pies – although these were regarded with such extreme derision by people in the village it may be the re-telling that I remember. There was certainly a recipe for Woolton Pie in war-time cookery books, which involved vegetables and no meat. Those sold in the Parish Room did contain something resembling meat, so perhaps were not true Woolton Pies. They were however unmistakably government issue! My mother was a great radio fan, and listened to *Workers' Playtime* and *ITMA*. Her mother could do a mean imitation of Gracie Fields, singing 'Sally, Pride of our Alley', and loved the *ITMA* catchphrases like 'Shall I do you now sir?' and the immortal words of Mona Lot, 'It's being so cheerful as keeps me going.' I do still use 'Don't forget the diver', although it is to the increasing incomprehension on the part of any listeners.

Knapton village should have been unthreatening to my mother, familiar as it was to her and to me. But one night she forgot to put up the blackout. There was a terrifying tap on the windows and the face of Mr Fawkes, Special Constable, could be seen in the darkness mouthing, no doubt, 'Don't you know there's a war on?' For a very short time we had a land-girl named Sonia billeted on us. I have no memory of how long she was there, or why she left, but the war was full of unexplained events in any case.

When it finally ended VE Day was celebrated in the village with a barn dance. We went along to take flowers, my arrangements of marigolds in a jam jar, which unsurprisingly were placed behind a door jamb. We also went down to the dance itself for a short time and I can remember seeing one of the most glamorous girls in the village, Thelma Smith, whirling round the dance floor and looking wonderful. When we came back, in the half dark, some soldiers in uniform walking down the street asked my mother the way to the dance and in reply she screamed and ran indoors, which was not reassuring. Small wonder then – as I mentioned before – that when the General Election result was announced in July 1945 and my mother said 'They've got rid of Mr Churchill', I was plunged again into dread, believing that this meant that the war was not over after all.

For Llewellyn Kirk (b. 1930), the moment when his father was called up is still vivid in his mind. *'My father Robert Kirk was in the 5th Battalion TA Norfolk Regiment. I was with him when he worked for Geaves, the farmer in Mundesley. We were in the harvest field and a dispatch rider came and told him he had been called up, two weeks before war was declared … The battalion moved to Weybourne* [on the North Norfolk coast]. *They thought the Germans would invade there, since there were no cliffs. They shot a plane down, and it contained maps and photos of all the trenches and gun emplacements in the area. So that was what the airship had been doing over Norfolk! So they all had to be changed.*

'After a while my father was transferred to the 1st Battalion as a sergeant. He was lucky as the 5th got taken to Singapore. He was sent to Chelsea Barracks in London with the Guards. They got bombed badly and his nerves went. After being in Shenley Hospital he was discharged from the Army and any other military service.

'He worked for Miss Robinson for a while. Then he joined the Home Guard in Knapton and got made up to Second Lieutenant. I used to go

round with them as Chief Scout. Other villages used to be the enemy, so I'd hide in the hedge and run back and tell the Knapton crowd that they were coming.'

Llewellyn had been given *'a rusty First World War sword by a neighbour, Lou Watts. I used to take it to bed with me to protect my mother from the Germans during the time my father was in the Army. When he came home we went to Mundesley beach and I went to jump on a heap of sand. He caught me just in time: it was a German mine washed ashore. The coastguards cleared the beach and blew it up with rifles.'*

Willie Wild (1913–83) wrote down some of his memories of serving in the Knapton Home Guard in the Second World War. *'We had been told over the radio that an announcement would be made at 11 a.m. by the Prime Minister, Neville Chamberlain. We waited for that time to come and he finally said, "We are at war with Germany." We wondered what would happen next. There were to be no car hooters, no church bells, no lights showing after dark. I had to make black-out frames to fit all windows, which were held in place with large wooden buttons. It was not long before gas-masks were handed out to all Knapton people in the then church rooms* [the Parish Room].

'All able-bodied people not called up for military service were expected to join one of many other services in civil life. Ladies played a big part as well as being housewives.

'I was a farm worker so was exempt from war service. I became a member of the Home Guard, today called "Dad's Army". We did night watch in Knapton, at a post we called S. church, and at Bacton Wood Mill [a sheep farm], *9 p.m. to 6 p.m., back to work at 7 a.m., transport, cycles.*

'Sunday a.m., practice with regular Army at Runton Range, cleaning Lee Enfield guns full of grease, Worstead sandpit, drive rounds overhead.

'Most sign posts were removed. What is now the Bacton gas site was one large field and trenches were made across it in both directions to stop enemy planes from landing.

'In September [1939] *a large number of evacuees came to Norfolk from London. My wife and I took in a lad about nine from the East End. By name he was Ronnie Wright. He was not socially groomed as you are*

today. His table manners were nil but soon improved. We lived in a small cottage and when our daughter was born in August 1940 there was no room for Ronnie so he went back home. We knew nothing of his mother, as an aunt came to collect him, and took him home without a word of thanks.

'But the war carried on. I saw planes in the sea and several on land, and bullet cases falling all around while I was at work. Italian prisoners of war were brought to the farm picking potatoes. The person in charge was a Mr Moxen, who after the war had a hairdressing shop in King's Arms Street in North Walsham.

'The Army were also brought in to help with the harvest. I was sorry for them as they had no idea how to use a fork (not their fault) and they soon had blisters on their hands.

'I saw thousands of planes go out to raid in the early morning, and when they came home in the afternoon we could stand on the cliff top and look from left to right, planes as far as anyone could see.'

Queenie Bane (Wild) (b. 1917) was a wartime bride. Her daughter-in-law June Wild writes: *'Queenie married Sidney Wild on a wet and windy afternoon in February 1941, at Knapton church. She wore a navy coat with a tie belt, and navy hat and a patterned dress. Queenie's sister, Marjorie, was the bridesmaid.*

'Because of the war it was a shortened service and no bells could be rung. From the church they went to the Parish Room for the reception for family and close friends. The family had all helped to make sandwiches for the guests. While they were in the Parish Room planes could be heard in the distance, so the reception did not last long as everyone wanted to get home safely.

'During the war Sidney was in the Royal Engineers on the inland waterways in London. He would get home on leave for one or two weeks.

'Queenie and her family would have the wireless on during an air raid, but they purposely did not listen to the news during the war.'

Olive Wild (Webster) (b. 1919) also married early in the war. *'I got married in October 1939 and was one of the first group to register for work in ammunitions or on the land. I went to work for Mr Harold Kidner, who farmed at Easton Lodge and Colton (near Norwich). It was where my late husband Vic was working as a tractor driver.*

'One of the jobs I had to do was getting docks out of the cornfields with a short-handled two-pronged fork. I then had to put them in a bag which I carried on my back. I worked from 9 a.m. to 4 p.m. with a half-hour break for lunch, which was red beet sandwiches.

'Less than a year later Mr Kidner asked me if I would like to be cook at the house. Two servants had been called up and he knew I loved cooking. I worked the same hours. I would pluck and dress pheasants as well.

'When the Kidners were away on holiday, and the nanny and children were left at home, Vic and I would sleep at the house. We thought we were in heaven as the house had electricity and our cottage did not. We were there for six years, until my daughter Ann was born.

'I remember the blackouts, food and coal rationing and clothing coupons. Used to do a lot of knitting. When the butcher came round we would be allowed a half pound of sausages! We kept chickens for eggs and meat, and would make a lot of meals with potatoes and rice. Sometimes when we had run out of rations we just had toast for our main meal.'

Nancy Miller (Lynch) (b. 1932) writes of the war: 'I do not remember much happening. At night when Norwich was being bombed we could see burning and once a bomb landed in a field near Knapton, on the Mundesley Road. The crater was huge but only damaged the field. We shared a dugout with Mr and Mrs Walter Watts when the raids were on and had biscuits and drinks and blankets to keep us warm.

'My father was in the Home Guard so he would walk the village to make sure everyone was safe. So many children were evacuated from London that we had to split the school day. Mornings were for us and the afternoons for the evacuees.'

Roger Dixon (b. 1933) has slightly different memories of the school-sharing arrangements from Nancy's. 'We used to use the school alternate days with the evacuees. We would be in the school one day and the Parish Room the next. Miss Doughty the infant teacher was getting nowhere with teaching me my sums. Then along came a teacher evacuated from London, a Jewish lady named Miss Cohen. She managed to get through to me and I began to understand. If we were kept separate, how I came to be taught by Miss Cohen I cannot remember.'

Kathleen Johnson (Suckling) (b. 1936), whose mother was headmistress of Knapton School, writes: *'One group of evacuees arrived in Knapton from Bethnal Green very early in the war. We took in twin girls. (Their brother, who had left Liverpool Street on a different train, ended up in North Walsham.) Their teacher came with them and their lessons were held in the Parish Room. After quite a short time, with the threat of a German invasion, Norfolk was considered too dangerous a place for these London children, and so they were moved on. My mother thought that if Norfolk was too dangerous for Londoners it was too dangerous for me so I was sent to Yorkshire with my grandmother to stay with relatives. We were there for almost a year and I came home with a very broad Yorkshire accent.*

'In 1944 with the flying bomb raids on London we had more evacuees in the village. I can remember one or two older girls joining our classes. I can remember one girl quite clearly as she had a serious problem with BO and always smelled of boiled milk, poor thing. Also, a group of mothers with babies and small children arrived in Knapton. They had come from Leytonstone and were absolutely horrified and frightened in the village. No shops, no pubs, no street lights and wide open spaces. Within a very short time they decided it was better to die in London than die of boredom in Knapton. One family did stay and a lifelong friendship developed. Every year a large black London taxi was seen outside the house of Jack and Nellie Kirk as the London family enjoyed a country holiday. Nellie and the London lady remained friends until the end of their lives.'

Josephine Hourahane (Langham) (b. 1936) and her brother Edward were among the second wave of evacuees who came to Norfolk in 1944. She explains why. *'In the summer of 1944 German VIs and V2s were used to bombard the British mainland. My brother Edward and I were two of thousands of children moved from the war-torn London suburb of Worcester Park. We had an unforgettably long train journey with no stops, from Epsom to Stockport. Our billet there turned out to be unsuitable.*

'Luckily for us, our parents were old friends of Mrs Johnson, head-mistress of Knapton School. So when she heard of our problem she offered to have us join her family at the School House in Knapton. No more

sleeping rough in cupboards, home-erected Morrison shelters or school shelters. We loved the fresh air, open fields and especially Knapton School. Looking back over that year we considered ourselves very lucky evacuees. Our parents must have been very relieved to know we were safe and out of earshot of the dreaded air raid sirens.

'Knapton School was a lovely village school, red brick country design in a perfect setting in which to roam and play safely. Mrs Johnson was an all-round expert. She played the piano for all our singing, organised and taught us country dancing and PE. Her gardening skills she passed on to the boys especially; each had a plot to cultivate. I was very proud of the raffia and wool slippers I made in the craft lessons. I can still knit on four needles thanks to her. Of course she taught a whole range of subjects to a full class of mixed ages, seven to fourteen, and mixed abilities. But we all made progress. Before this regular teaching I had spent most of my school days in the air raid shelter.

'Before evacuation our lives were dominated by air raids, sirens, doodlebugs, gas masks and the all clears, but I cannot say I was ever frightened. As I was only three when war broke out I knew no other way of life. Our parents never left us on our own, neither were we hungry. My mother had to work when we were evacuated and among her many jobs was one in a bakery. So she would often send a parcel of various cakes and rolls to Knapton.

'We had to live on rations but had milk delivered from Mr Puncher, fresh vegetables from the garden and a weekly delivery of all other groceries from North Walsham. Friday was baking day.

'Valentine's Day was observed in the School House. There would be a knock at the front door. No one would be there, but there was a small gift left for all of us. We discovered years later that uncle Arthur (Mr Johnson) rigged up a scheme whereby he could rattle the letter box without leaving the back kitchen. We all thought it was Saint Valentine and were thrilled.'

Barbara Dixon (Jarvis) (b. 1938) was also one of the 1944 evacuees. She writes: *'I was only one year old when war broke out and until the age of six I lived in London and slept in a Morrison shelter. This was like a large metal table with wire round the sides, rather like a cage. I had a small bed made up on the floor to one side. I can remember lying there and looking through a small hole in the blanket to see the search-lights criss-crossing the sky over our house. I woke up one night when the house across the street was hit. It had a big hole in the roof and was on fire. There were a lot of people running up and down the street.*

'*I remember being taken to Liverpool Street station when I was six. I shall always remember the very high grey walls outside the station, but I had to no idea what was going to happen to me. My coat had a label with my name on. I also had my Micky Mouse gas mask in a little box on my shoulder. The train was full of children of all ages. Lots of us were crying and it was very noisy. My grandad gave me his favourite pencil, red one end, blue the other, so that stopped the tears. A bus full of us ended up at Paston Village Hall, where all of us children were taken to different homes. Mr and Mrs Dixon took me in. We lived in Paston for two years, then dad bought the Shop House in Knapton. We moved there when I was eight, and they adopted me, so I never went back to London.'*

June Wild (b. 1951) has kept letters and cards from her father Henry, which he sent home from his time in the Royal Artillery during the war. His first letter stated: '*I have arrived in France at last, but I cannot give you any address to write to, not yet. Please give my love to all at home, and tell them I am OK. Cigs, 50 Players for 20 francs, about 2s 3d. Some of the countryside here reminds me of home.*'

Like many soldiers, Henry kept a diary:

14 October 1944
France. People looking very untidy in regard to clothing, and the children underfed so they look very poor. We get on all right with them, they are always asking for chocs and sweets. Tonight free show given by ENSA.

16 October 1944
Sunday. Still no letters getting through from home. How is [their neighbour] *Harry Sexton? I bet he is sitting by the fire now with his* News of the World *and swearing about the War. I*

have just been after my morning cup of tea before dinner, as we get it issued every morning, as we can't buy tea outside the camp, can get fresh coffee but not much good. Wish I was going up to Trunch Crown for a pint.

24 October 1944

Belgium. The towns are nice and clean, plenty of stuff to buy, ice cream, tins of fruit. People friendly, a lot speak English, gave good welcome when we arrived.

11 November 1944

Holland. We had a parade here this morning, it being Armistice Day. Some of us were picked out to represent our regiment on the parade. It was quite a good do, the streets were packed with people and round the cenotaph.

21 November 1944

A lot of rain today, mud everywhere. There are no shops where I have been the last few places, what were houses and shops have been knocked about and the people cleared out, a lot of their stuff has been taken [by the Germans?]. *I shall have to try to get you a pair of those clogs the Dutch wear.* [He did.]

29 November 1944

I am writing this in a farmhouse, a few of us go in most nights as there is a nice fire going, a table where I can do some writing, and have a game of cards. The people of the house are in the same room and are OK to us.

9 December 1944

Letter and parcel arrive from home. Snow has started to fall. In the house where I am living there is a little boy, four years old, who since we have been here has been learning to speak English. He is doing OK. He tries to clean our boots for us, we are going to buy him a present for Christmas. He can smoke cigs all right, all the children can, out here.

21 December 1944

[No location given.] *All the people here are getting ready for Christmas, trees being taken in. Not much in the shops in the way of presents. What they have got is very expensive. People are looking forward to Christmas.*

Christmas Day 1944

I had a decent dinner today. Some cigars, fruit, chocs and sweets also in my ration. I spent the day with four of the boys, did our own cooking, everything worked out OK.

28 February 1945

I have met some boys from near home up this way. One had been home on leave, it was nice to see someone and be able to talk about the old district.

12 March 1945

I am on guard tonight, which is not so good, as there will not be much sleep. You are lucky to be able to get pork, we nearly always get mutton. I read in the papers that you are not getting so much rice, and that it cost you more.

18 April 1945

Coming up here today we had crowds of people to greet us as we have just cleared out Jerry from here.

26 April 1945

Get on well with the people in this part of Holland. They are always asking for cigs, chocs, and soap, the kiddies bring up eggs in exchange for them, that is how I get my suppers.

7 May 1945

Holland. Since I have been in Holland, I have been with the Canadian Army, some of the time it was rough.

25 May 1945

Germany. We must not have anything to do with the people, must not even speak to the children. If we are caught doing so we are put on a charge. [June notes that a later letter stated that they were now allowed to speak to the Germans.]

6 June 1945

Germany. We are looking after a lot of Russians, Polish, Dutch, French, and Belgians who were slave workers in Germany, men, women and children. Believe me, there are some bad cases among them, what a time they must have had here Every day we are seeing hundreds of people, walking, cycling, a few cars and lorries packed out, making their way back, at night sleeping by the side of the road.

3 August 1945
I have had an interview with an officer today, as some of us have to go on a course of carpentry and bricklaying for Civvy Street, ready for demob time.

Henry was demobbed on 22 October 1945. He came home. Three Knapton men commemorated on the War Memorial in the churchyard did not. They were Frederick Watts, Thomas Wood and Sydney Woollsey.

Like all other communities, Knapton was deeply affected by the war on the home front, although its near self-sufficiency in food, fuel and water supply, and entertainment, not to mention spirit, stood it in good stead. Strong leadership from Miss Robinson and Mrs Johnson, church and chapel leaders and others was also very much in evidence.

Food rationing had somewhat belatedly been tried at the very end of the First World War. As the threat of the Second World War loomed in July 1939 a government leaflet was issued, called 'Your Food in Wartime'. This advised householders to lay in stocks of canned meat, fish and milk, sugar, tea and cocoa, flour and suet and plain biscuits. Obviously with no fridges and freezers, and household budgets in most cases fully stretched, advice needed to be limited and low key.

The leaflet warned that soon after the outbreak of a war, certain foods would be brought under a rationing scheme – meat, bacon and ham, sugar, butter and margarine 'in the first instance'.

Identity cards were issued in September 1939, 46 million in total. Failure to produce your card was an offence. The leaflet explained that people would need to apply for ration books, one for each member of the household, by taking their identity cards to a local Food Office. They then had to register with a retail shop for each of the rationed foods. My own family registered with Rusts, grocers in North Walsham where they had always dealt, and with Bloom's the butchers, who had for years done business with our family.

Rationing began in January 1940. The rations allowed in the first instance were four ounces of bacon or ham, four ounces of butter and twelve ounces of sugar per person each week. Meat was rationed according to value, 1s 10d per person per week, which explains why sausages and offal were highly sought after, as you got more for your money and ration. People in manual occupations were allowed more rations. Children under five were eligible for free orange juice and cod liver oil. Malt was also issued to children thought to be in need of extra nourishment. I can still remember the taste of the orange juice which came in flat rectangular bottles with a blue label. Apparently the juice used the peel and pith of the orange as well as its flesh and juice, and it had a distinctive and not unpleasant flavour. The same could not be said of cod-liver oil, which was rammed down the protesting throats of small children in millions of households across the country.

A points system was also introduced. This applied mainly to tinned goods: a tin of salmon might be thirty-two points, whereas a tin of pilchards might be two points. Kathleen Johnson (Suckling) (b. 1936) writes: *Jill Watts's mother frequently joked about Sunday tea. She often came to our house for this meal as her husband was serving in the Royal Marines and with a small baby she enjoyed the company. She told me many times how she and my grandmother would have long discussions as to what they would prepare for the meal. In the end it was usually tinned pilchards, as nothing else was available.'*

In 1942 sweets and chocolates were rationed. There was a points system which in theory allowed people to choose what they preferred. Chocolate was either milk or plain, and that was that. In practice the whole idea of choice between different kinds of food was, in my recollection, something which only gradually returned after the war. Thus butter, margarine, tea, cheese and even biscuits, were, I thought, generic terms. It was the arrival of Stork margarine in the shops in the early 1950s that made me realise they were not, and that there were in fact different makes of tea and marge, and even different kinds of cheese, not just red, white and processed.

Beer and bread were not rationed during the war, although the price of beer increased enormously. Bread was put on the ration for a couple of years in 1946, as is explained elsewhere in this book, causing absolute fury among housewives and the population in general. Many disliked the wartime loaf, which used a wholemeal flour. There is no doubt, however, that it was more nourishing and healthy than over-refined white flour, although it has taken many decades for it also to be regarded as more fashionable.

The whole matter of feeding the nation in wartime was obviously of vital importance, given the interruption of imported food supplies on which the nation had been allowed to become over-reliant before the war. It was Lord Woolton as Minister of Food who presided over the great structure of the Ministry of Food, which by 1943 was employing 50,000 civil servants. Lord Woolton gave freely of his culinary advice to the housewife, in the form of exhortation and even recipes. This was Big Government.

In 1942, for example, the Ministry of Food made it clear that Christmas pudding and mince meat would have to be made with prunes, potatoes, carrots, stale breadcrumbs, apples and spices, instead of the usual ingredients. Such variants are uncannily similar to the achingly fashionable recipes printed in the Sunday supplements of the early twenty-first century. Others are not. A recipe was issued for making almond icing, with haricot beans, almond essence and a knob of butter. Kathleen Johnson recalls a substitute for royal icing: '*Whisk one egg white with one tablespoon of Golden Syrup in a bowl over gently boiling water until the mixture is thick and fluffy. Allow to cool slightly. Colour if desired, and spread roughly over cake.*' She remembers making mock cream to serve with the Christmas pudding: '*Use one cup of fresh milk and one tablespoon of cornflour to make a blancmange. Allow to get quite cold. In another bowl, beat 2oz of butter and 1 dessertspoon of sugar to a cream. Add the blancmange little by little until all mixed together. Flavour with a few drops of vanilla essence.*' Kathleen continues, '*I much preferred Household Milk (dried milk which came in tall silver and blue tins) mixed to a thick cream. We also used to whisk evaporated milk until thick, and for special occasions set it with a little gelatine.'*

Lord Woolton also gave his name to the Woolton Pie, which was issued by the government as a nourishing convenience food. I can remember Miss Robinson coming to our house to tell us about the pies, which were to be sold for 4d or 6d at the Parish Room, and to exhort us to buy. We went to look, but my mother could not bring herself to go further than buying a couple of sausage rolls. The pies were also available at White House Farm, as Llewellyn Kirk remembers: *'We had a pie each week as it was on ration. We found a piece of wire in one and my mother took it back but they would not change it.'*

Other wartime foods, like Spam, were much more popular. Even now, I think of Spam fritters with some longing, although whether the reality would live up to the memory is not something I would risk. Kathleen Johnson has a different nostalgic memory, of *'a savoury fritter mix, called Frizettes, I think. Water was added to the powder and the mixture made small pancakes which were fried with bacon and eggs. I thought them absolutely delicious but have never met anyone else who remembers them. Some years ago, I was taken to a small restaurant in Nice to sample the local delicacy, pancakes made with chickpea flour. The flavour was just as I remembered Frizettes.'*

The BBC radio programme *The Kitchen Front* dispensed advice on making food go further and on using up leftovers. The Ministry of Food even devised a board game for 'women fighting on the Home Front'. Frank Meeres, writing in *Norfolk in the Second World War*, says: *'The game is something like snakes and ladders ... A player soars upwards for serving a healthy meal every day. She crashes for wasting bacon rinds and trimmings. Points are scored for "eating lots of vegetables" or lost for "refusing to eat oatmeal porridge".'*

Food was not the only staple to be rationed. Clothes too were the subject of a points system. In 1942 the 'utility' concept was introduced by Hugh Dalton. It was later also applied to furniture and pottery. The object was to make sure that standardisation throughout the industries would enable them to provide enough supplies to meet demand. Thus as far as clothes were concerned there were to be short skirts, a restricted number of styles and colours, and a reduction in the numbers of buttons on garments. Pamela Dixon (Garnham) (b. 1935) writes: *'During the war most of my clothes were made by hand. We used to cycle to Gimingham to a lady who did dressmaking to get dresses made. My toys and dolls were knitted, and faces embroidered on. My uncle made me a large dolls' house with furniture which turned out to be much too large for the house!'*

I was really too young during the war to remember any concern about clothes, or the lack of them. Photographs reveal that I was exclusively dressed in hand-me-downs as most other children would have been, in my case from my older cousins, and sometimes refurbished by one of my aunts who had been apprenticed as a dressmaker in North Walsham.

Petrol rationing was introduced in September 1939. Private users were rationed to 1,800 miles per year, but in 1942 petrol was only available for essential users. Rationing continued until well after the war and while this was undoubtedly very difficult for some, for many in Knapton it was the least onerous of wartime deprivations, as they did not have a car anyway.

Eventually the war ended. The peace brought with it new problems. But Pamela Dixon will never forget the first Christmas after the war. *'We went to Malvern on the train to visit my aunt. We had to sit on our suitcases in the crowded corridor for hours, changing trains at Birmingham and again at Worcester, the last few miles to Malvern in a small train called Tin Lizzy. I will always remember standing on Malvern Common on Christmas morning to listen to the bells from all the little churches in the area, one which played carols. This was so memorable because all the bells had been silent during the war.'*

The village celebrated the end of the war with, of course, a Social. June Wild has kept the invitation sent to her parents for the event: *'WELCOME HOME. The people of Knapton invite you and your family to a Social, in Knapton Parish Room at 7 o'clock, on Saturday, 8 June 1946. The enclosed is a small token and our welcome.'*

With what was obviously a gift from the people of Knapton to their sons and daughters returned safe from the war, Knapton entered the challenges of peace.

APPENDIX 1: OCCUPATIONS

In 2007, contributors and others involved in the publication of *Knapton Remembered* provided details of their fathers' and mothers' occupations and of their own subsequent careers.

Name	Parents' Occupations	Own career
Philip Almey	Farmers	Farmer
Queenie Bane	Father farm labourer	Domestic
Grace Burlingham	Father farm labourer; mother home and farm work	Nanny, boatyard, care assistant
Ivy Burlingham	As above	Housewife, hairdresser
Andrew Claydon	Father farmer	Tenant farmer
Neville Coe	Father gardener, road man; mother home help	Boat builder, Bacton gas site
Pamela Dixon	Father poultry farmer; mother shop and post office	Sub-postmistress, guest house owner
Barbara Dixon	As above	Fashion retail
Roger Dixon	Father motor mechanic; mother daily help, farm work	Teacher, curate, vicar, rural dean
Nellie Dixon	Father gardener; mother pub licensee	School cleaner, dinner lady
Meryvn Fawkes	Father gardener; mother seasonal fruit-picking	Apprentice carpenter, coach driver
Roy Fawkes	As above	Motor mechanic, coach driver
Gordon Harrison	Father station master	Building trade

Kathleen Johnson	Father poultry farmer; mother head teacher	Home economics teacher
Llewellyn Kirk	Father farm worker and gardener	Coach builder, carpenter
Maureen Kirk	Father agricultural engineer; mother dinner lady	Banking (Barclays and HSBC)
Josephine Langham	Father dental technician; mother various jobs	Teacher
Edward Langham	As above	Director, Canadian Space Agency
Anne Lee	Mother housewife and widow	Teacher
Phyllis Meffin	Father farm worker	
Sam Meffin	As above	Crane driver
Michael Miller	Father farm worker	Agricultural worker
Ray Pearman	Father cowman	Cowman
Willie Puncher	Father farmer	Farmer
Barbara Puncher	Father engineering works, farm work, gas site	Catering assistant
Joan Puncher	As above	School cook
John Rayner	Father painter and decorator	University professor
Jacqueline Skippen	Father painter and decorator	Secretarial work
Ruth Steward	Father farm worker; mother housework for others	Nursery nurse
Mary Steward	As above	Child care
Janet Steward	As above	Residential care: children, aged, homeless
William Stubley	Father stockman; mother cook	Royal Navy and MOD consultant

Gillian Watts	Father cattle dealer and poultry farmer	Teacher, MP, Minister, Peer
Josephine Watts	Father carpenter	Secretarial, shop manager
Dorothy Wild	Father gardener	Shop work, nursing, councillor
June Wild	Father carpenter; mother cleaner	Hairdresser
Brian Wild	Father farm worker; mother domestic work	Gardening, newspaper round
Richard Wild	As above	Bricklayer
Malcolm Wild	As above	Police officer
David White	Father pigman, builder's labourer	Insurance (Norwich Union)
Sylvia White	As above	Land work
Brenda Wilkins	Team-man	Shop work, domestic service
Shirley Wright	Father farm worker	Secterial, then Registrar of Births, Marriages and Deaths
John Wright	As above	Carpenter and builder
Cecil Yaxley	Father farm worker; mother domestic work	RAF

APPENDIX 2: A NOTE ON THE VALENTINE TRADITION IN NORFOLK

Several of our writers have written about the celebration of Valentine's Day. This seems to be peculiar to Norfolk, and is described as such by John Glyde in *Folklore and Customs of Norfolk*, first published in 1872:

> In Norwich and the towns of Norfolk the celebration of St Valentine is somewhat peculiar and demands a notice at our hands. It is customary at Norwich for valentines to be received, not on 14th February as in other districts, but on the evening of the 13th, St Valentine's Eve. Another peculiar feature connected with this festival in Norfolk is that the valentine, instead of being an ornamental billet-doux, is some article of intrinsic value ... Tradesmen anxiously obtain all kinds of novelties for the season, and many of the shops most noted for the variety of their stocks are literally besieged by customers on Valentine's Eve. The mode of delivering these valentines is also peculiar. The parcel containing the valentine is placed on the doorstep on Valentine's Eve, and a thundering rap being given at the door, the messenger takes to his heels and is off instantly. Those in the house, knowing well enough the purpose of such an announcing rap, quickly fetch in the various treasures. Where there is a young family, the raps are likely to be frequent, and the juveniles get into a perfect furore of excitement on such evenings.

In March 2009 Janet Steward (Munro) (b. 1940) wrote to the *Eastern Daily Press* asking for readers' recollections of Valentine's

Day customs. She had personal replies from fifteen readers of the paper, whose circulation is largely limited to Norfolk and North Suffolk. All of them recount memories of celebrations of Valentine, whom they variously call Jack Valentine, Mr Valentine, Frank Valentine, Old Mother Valentine, Father or Old Father Valentine, Johnny Valentine and Jimmy Valentine. All are from people born and brought up in Norfolk – with one exception, from Halesworth in Suffolk.

Mrs Morton from Hellesdon, near Norwich, writes: 'My father, who would have been ten years old in 1900, told me how as boys on Valentine's night he and his friends would ring doorbells and run away, tie door handles together, leave a parcel on the end of a string and twitch it away when the door was answered, or even worse, leave a box filled with manure on some poor person's step. My father never told me what retribution if any came their way!'

Mr Yarham of Fulmodeston, near Fakenham in Norfolk, was brought up in New Holkham. He writes: 'These customs were kept up in many parts of North Norfolk at least until the late 1950s and at least in some families, for even longer. In these parts, however, we knew nothing of Jack Valentine, it was Old Mother Valentine who was the supposed giver of the anonymous small gifts which we children would find left on the step when we answered the door to her knocking … My own daughters, who were born in the mid/late 60s believed in Mother Valentine long after they had ceased to believe in Father Christmas! … In New Holkham where I lived as a boy, the early part of the evening was devoted to the giving and receiving of real presents, then came the fun of "snatch Valentines", brooms positioned so as to fall on you when you opened the door, and other such practical jokes. One year a Valentine sent from doorstep to doorstep along the row of cottages at Quarles Farm consisted of a shoebox containing a few fly buttons and a note proclaiming, "We have done those things we ought not to have done, and left undone those things which we ought to have done up!" My wife spent her childhood in Fulmodeston, and after school on Valentine's Day the children in Barney and Fulmodeston would go from door to door, singing for sweets and pennies: "Good Old Mother Valentine / God bless the baker / You be the giver / I'll be the taker / If you want to hear us sing / Open the door and let us in." This was in addition to the fun of Mother Valentine's visits in the evening.'

In our household, there was no celebration of Father Valentine, partly perhaps because my mother came from Sheffield. My father and his family were from Norfolk, but not much given to celebrations apart from Christmas. I do remember, however, Pamela and Barbara Dixon banging on our door and leaving a present on one Valentine's Eve, explaining the next day that Old Father Valentine had called. The custom obviously loomed large in the memories of many of the contributors to this book, however, since they devote as much space to Valentine as they do to Christmas.

BIBLIOGRAPHY

Amis, Arthur, *From Dawn to Dusk* (Simac Marketing, 1992)

Ashwin, Trevor, and Davison, Alan (eds), *An Historical Atlas of Norfolk* (Phillimore, 2005)

Blythe, Ronald, *Akenfield* (Allen Lane, 1969)

Edwards, George, *From Crow Scaring to Westminster* (Larks Press (new edition), 2008)

Edwards, Noel, *Ploughboy's Progress* (Centre of East Anglian Studies, 1998)

Glyde, John, *Folklore and Customs of Norfolk* (reprinted by EP Publishing Ltd, 1973)

Grapes, Sidney, *The Boy John* and *The Boy John Again* (Norfolk News Co Ltd, 1958)

Groves, Reg, *Sharpen the Sickle* (Merlin Press (new edition), 1981)

Hennessy, Peter, *Never Again* (Jonathan Cape, 1992)

Hennessy, Peter, *Having It So Good* (Allen Lane, 2006)

Kelly's Directories of Norfolk of 1892, 1922 and 1933

Mee, Arthur, *Norfolk* (Hodder and Stoughton, 1940)

Meeres, Frank, *Norfolk in the Second World War* (Phillimore, 2006)

Norfolk Federation of Women' Institutes, *In Living Memory* (1971)

Paston 2000 (published to mark the Millennium by a group of people in Paston, 2000)

Pevsner, Niklaus, *North-East Norfolk and Norwich* (Penguin, 1962)

Shephard, Gillian, *Shephard's Watch* (Politicos, 2000)

Shephard, Gillian (ed.), *Knapton Remembered* (Larks Press, 2007)

Smith, Graham, *Norfolk Airfields in the Second World War* (Countryside Books, 1994)

KNAPTON REMEMBERED
Edited by Gillian Shephard

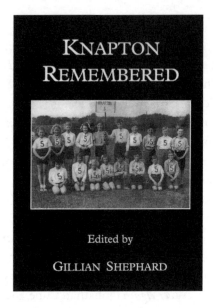

These are the memories of some of the people who lived in
Knapton from the 1930s to the 1960s and
attended Knapton School.

Knapton was not a prosperous village, but its children were
blessed by an inspirational head teacher, Mrs Johnson, the strong
and generous leadership of Miss Robinson of Knapton House,
and the influence of its two flourishing churches.

The sense of community and the rhythm of the farm year
permeate every page of this book, which has been
produced by the efforts of some seventy people who are still in
touch with each other.

176pp paperback • £10.00
www.booksatlarkspress.co.uk